HO! FOR THE BLACK HILLS

Capt Jack Crawford.

HOUSEWORTH'S Celebrities, 12 Montgomery St., San Francisco

CAPTAIN JACK CRAWFORD

Ho! For the Black Hills

REPORTS THE BLACK HILLS GOLD RUSH AND GREAT SIOUX WAR

EDITED BY PAUL L. HEDREN

SOUTH DAKOTA
STATE HISTORICAL SOCIETY PRESS *Pierre*

This publication is funded, in part, by the Deadwood Publications Fund provided by the City of Deadwood and the Deadwood Historic Preservation Commission.

Library of Congress Cataloging-in-Publication Data
Crawford, Jack, 1847–1917.
Ho! For the Black Hills : Captain Jack Crawford Reports the Black Hills Gold Rush and Great Sioux War / edited by Paul L. Hedren.
p. cm.
Includes bibliographical references and index.
ISBN 978-0-9846505-0-7 (cloth)—ISBN 978-0-9852817-8-6 (pbk.)
1. Crawford, Jack, 1847-1917—Correspondence. 2. Black Hills (S.D. and Wyo.)—Gold discoveries. 3. Frontier and pioneer life—Black Hills (S.D. and Wyo.) 4. Dakota Indians—Wars, 1876—Personal narratives. 5. Cheyenne Indians Wars, 1876—Personal narratives. I. Hedren, Paul L. II. Title.
F657.B6C73 2012
978.3′9—dc23 2012011477

The paper in this book meets the guidelines for permanence and durability of the committee on Production Guidelines for Book Longevity of the Council on Library Resources.

Cover image: *Captain Jack Crawford*, © 2011 Thom Ross
Frontispiece: Captain Jack Crawford traveled with Buffalo Bill Cody's Combination Show in mid-1877. *Houseworth & Co. Photographers. The Bancroft Library, University of California, Berkeley*

Please visit our website at www.sdshspress.com

Printed in the United States of America

For WATSON PARKER,

friend and raconteur

in the spirit of

Captain Jack Crawford

CONTENTS

PREFACE

"Ho! For the Black Hills" headlined many a story about the Black Hills gold rush in the *Omaha Daily Bee* in 1875–1876 and seems an apt title for a book of gold-rush letters written by a character as colorful as the saga itself, Captain Jack Crawford. The self-proclaimed "Poet Scout of the Black Hills," Crawford was known to friends and acquaintances as Captain Jack, or simply Jack, and he was a William F. "Buffalo Bill" Cody protégé through and through. He came West from Pennsylvania in 1875 as news of the new El Dorado was spreading throughout the land. In Omaha, Nebraska, he landed a job as a Black Hills correspondent for the *Bee*, and for about a year, he roamed the Hills, prospecting some, exploring widely, immersing himself in community affairs, and sending detailed letters to the newspaper telling of these exploits. In the midst of this great adventure, Crawford himself seemed to be torn between the business of the gold rush and his responsibility to his editor, Edward Rosewater, on the one hand, and the lure of Cody's world on the American stage, on the other. Crawford was a born raconteur and entertained casually in the saloons of Custer City and around campfires. He had met Buffalo Bill in Pennsylvania, and their paths crossed several times in 1876 before joining on the Sioux war trail that fall. As it turned out, the dutiful, letter-writing, poet scout of the Black Hills had not yet realized his true calling.

I learned of Captain Jack Crawford's letters through Darlis Miller's exceptional biography of Crawford, *Captain Jack Crawford: Buckskin Poet, Scout, and Showman.* Miller demonstrated that this colorful but now almost-forgotten figure had indeed been a prospector, author of books of poetry, and lyceum performer. In his stage performances, he had featured and reflected upon a wealth of experience gained during the Civil War, as an adventurer in the goldfields of the Black Hills, Canada, and Alaska, and as a genuine army scout during the heady days of the Indian wars, most particularly the Sioux war of 1876. During Crawford's Black Hills exploits, he worked primarily as a paid correspondent for the *Daily Bee*, Omaha's leading newspaper at the time, and penned lively accounts from Custer City or Deadwood almost weekly. In those letters, Crawford recounted his explorations and prospecting in the gulches of the central and northern Hills, his adventures on the trails linking Sidney and Cheyenne with Custer City, and his deeds as a town-builder, promoter, and Black Hills Ranger. As well, his correspondence brimmed with notes and commentary on the characters he befriended, and sometimes squabbled with, who almost always seemed every bit as colorful as he was. Darlis Miller made artful use of Crawford's letters as she fashioned her biography but was never specific about them, confessing almost as an aside that perhaps some thirty existed. She later told me that she harbored her own notion of preparing them for publication, as I am doing here, but never got around to it.

Clearly, Jack's letters had caught my attention, especially after I moved to Omaha, where the Union Pacific Railroad, Crook's House at Fort Omaha, the timeworn Prospect Hill Cemetery, and the venerable but now defunct *Daily Bee* still resonate distinctly, and all with palpable connections to Captain Jack Crawford and his captivating exploits on the northern plains in the 1870s. Beyond Miller's book, I had encountered Crawford on a number of other occasions. I knew of Captain Jack's participation in the Sioux war, where he was especially remembered for carrying dispatches for the *New York Herald* about the Slim Buttes fight. I knew Crawford as a friend and then rival of Buffalo Bill Cody. I had collected some of Crawford's books of poetry, though I took no particular fancy to them other than acknowledging that he had things to say in verse about Wild Bill Hickok, George Armstrong Custer, General Crook, and gold. I was quite unaware of his role as a pioneer Black Hiller other than what Miller had reported. But I had a notion that this project was worth pursuing and that maybe an article or even a book might result.

My initial step into Crawford's world began with a methodical reading of the *Omaha Daily Bee* for the years 1875 through 1877, during which I discovered a sound newspaper with a strong local and regional voice. In the microfilm reel for 1875, I read substantial coverage of the developing Black Hills gold rush and so-called Dodge Expedition and saw occasional references to Jack Crawford, or J. W. C. (he was not yet Captain Jack), but little in any Black Hills context. I copied much, including two long letters to the *Bee* from the Dodge Expedition signed simply "Ned." One letter contained lines of verse, and I was suspicious. Early in the microfilm reel for 1876, I came across the first Captain Jack letter, duly signed, long, and explicit. And for ten months thereafter, Crawford's letters kept appearing. My photocopying bill at the Omaha Public Library reached hundreds of dollars as I not only copied more than forty Crawford letters but also virtually everything else related to the Black Hills gold rush and the Indian war that erupted in direct consequence. I found and copied Black Hills letters from Crawford in other newspapers, too, along with those he wrote about the Sioux war after he wrangled an invitation from Cody to join General George Crook "at the front," just in time to participate in the horrendous Starvation March and Battle of Slim Buttes.

After transcribing the letters and fashioning a sense of how they might be presented, I dropped my friend Nancy Tystad Koupal, director of the South Dakota State Historical Society Press, a note, half wondering about and half selling a book prospect that showcased Crawford's letters from the gold rush and Sioux war. She invited me to send a selection of letters for examination, which I immediately did, and her response thereafter was quick and enthusiastic, and my effort gained new purpose. We both saw an original and compelling new voice on two intriguing, almost timeless story lines from the 1870s: the remarkable Black Hills gold rush and the equally stirring Great Sioux War. In both instances, Crawford's letters were no humdrum of dates, time, and weather but were rich with particulars of events, encounters, geography, friends, acquaintances, and opinions, all gained as he experienced two of the most dramatic sagas to occur in Dakota Territory and on the northern Great Plains.

NOTES ON EDITING

In transcribing Crawford's letters to the *Bee* and other newspapers, I aimed to produce literal copies of texts as they appeared on the printed newspaper page. Jack's writing style was delightfully clear and straightforward and lacked almost all pretension. His few quirks and impositions were more reflections of the time, it seemed, than any compromise on the rules of English. He occasionally wrote in haste, and his letters sometimes had a stream-of-consciousness quality about them, but his story line was never impaired. I did not regularize Crawford's various spellings of surnames and place names, which I found charming and not at all bothersome. Crawford's editor in Omaha, Edward Rosewater, obviously exercised the same light hand in typesetting the incoming letters. I did silently correct occasional obvious typographical errors that seemed much more attributable to the *Bee* than to Crawford. And I eliminated the newspapers' story subheads, which were of their creation, but I did use the newspapers' headings and signature styles. Where I could not decipher blackened or blotched microfilm that obscured occasional words, I indicated so with brackets, and my few insertions are also within brackets. Finally, I chose to present the letters in the order in which Crawford wrote them, not in the order in which they appeared in newspapers (I address issues of irregular postal service several times in my introductions).

In presenting Captain Jack's letters to the *Bee*, the *Sidney Telegraph*, the *Black Hills Pioneer*, and the *New York Herald*, I have provided contexts and background in chapter introductions and have added few emendations to the text. I particularly highlighted within these various chapter openings a number of characters that figured regularly in the letters, but Crawford's correspondence was replete with names of individuals, many of whom were transitory, and I was selective. Where identity seemed clear, I have provided the person's first name and the correct spelling of the name at first mention, either in the chapter introduction or in brackets.

I have also provided a general introduction that sets up the book, giving pertinent information on the matter of gold in the Black Hills and the leading character in this narrative, Jack Crawford, the highly imaginative but still budding "poet scout." Necessary background concerning the Great Sioux War, particularly in its Black Hills context, can be found at the beginning of Chapter 7. Although there is a certain sameness to the way others before me have related these histories, I tried to breathe freshness into my versions and use some new sources, particularly the *Omaha Daily Bee*, which for too long has been unheralded as a rich repository of information. Crawford's letters themselves segmented quite nicely, and I have presented them accordingly, with some sections containing more letters of like content than others. And I added one essay that specifically explores the story of Jack Crawford's ride from the Slim Buttes battlefield to Fort Laramie, his one unique contribution to the Sioux War story. Sources on the ride conflict, and it has long needed, I believe, a fresh telling.

The majority of photographs illustrating this book are images by the renowned stereographers Daniel S. Mitchell and Stanley J. Morrow, who came to the Black Hills in mid-1876 and spent the summer photographing its diggings, communities, businesses, and characters, including in Mitchell's case his friend Captain Jack. Mitchell and Morrow produced a remarkable body of work, and between Crawford's letters and these photographs, it can honestly be said that this book presents the way it was in Custer City and the Black Hills in 1876, encompassing the rumors, the violence, and the hopes and fears of its inhabitants. I have not clouded the immediacy of Crawford's actual accounts with explanatory notes that explore the nature or source of rumors or exaggerations. The reader is advised to consider these letters as primary documents that represent one man's observations, knowledge, and point of view, and they have to be compared with other primary sources with which they may conflict. Nor have I tried to place all of Crawford's locations within the modern landscape of the Black Hills, although I have supplied two maps that should aid readers in locating themselves within both eras.

ACKNOWLEDGMENTS

Many friends and colleagues were gracious with their time and talent and fully abetted this personally fascinating chase of Captain Jack Crawford through the Black Hills and Sioux Country. I am especially grateful for the kindnesses rendered by Darlis Miller, emeritus professor of history at New Mexico State University, Las Cruces, and author of an essential biography of Captain Jack. Darlis warmly encouraged my interest in the project, answered innumerable email queries, and repeatedly ferreted out and copied useful source materials originally used in the biography and now reposing among her papers in the university's archives.

Nancy Tystad Koupal in Pierre was equally supportive in many different ways, encouraging the book from the time of my first communication with her, tipping me to funding sources that supported research travel, accommodating several requests in matters of production, skillfully editing the manuscript with the extraordinary but common-sense flair for which she is renowned among history professionals, and sharing all along my sense of the tremendous worth of these Crawford letters from Custer City, Deadwood, and the Sioux war.

David Wolff, history professor at Black Hills State University, Spearfish, a foremost authority on the mining history of the Black Hills, read a near final draft of the manuscript and offered many insightful comments and posed some challenging questions, closing with the coy caveat that I was welcome to ignore as much or all as I wished. But I did not ignore much and truly believe in consequence that my introductions are sharper and more fully rounded because of his insights and curiosity. Moreover, David and I both suffer bouts of gold fever, love trails history, and enjoy enticing each other with tales of big placer nuggets, deep trail ruts in Buffalo Gap, Red Canyon, or wherever, and other wonders and intrigues of the historic Black Hills.

Robert Kolbe of Sioux Falls, a foremost collector of Black Hills and Dakota photographica and an authority on camera artists like Mitchell, Morrow, and Illingworth, kindly lent images from his collection for use in the book and joined me in interpreting some of the obvious and unobvious in those early Black Hills views. We particularly studied the proclaimed "first photograph of Deadwood" preserved in the collections of the Adams Museum and came away agreeing that it is indeed so (*see* page 190).

My long-time friend Jim Brust, M.D., of San Pedro, California, was an early supporter of the project and took time on my behalf to explore and report on the Jack Crawford collection in the Autry National Center in Los Angeles. The Autry possesses a number of remarkable Crawford artifacts; photographs of several central to this story are reproduced in the book.

Archivists and librarians at the Nebraska State Historical Society in Lincoln and W. Dale Clark Main Library, Omaha, were particularly helpful throughout the project, making accessible microfilm reels of the *Omaha Daily Bee*; maintaining for the public, at considerable cost I am told, genuine old-style microfilm readers and reader-printers; and cordially handling inter-library loan requests. I am especially pleased to recognize Andrea Faling and Matt Piersol of the Nebraska State Historical Society and Lynn Sullivan and Andrew Ireland of the Omaha Public Library for their many courtesies.

Among other librarians and archivists, I am grateful to Abby Hoverstock, Denver Public Library; Jeanette Chaney-Moodie and Carol Hauck, Deadwood Public Library; Crystal Mensch-Nelson, Dakota Territorial Museum, Yankton; and Gary Rosenberg, Douglas County Historical Society, Omaha, for help rendered on my unannounced visits.

The photographs in this book came from many additional sources, and I am pleased to acknowledge the assistance of Laurie Langland, Dakota Wesleyan University, Mitchell, South Dakota; Linda Hein, Nebraska State Historical Society; Marilyn Kim and Alyssa Brust Lebetsamer, Autry National Center; Darrel Nelson and Rose Speirs, Adams Museum, Deadwood; Larry Ness, Yankton, South Dakota; Jim Crain, San Antonio, Texas; Lorna Kirwan and Daniel Wikey,

Bancroft Library, Berkeley, California; Bill Gonzalez, The Durham Museum, Omaha; Sean Campbell, Mack Frost, and Mary Robinson, Buffalo Bill Historical Center, Cody, Wyoming; Paul Horsted, Custer, South Dakota; and Reid Riner, Minnilusa Historical Association, Rapid City, South Dakota.

As always, friends and associates lent support, ran interference, opened doors, provided tips, and encouraged the project in innumerable ways, and I am pleased to recognize Jim Potter, Chadron, Nebraska; Jim McLaird, Mitchell, South Dakota; Barbara Case, Redondo Beach, California; Ephriam Dickson, Salt Lake City; Paul Andrew Hutton, Albuquerque; Jerry Greene, Arvada, Colorado; Tom Buecker, Lincoln, Nebraska; Marv Kaiser, Prescott, Arizona; Sandra Lowry, Fort Laramie National Historic Site, Wyoming; Thom Ross, Santa Fe, New Mexico; Jim Aplan, Piedmont, South Dakota; Jeff Barnes, Omaha; Eli Paul, Kansas City; Marc Abrams, Brooklyn, New York; Jack McDermott, Rapid City; Bill and Nadya Henry, Florence, Oregon; Brian Dippie, Victoria, British Columbia; Louis Kraft, North Hollywood, California; and Steve Friesen, Buffalo Bill Museum, Denver.

Attempting to understand the geography of Black Hills landmarks and trails led to interesting exchanges with John Hedren, Deephaven, Minnesota; Tom Farrell, Wind Cave National Park, South Dakota; Lonis Wendt, Vivian, South Dakota; Peggy Sanders, Hot Springs, South Dakota; and David Wolff, and I hope the maps in this book are at least reasonably accurate; if not, I am to blame.

A number of South Dakota State Historical Society staff members particularly shepherded the project, and I am pleased to acknowledge Ken Stewart and Matthew Reitzel in the State Archives, and Patti Edman, Rodger Hartley, and Martyn Beeny in Research and Publishing for their innumerable courtesies, whether discussing sources, ferreting out the treasured original 1875 French Creek claim book, wrangling photographs, or making maps. This crew and all those at the State Historical Society in Pierre personify public service of the highest order.

Along the way, I was the grateful recipient of a research grant from the South Dakota Humanities Council that permitted important travel and helped to cover photographic expenses. Sherry DeBoer, Stephanie Horsley, and Evan Phillips of the council, and Ron

Woodburn of the Capital University Center Foundation of Pierre, my South Dakota sponsor, were exceedingly cordial and expeditious in handling this welcome support.

My daughters, Ethne and Whitney, and wife, Connie, accommodated again another history chase. It is what I do these days, and almost all I do. Fortunately, these women share my enthusiasm for the Black Hills. Our individual reasons might differ slightly, but it is one of those things we enjoy together, and for that I am exceedingly grateful.

To one and all, thank you very much.

Paul L. Hedren
Omaha, 10 September 2011

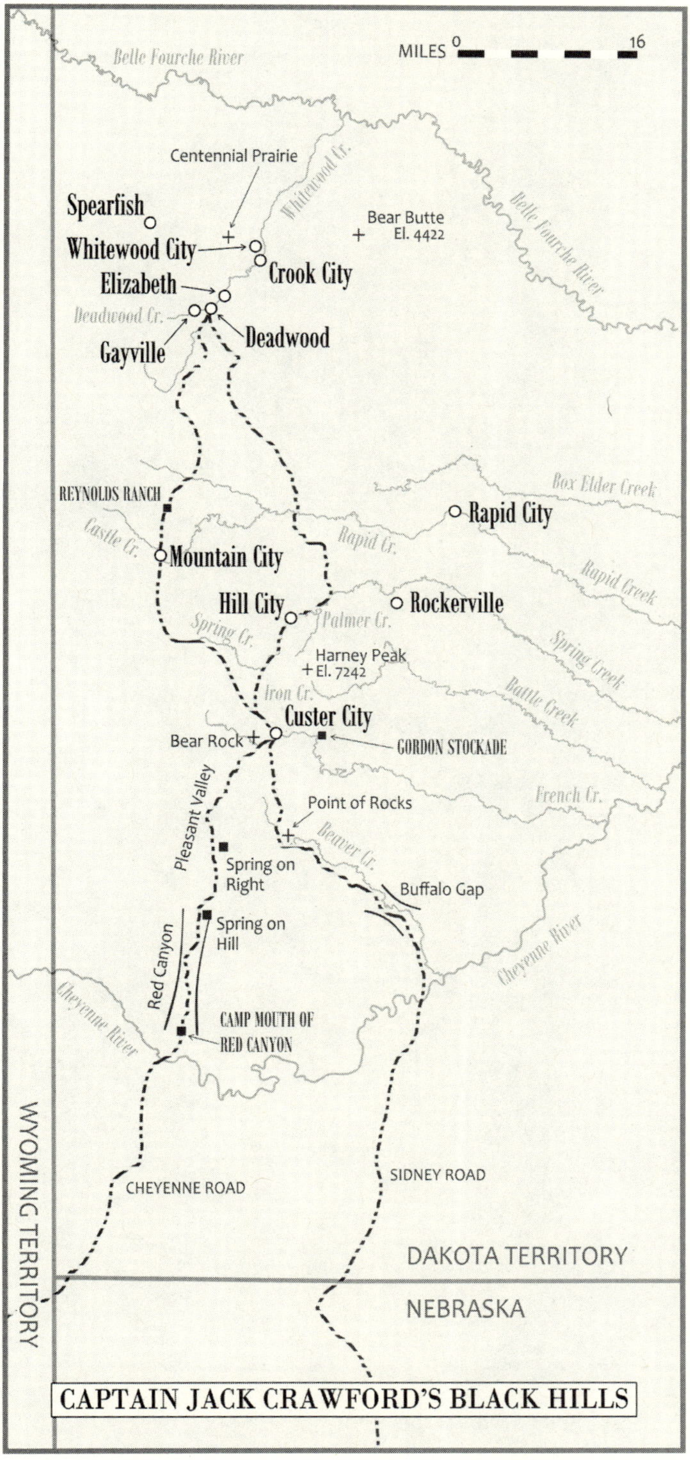

CAPTAIN JACK CRAWFORD'S BLACK HILLS

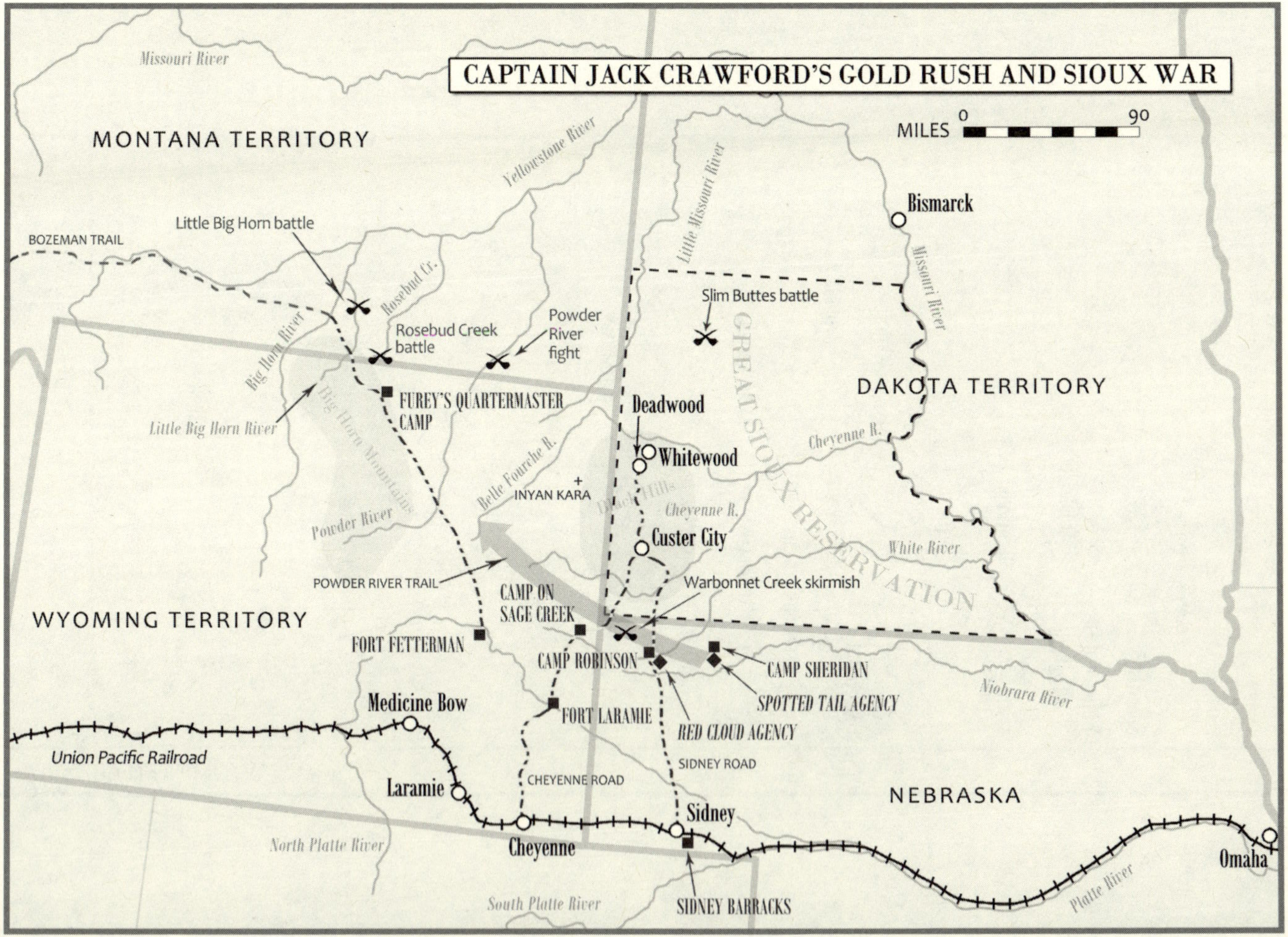
CAPTAIN JACK CRAWFORD'S GOLD RUSH AND SIOUX WAR
MILES 0 90
MONTANA TERRITORY
DAKOTA TERRITORY
WYOMING TERRITORY
NEBRASKA
Missouri River
Yellowstone River
Little Missouri River
Bismarck
BOZEMAN TRAIL
Little Big Horn battle
Rosebud Cr.
Big Horn River
Rosebud Creek battle
Powder River fight
Slim Buttes battle
GREAT SIOUX RESERVATION
FUREY'S QUARTERMASTER CAMP
Little Big Horn River
Big Horn Mountains
Deadwood
Whitewood
Cheyenne R.
Belle Fourche R.
INYAN KARA
Powder River
Custer City
White River
POWDER RIVER TRAIL
Warbonnet Creek skirmish
CAMP ON SAGE CREEK
FORT FETTERMAN
CAMP ROBINSON
CAMP SHERIDAN
SPOTTED TAIL AGENCY
Niobrara River
Medicine Bow
FORT LARAMIE
RED CLOUD AGENCY
Union Pacific Railroad
SIDNEY ROAD
CHEYENNE ROAD
Laramie
Sidney
Cheyenne
North Platte River
Omaha
Platte River
South Platte River
SIDNEY BARRACKS

INTRODUCTION

CAPTAIN JACK AND THE BLACK HILLS GOLD RUSH

Two commanding energies converged in the Black Hills in the mid-1870s. One was the irrepressible lure of the nation's newest El Dorado, which drew thousands of Americans to the placer-rich gulches lacing the mountainscape of southwestern Dakota Territory. The other was an effervescent, twenty-eight-year-old Pennsylvanian, John Wallace Crawford, drawn to the Dakota diggings to prospect, take pleasure in an extraordinary adventure, and report for the *Omaha Daily Bee*, one of the region's leading newspapers. These energies intertwined for nearly a year. The gold fields proved notable, especially in the wake of the economic chaos associated with the Panic of 1873, and Crawford, among the earliest of Black Hillers, carved a meaningful and marketable name for himself as a reporter, as a genuine plainsman and scout, and as a raconteur in the mold of Buffalo Bill Cody, Wild Bill Hickok, and Texas Jack Omohundro.

Crawford, indeed, found his way to the Black Hills diggings not once but twice in the earliest days of the rush, tagging along with the close-quartered government surveying expedition of 1875—the so-called Dodge or Jenney Expedition—and returning early in January 1876 for six additional months of reporting, prospecting, and Black Hills adventure. Central to Crawford's story were his letters to the *Omaha Daily Bee*, some thirty-five in all, plus five more to other newspapers. Each letter richly and candidly detailed the worth of the gulches, the hardships of travel to and from the Black Hills; the art, sometimes luck, of surviving there; struggles with governance in the fledgling communities; and the perils posed by weather, outlaws, and American Indians. Along the way, the seemingly ever-genial Crawford befriended miners, businessmen, fellow reporters, and showmen. When beckoned in mid-summer by none other than William F. "Buffalo Bill" Cody to join Brigadier General George Crook's Indian campaign then underway, he seized that opportunity as well. Crawford arrived in the sprawling army camp on Rosebud Creek, Montana, in time to experience and report the grueling Starvation March and Indian fight at Slim Buttes. As a guide for Crook and messenger for newspapermen, Crawford ushered important dispatches through Indian country and the Black Hills to the nearest telegraph terminal on the Fort Laramie road. Crawford's amazing letters recounting these high adventures in the gold country and on the Sioux war trail comprise a vibrant and almost unknown account of this fascinating time in the American West.

Notions of gold in the Dakota Black Hills had persisted throughout the entire nineteenth century. Just before the time of the Lewis and Clark Expedition (1804–1806), French-Canadian fur trader Régis Loisel reported to Spanish authorities in New Orleans that gold could be found in the distant Black Hills, a vaguely understood landscape he called the Costa Negra, at the head of the Rio Que Corre, the "River which runs," or the Niobrara. This knowledge had been gained from Indians during Loisel's ascent of the Missouri River in 1803. From time to time thereafter, other trappers, traders, and errant explorers also mentioned gold in the Black Hills, but the scattered tales never sparked any particular interest beyond the simple mention. Several shadowy prospecting parties explored the Black Hills at mid-century, one in 1852 and another in 1863, and each supposedly carried out gold, but, again, neither episode triggered much interest or any follow-up action, and little is known today of either expedition.[1]

At almost the same time, Indians were supposedly bartering gold for trade goods at places like Fort Pierre on the Missouri River and Fort Laramie on the North Platte River in Wyoming, and the "Indians having this gold were always from the Black Hills country," or so it was said.[2] While it seems improbable that Indians were actually recovering placer gold themselves, perhaps such gold was purloined from early miners, death seeming the standard fate of most of these obscure early prospectors. Or perhaps Indians handled gold-speckled quartz. An individual by the name of J. C. Wilcox, bound for the Black Hills during the rush in 1876, penned an interesting letter to the *Omaha Daily Bee.* He asserted that while at Fort Laramie in 1859 he had heard from French fur trappers of places in the Black Hills where Indians chipped off gold-bearing quartz visible in the rocks. Wilcox's story is uncorroborated, but gold visible in quartz was later not an entirely unknown phenomenon in Deadwood Gulch and elsewhere.[3]

Two formal government-sponsored surveying expeditions circled the Black Hills at mid-century, mostly noting such features as rivers and prominent geological landmarks on the margins. Both surveys, Gouverneur K. Warren's expedition in 1857 and William Raynolds's exploration two years later, reportedly found traces of gold, but neither party measured whether it existed in paying quantities, and the discoveries in both instances were downplayed in formal reports. When prospectors finally openly entered the Black Hills in the mid-1870s at the commencement of the great rush, evidence of earlier prospecting was supposedly commonplace. Miners reported finding old prospectors' holes in which large trees were now growing, scattered weathered sluice boxes, timbered shafts, rusted shovels and picks buried deep in stream gravels, remnants of cabins, and skeletons of white men, including one skull supposedly having at its side a pair of silver-bowed spectacles.[4]

Citizens in Yankton, in the southeastern corner of the newly established Dakota Territory, agitated fervently throughout the 1860s and early 1870s for additional surveys of the Black Hills, but every movement toward that end was thwarted by the United States Army and the complications posed by travel into the land of the Lakotas, or western Sioux. A series of military campaigns against the Sioux in Dakota and Wyoming in the wake of hostilities following the Minnesota Uprising in 1862 and the Sand Creek Massacre in 1864 had turned Sioux Country into an intimidating landscape. Farther west in the mid-1860s, travel to the Montana gold fields on the Bozeman Trail had spawned open hostilities with the Lakotas that largely closed travel on that road. The end of the so-called Bozeman Trail or Red Cloud's War further isolated the Black Hills, which were included in the Great Sioux Reservation created for the Lakotas by the Fort Laramie Treaty of 1868. The new reservation encapsulated all of Dakota Territory south of the forty-sixth parallel of north latitude and west of the Missouri River. Despite a continuing clamor from citizens of Yankton and nearby Sioux City, Iowa, for the government to investigate the rumored gold, travel to the Black Hills remained virtually impossible until well into the 1870s, and it was illegal after the 1868 treaty made the area a vital quarter of the formally established Sioux reservation.[5]

But other forces aligned in 1874, driven mostly by the Panic of 1873, which wracked the nation with calamitous unemployment and economic despair. The military finally authorized an exploration for the purposes of surveying the Black Hills for the site of a new military post, an action permitted in Article Eleven of the 1868 Fort Laramie Treaty.[6] For four weeks in July and August 1874, Seventh Cavalry troops, under the command of Lieutenant Colonel George A. Custer, ambled the Hills. They noted abandoned Indian camps on the trail, the vast agricultural potential of the region, the abundance of wildlife, and, indeed, a logical site for a new military post that might one-day buffer the inevitable pioneer tide from Indian opposition. Custer's crew included scientists, engineers, a photographer, and two practical miners who prospected the Hills carefully, often citing the broad distribution of gold-bearing quartz. Along French Creek in the heart of what is the modern-day city of Custer, on 30 July 1874, Horatio Nelson Ross washed color from dirt taken from the side of the stream and showed it to his commander and other officers. The yield was modest, estimated at perhaps five- to seven-cents per pan, but the men continued prospecting on French Creek, and color abounded. The camp moved down French Creek several miles in search of fresh pasturage, and on 2 August, Ross and his partner, William McKay, panned excellent color in the loose creek soil, estimating a yield of thirty-five cents in dust to three pans and perhaps a dollar a pan in more difficult soil.[7] Ross and McKay dug a prospecting hole about as long and wide as a human grave and about six feet deep and found pay dirt "from the grass roots down."[8]

Spurred by Custer himself, news of the gold discovery spread rapidly. In early August, Custer dispatched one of the expedition's civilian scouts, Charley Reynolds, down Red Canyon to Fort Laramie, then the nearest telegraph connection, carrying the commander's report for Lieutenant General Philip H. Sheridan, commander of the military Division of the Missouri in Chicago. Custer affirmed gold in paying quantities. Reynolds also carried a mail bag brimming with other letters and newspaper dispatches. Within days, the nation's newspapers bellowed reports of a great gold discovery in the

Horatio Nelson Ross and William McKay found gold in Golden Park, three miles east of present-day Custer, on 2 August 1874, "from the grass roots down" and helped precipitate the Black Hills gold rush. *William Illingworth photograph. Minnilusa Historical Association at the Journey Museum, Rapid City, S.Dak.*

Black Hills, the new "Land of Promise." In his own report, Custer was coyly circumspect about the richness of the discovery and urged that no opinion be formed. Still, the news of gold was electrifying, and this time the nation paid heed.[9]

Before Custer's expedition departed its French Creek camp, the first-ever miners meeting was held in the Black Hills, convened on 5 August around an evening campfire in the expedition's wagon corral. A few teamsters, cooks, soldiers, and miners participated, staking twenty-one claims in the newly proclaimed District No. 1 of Custer's Gulch. Ross held the discovery claim, and twelve claims were recorded below Discovery and eight above, to be worked, they all agreed, "as soon as peaceable possession can be had of this portion of Dakota Territory by the General Government." The participants declared themselves the Custer Park Mining Company and posted a notice of their claims on the inside of an empty hard-tack crate, which they placed upside down on the discovery claim. Thus were mining interests inaugurated in the Black Hills, irrespective of the illegalities of whites claiming lands within the bounds of the Great Sioux Reservation.[10]

Even as news of the gold discovery spread from coast to coast in mid-August, another survey of the Black Hills commenced, this one not aimed at seeking gold but at locating suitable permanent homes for the Red Cloud and Spotted Tail Indian agencies, or perhaps a single place for both of them. These two agencies were temporarily located on the White River in Nebraska. Organized by Reverend Samuel D. Hinman, an Episcopal priest, missionary, and Indian-rights activist, and provided with a small military escort from the Fort Laramie garrison, the impromptu survey traveled many of the same trails that Custer had in the central and southern Hills. Just weeks apart, the two expeditions saw many of the same sights, climbed the same mountains, and panned the same streams. But instead of issuing an optimistic report on the varied matters of worth in the Black Hills, Hinman found the Hills bleak and sterile, except for the obvious timber. Moreover, Hinman found no evidence of mineral wealth, despite the presence of several experienced miners with his party. Hinman contradicted Custer point for point but was ignored, his findings generating no publicity whatsoever and his report buried in the 1874 annual Report of the Commissioner of Indian Affairs. Despite Hinman's conscious effort, the Black Hills gold rush was not to be deterred.[11]

The invasion of the Black Hills commenced almost as soon as Custer took up the trail for his home at Fort Abraham Lincoln, near Bismarck on the Missouri River. By early-September 1874, a well-publicized expedition was forming in Sioux City, intent on entering the long-anticipated gold fields. Respecting the fact that this reservation land was off-limits to whites, General Sheridan mobilized troops from the garrisons at the Lower Brule Agency and Fort Randall on the Missouri River to patrol likely routes to the Hills. He thereby put in motion a frustrating exercise of evasion, capture, eviction, and return played out between mining parties and the army throughout some of 1874 and almost all of 1875. The first civilian expedition to enter the Black Hills, led by John Gordon of Sioux City, reached Custer's French Creek campsite on 23 December 1874. The party noted Ross's prospecting hole and erected a formidable stockade just below it that enclosed six cabins. Winter had begun, and prospecting was therefore limited, but the men found good color while digging the stockade postholes and well. Gordon reported that members of his party found prospects as high as fifteen cents to the

Many early Black Hills photographers documented the Gordon Stockade. This important gold rush landmark was located three miles east of Custer City on French Creek. It served as a residence and refuge throughout the boom. *D. S. Mitchell photograph. Jim Crain*

pan and projected that miners working sluices could make from ten to twenty-five dollars per man per day.[12]

In early February, Gordon departed the stockade that now carried his name, bound for Yankton and intent on organizing another party for the Black Hills. Newspapers followed his exploits closely, as did the army, which was already perplexed by his successful evasion of Indians and troops. Deployments from Fort Randall, Cheyenne River Agency, Camps Sheridan and Robinson, and Fort Laramie were mobilized but almost immediately hampered by winter weather. Finally in March, Captain John Mix led a column from Fort Laramie that found the miners, allowed them several days to collect livestock and pack possessions, and escorted them from the Hills. The well-publicized expulsion only served to incite additional interest in the gold country. Meanwhile, troops in northwestern Nebraska intercepted Gordon's second expedition in late May. The military burned his wagons and pushed the contents into a coulee, arrested Gordon, and escorted him to Omaha for prosecution. Charges were later dismissed. All the while, careful, diligent invaders were avoiding the military cordon. By mid-summer 1875, as many as six hundred miners were quietly but successfully prospecting French, Rapid, Spring, and Castle creeks in the central Black Hills.[13]

Even as miners quietly worked the gulches, the secretaries of the interior and war departments visibly stewed over the actual worth of the new gold country and the predicament they were in. The Black Hills were undeniably protected Indian lands, but they were also now the scene of an invasion that could scarcely be stemmed. The secretaries realized that if valuable mineral deposits existed within the Black Hills and Great Sioux Reservation to the extent alleged, an attempt to purchase or abrogate rights held by the Sioux would become a political necessity. And since Custer's expedition in 1874 did not determine such value—which was never its charge—another formal exploration would be necessary.[14]

While Custer's expedition had originated at Fort Abraham Lincoln northeast of the Black Hills in the army's military Department of Dakota, the 1875 survey was organized at Fort Laramie, southwest of the Hills in the Department of the Platte, the army's administrative boundaries giving way to the practical geographic and logistical realities of proximity and ease of supply. The new survey was dubbed variously the Dodge Expedition, referring to Lieutenant Colonel Richard I. Dodge of the Twenty-third Infantry who led the military escort of some four hundred troops, and also the Jenney or Newton-Jenney Expedition, referencing the two geologists who headed the scientific corps, Walter P. Jenney and Henry Newton, both of the Columbia School of Mines in New York City. For four months in the summer of 1875, this well-outfitted survey examined quartz outcroppings and panned the gravels of the central Black Hills.[15]

The expedition's miners readily found placer gold, and Dodge, Jenney, and Newton admitted that miners could make wages. But the miners found no rich bonanza either, and ultimately the reports from the 1875 expedition bordered on discouraging. Along French Creek, Jenney noted that water was in short supply for much of the year and that the shallowness of the stream and its slow rate of fall in the valley would make working placer deposits difficult. Dodge predicted that large investments in hydraulic equipment would be required to make these placers pay.[16] Even Moses "California Joe" Milner, one of the expedition's civilian scouts, acknowledged that while there was gold from the grass roots down, there was "*more gold* from the grass roots *up*," focusing on the lush agricultural potential of the countryside.[17] Jenney expressed the same sentiment. "There is gold enough to thoroughly settle and develop the country," he admitted, but concluded, "after the placers are exhausted, stock-raising will be the great business of the inhabitants."[18]

The civilian miners and exuberant soldiers working alongside the expedition's scientists, however, were undeterred. Dodge's soldiers got especially caught up in the excitement of discovery on French Creek and for several days worked with pans and rockers and proved themselves adept miners. Jenney reported rather matter-of-factly that recoveries of sixteen to twenty-six colors per pan were common in the beginning. One soldier found a piece of gold worth twenty cents, and another discovered a small nugget weighing a pennyweight, worth ninety-seven cents.[19] At the same time, the nation's newspapers openly derided the cautious opinions of the Columbia professors. In one instance, a correspondent for the *Omaha Daily Bee* charged, "While Prof. Jenney has stated *officially* that he could only find *one cent* to the pan, old miners panned out from 11¢ to 35¢ right under his nose, so to speak."[20] The Black Hills gold rush merely gained momentum.

As spring 1875 gave way to summer, news from the diggings took a new turn. At first, feature stories appearing in the region's newspapers consisted of near-verbatim copying of the expeditions' reports or promotional pieces that editors fabricated to position their communities as outfitting and gateway centers for the anticipated boom. While such promotional stories never disappeared from the Bismarck, Yankton, Sioux City, Omaha, Sidney, and Cheyenne newspapers, reports from actual Hillers writing letters home or articles derived from face-to-face interviews began to complement them. Occasionally these letters had a "busted" tone, coming from a dis-

Brigadier General George Crook, shown here in January 1877, commanded the United States Army's Department of the Platte and played critical roles in the Black Hills gold rush and subsequent Great Sioux War. He and Crawford crossed paths often in 1875 and 1876. *D.S. Mitchell photograph. Paul L. Hedren*

gruntled Argonaut who found little or no gold and talked of exaggerated prospects, arduous work, intolerable weather, and threats from Indians.[21] But far more common were letters extolling the richness of the diggings. One of the men with Jenney wrote that miners "are panning about ten dollars a day each, and think that when they get their sluices and rockers fixed it will pay from $40 to $50 per day."[22] Another early eyewitness reported miners making from $10 to $75 per day.[23] As the months passed, such accounts grew more specific and ever more enticing.

The army, meanwhile, continued its policing efforts, deploying troops to the gold country from as near as Camp Robinson, Nebraska, and as far as Fort Randall in southeastern Dakota Territory near Yankton. When miners were found, the soldiers escorted them to "civilization" (sometimes Fort Randall and the Missouri River; other times Sidney Barracks, Nebraska, and the Union Pacific Railroad; or more commonly Fort Laramie or Cheyenne). Chasing miners was fitful duty, and civilians proved adept at avoiding contact or, if cornered, at returning to the diggings with surprising speed. Dodge did little to participate in the evictions, focusing intently on the surveying work at hand. The result was ineffectual policing locally and a testy political imbroglio for the Ulysses Grant administration, especially on the eve of its dispatching commissioners to the Sioux agencies to negotiate for the purchase of the Black Hills. To gain some measure of control over the situation, Sheridan ordered Crook to visit the Hills personally and do whatever was necessary to expel the miners, particularly before the new commission commenced its work.[24]

Crook's mission to the Black Hills in July 1875 was a good show but achieved only modest results. He readily made his way to and explored the gold country, traveling from Omaha by way of Fort Laramie. To announce his intent, he liberally tacked a broadside proclamation on trees throughout the diggings that ordered the miners to convene, document their claims, and depart. Crook conversed with prospectors at every turn, expressing his reluctance at having to execute such an unpleasant duty, explaining and defending the government's difficult position, and cajoling all to go peaceably. The proclamation set a departure date of 15 August, but Crook first urged miners to assemble on French Creek no later than 10 August to draft resolutions that would secure their discoveries for the day when the country could be reoccupied. Many miners heeded Crook's directive and departed with him in mid-August, but the general acknowledged that some chose to dodge the troops. To harass and corral the unwilling, Crook detailed two companies of Ninth Infantry, commanded by Captain Edwin Pollock and drawn from Dodge's column, to establish a winter outpost called Camp G. H. Collins, where Custer City would blossom a few months later. The assembled miners had voted on the name Custer City before departing with Crook. The general also permitted seven miners to remain behind to guard personal property until the Black Hills were opened legally.[25]

After Crook departed, diggings and gulches continued to pulse with activity, despite Pollock's attempts at exercising his duty. The lingering bustle of the Dodge Expedition, which remained in the Hills into early October and shuffled a constant stream of men and wagons between that command and Pollock's camp on French Creek, was hubbub of one sort. Another was the fairly steady flow of military traffic (wagons and cavalry) between Pollock's camp and Fort Laramie as supplies were forwarded to support the presumed winter-long occupation. The small clutch of miners that Crook permitted to remain behind, ostensibly to guard prospecting equipment, and the continuous if quiet arrival of other miners evading the loose military cordon added another dimension to the commotion. While several hundred miners supposedly accompanied Crook from the Black Hills on 15 August, geologist Walter Jenney estimated that as many as one thousand to fifteen hundred men were actually working the placer gulches at the time. And then almost at once, circumstances changed dramatically. In late November, Pollock's two infantry companies unceremoniously withdrew from their Custer City camp and returned to Fort Laramie. Hillers may have sensed the changing situation, but they were doubtless unaware of matters on the national scene that had worked to the direct benefit of those still toiling in or seeking the gulches of the Black Hills.[26]

The attempt to purchase the Black Hills from the Sioux had proved a resounding failure. In September, government commissioners met with Red Cloud, Spotted Tail, and other headmen from the Oglala and Brulé bands residing along the White River in Nebraska to haggle over the worth of the Hills, but they were frustrated in attempts to reach a purchase agreement. In light of that failure and the ever-pressing demands to open the Black Hills, President Grant

Placer miners worked diggings and a sluice on the banks of French Creek in the vicinity of Custer City during the time of Dodge's expedition to the Black Hills in 1875. *Albert Guerin photograph. J. Leonard Jennewein Collection, Dakota Wesleyan University Archives, Mitchell, S.Dak.*

convened a small, unpublicized gathering in the White House on 3 November, attended by his secretaries of the interior and war, the commissioner of Indian affairs, and Generals Sheridan and Crook. Those present acknowledged the government's moral and legal obligation to protect the integrity of the Sioux reservation, a task made nearly impossible by the uncontrollable invasion and the mounting pressure to open the new gold country. Crook recounted his face-to-face meetings with miners, who had argued that it was their sovereign right as citizens to go and do as they pleased. In spite of the failed commission, Grant ultimately committed to a policy favoring the miners and all that that implied. Standing orders forbidding the occupation of the Black Hills were not to be rescinded, he cautioned, but the military would henceforth no longer obstruct such incursions. In short order, Pollock and the army were withdrawn from the interior and periphery of the Black Hills, and the steady if quiet gold rush became a frenzied tide.[27]

Illegal though it was, the rush was on, and it brought with it a colorful cast of genuine larger-than-life "characters," a wonderful Who's Who of the American West. Military officers like Custer, Dodge, and Crook played significant roles in the initial discoveries and, of course, already enjoyed illustrious reputations then and after. Boosters and pioneers like John Gordon, Charles Collins, and Annie Tallent, the latter heralded as the first white woman in the Black Hills, earned their reputations in the earliest days of the gold rush. The first black woman in the Black Hills had been Sarah Campbell, a cook accompanying Custer's 1874 expedition who was among the initial claimants on French Creek. Equally intriguing were monikered characters like Moses "California Joe" Milner, a notable plainsman, "Buckskin Jack" Rand, a Hiller noted in Sioux City for his unique dress and audacity in planning for and participating in the early rush; Martha "Calamity Jane" Canary, a harlot who actually wrangled a job as a teamster in the manly world of the Jenney Expedition; and "Colorado Charley" Utter, James Butler "Wild Bill" Hickok's pal.[28] This distinguished lot continued to swell as the gold rush gained momentum, the trails and gulches luring many with national prominence—Wild Bill Hickok himself, thespian Jack Langrishe, musician "Banjo Dick" Brown, Major Edward Wynkoop, and others. And the Hills also lured John Wallace Crawford, known initially to a few merely as "Ned," but soon enough to the nation and world as "Captain Jack, the Poet Scout of the Black Hills."

For all the notoriety Captain Jack Crawford earned as a plainsman and in a long life of letters as a published poet and thespian, little is known about his formative years. Born in Northern Ireland on 4 March 1847 to an impoverished family in an impoverished land, he and his siblings were left with an uncle when his parents emigrated to the United States, separately, in the mid-1850s. Young Crawford crossed the Atlantic, too, in 1861 and connected with his mother in Minersville, Pennsylvania. Crawford's father was absent, again, his departures from the family a common and trying occurrence. This time he had heeded President Abraham Lincoln's call for volunteers at the onset of the Civil War. Jack, meanwhile, took work in one of the anthracite coal mines of eastern Pennsylvania as a slate picker, one of the dirty, hazardous jobs available to young boys. Over the next several years, Crawford's employment varied but never strayed outside the dangerous work associated with the coal mines.[29]

Jack's father John was seriously wounded in the Battle of Antietam on 17 September 1862 and was discharged and returned home early in 1863 after a long hospital convalescence. A year later, he and Jack attended a local celebration in nearby Pottsville occasioned by the return of his regiment on furlough, and both father and son were drawn into the patriotic fervor coloring the event. John, encouraged surely by soldier comrades, reenlisted in his old outfit, the Forty-eighth Pennsylvania Volunteer Infantry, on 26 February 1864, and Jack enlisted on 7 March, a few days after his seventeenth birthday. Both Crawfords were assigned to the same company. Enlistment records provide a few scant details about Jack at this youthful age: height, five feet five inches; eyes, blue; hair, brown.[30]

Within weeks, the Forty-eighth Pennsylvania Volunteers returned to the war, joining Ambrose E. Burnside's Ninth Corps attached to Grant's Army of the Potomac. Young Jack's introduction to army life was brief and largely gained in transit as the regiment passed through Washington and on to Virginia, where it participated in the Battles of the Wilderness and Spotsylvania in May. During the latter engagement, both son and father were injured, Jack receiving a serious bullet wound in the right hip, and John a reeling head blow that fractured his skull. Jack was first tended at a field hospital in Fredericksburg and then Washington. He was eventually evacuated to the Satterlee General Hospital in West Philadelphia, one of the largest Union hospitals of the Civil War, particularly remembered for the nursing care provided by the Catholic Sisters of Charity.[31]

Young Crawford's convalescence was long and excruciating, doctors initially believing that his condition was precarious and near hopeless, but it was also life changing. After being bedridden for over nine weeks, Jack gradually mended and regained his mobility, though he ever after walked with a slight limp. This period of recovery is most significant, however, for the fact that one of the attending nuns encouraged the illiterate seventeen-year-old to learn to read and write and then served as his personal tutor. Jack proved an eager student despite the painful wound, and his first letter to his mother supposedly opened with the salutation "Deer Mother" and closed with "Yure woonded Sun." Jack recounted this transforming episode in his poetry collections and on the stage for the remainder of his life.[32]

Refusing an offered discharge from the army, Jack Crawford rejoined his regiment in November 1864 in time to participate in the protracted siege of Petersburg, Virginia. There he was wounded again, in the left foot, and evacuated to the field hospital at City Point on the James River that also served as General Grant's headquarters. In the waning days of the war, President Lincoln visited Grant at City Point and toured the hospital, where he shook young Crawford's hand. There, too, Jack penned new words to an old tune, "The Old Virginia Lowlands." To his pleasant surprise, the song became something of a regimental favorite. By the time Jack Crawford rejoined his regiment in late April, the war was over, and he and fellow soldiers were eventually mustered out. Jack returned home to his mother and struggling father, but he was a changed young man who had experienced the viciousness and suffering of war and was himself a twice-wounded veteran. Ever after, Crawford's bond with the veterans of the Civil War became, as one biographer noted, something of a religion to him as he tirelessly championed their causes and extolled their patriotism.[33]

In the late 1860s, Crawford settled into a working-class life, intermittently laboring in the coal mines, playing local baseball, and participating in the affairs of the Good Templars. Alcoholism was a continuing misery in his father's life, and on his mother's deathbed in 1867, Jack pledged his personal abstinence, doubtless spurred by his father's abuse and his mother's and family's anguish. Jack resisted drink ever after, even as he participated in the spirituous worlds of mining camps, Indian campaigns, and the American stage.[34]

Jack married young Maria Stokes in October 1869. The couple had known each other for several years, and were both active in the Girardville Good Templars. Jack was then postmaster of Girardville, a small town some ten miles north of Minersville and Pottsville. To this marriage came a daughter in 1870 and son in 1871, but it also bore signs of the younger Crawford's own wanderlust. He resigned his postmastership in mid-1871, about when his father died of complications from his second war wound, and dropped from the public record for several years. While Jack Crawford's marriage was never dissolved, it had the appearance of being one in name only, although two other children were born to it.[35] Crawford, mostly silent about these years, allowed that it was then that he "struck out for the wild West."[36]

Crawford's biographers have speculated about the roots of his fascination with the American West, suggesting the influence of dime novels, so many of which featured lurid Western themes, and of regular news from the West, which in the 1870s was still Indian country. It was the era of transcontinental railroads, buffalo hunters, and Custer in the Black Hills. During this unique time in America, actual Western personalities became stage heroes, a phenomenon, actually, with a long history in the American theater but brought to new focus in the embodiment of popular public figures like Buffalo Bill Cody, James Butler "Wild Bill" Hickok, and Christopher H. "Kit" Carson, who proved that buckskin and gunsmoke were the proper ingredients for box-office acclaim and success. In fact, a local appearance of Buffalo Bill's Combination Show may have piqued Jack's interest in the West. Cody brought his melodrama, *Scouts of the Prairie*, starring himself and John B. "Texas Jack" Omohundro, to the Pottsville theater in late May 1873. He returned to Pottsville with a new play, *Scouts of the Plains*, in mid-December of the same year. The new feature again starred himself and Texas Jack, but it also added Wild Bill Hickok as himself. Pottsville was the largest town in Crawford's neighborhood, and whether or not he attended these performances is unknown, but it is not improbable. By early 1876, Crawford had adopted for himself a Cody-Omohundro-Hickok-like persona, and he had to have been exposed to it somewhere. Moreover, Crawford, Cody, and Hickok would soon literally cross paths on one of the roads leading to the Black Hills.[37]

Twenty years later, in 1896, a former *Omaha Daily Bee* colleague wrote a recollection of Crawford, likely on the occasion of the Poet Scout's passing through Nebraska on his national lyceum tour that year. It offers a reflection on the twenty-eight-year-old at the time of his first appearance in Omaha in 1875. "He was in the depths of misfortune, friendless and alone," remembered John Harwood Pierce, who, bearing the *nom de plume* "Ranger" would join him in reporting on the Black Hills gold rush a year later. Crawford carried a letter of recommendation from Pennsylvania governor John F. Hartranft, the former commander of his Pennsylvania infantry brigade, dated 8 May 1875, and that date helps establish Crawford's initial venture

At the time of Jack Crawford's arrival, Omaha, Nebraska, was a substantial city. One of its prominent structures in 1875 was the "Cow Shed," visible in the right foreground covering the railroad tracks at the Union Pacific depot. *KM3TV/Bostwick-Frohardt Photograph Collection, Durham Museum, Omaha, Nebr.*

into the West and his arrival in Omaha. While the letter apparently had not yet opened any meaningful opportunities for Crawford, he wrangled a job as a watchman at the office of the *Omaha Daily Bee*, then Omaha's newest newspaper. One evening, Crawford vigorously fended off vandals at the newspaper office. Impressed with Crawford's fearlessness, and learning that he had talent with both pen and revolver, the owner and editor of the *Bee*, Edward Rosewater, outfitted him at a reported "considerable expense" and dispatched him to the Black Hills as a field correspondent. The Dodge-Jenney Expedition was just then organizing at Fort Laramie. Crawford's first adventure in the West was about to begin.[38]

1

WITH THE DODGE EXPEDITION, JUNE–AUGUST 1875

After Jack Crawford joined the Dodge Expedition in June 1875, he told his *Omaha Daily Bee* readers virtually nothing about himself or his travels from Omaha to Cheyenne, northward to Fort Laramie, and northward again to Camp Jenney, located on Beaver Creek near today's Newcastle, Wyoming. Dispatched by Edward Rosewater, owner-editor of the *Bee*, Crawford quietly found his way to Fort Laramie, where he apparently connected with a supply train captained by Andrew Burt of the Ninth Infantry. He ultimately reached the expedition on 23 June, when it was encamped on French Creek in the heart of the Black Hills. The movement of such supply trains between Fort Laramie and Dodge's camp was fairly routine throughout the long course of the 1875 exploration. From French Creek, Crawford wrote his first letter to readers of the *Bee* on 28 June.[1]

The precise nature of Crawford's role with the expedition, if any, is unstated in his correspondence and cannot be found in the historical record. If he viewed his duties as a newsman foremost, he certainly was the least heralded of that lot and, without a doubt, the least experienced. Among the professional journalists accompanying Dodge's expedition were Rueben B. Davenport, filing for the *New York Herald*, and Thomas C. MacMillan, writing for the *Chicago Inter-Ocean*. Several officers also doubled as reporters, including Second Lieutenant John G. Bourke, Third Cavalry, writing for the *San Francisco Alta California* and *Cin-*

cinnati Gazette; Captain Burt, filing for the *New York Tribune*; and Acting Assistant Surgeon J. R. Lane, contributing to the *Chicago Tribune*. Dodge, himself a meticulous diarist, mentioned all but Crawford. Neither Dodge nor other participants mentioned the *Bee* as a source of news from or about the expedition, despite the professional and personal interest surely existing among the staff officers of the army's Department of the Platte, headquartered in Omaha, which broadly oversaw Dodge's survey.[2]

That so many correspondents, formal and informal, reported on this expedition for newspapers from coast to coast speaks to the nation's growing fascination with the Black Hills. During Custer's exploration the year before, reporters from Saint Paul, Chicago, and New York had accompanied the expedition but largely focused their reports on the survey work. The new crop of writers provided readers with detailed descriptions of this still largely unknown territory, as well as speculations concerning its probable mineral wealth. The Black Hills possessed geological wonders, bountiful and diverse flora and fauna, and valuable ores, to be sure, but also great peril. It was Indian country, where trespass by whites was unlawful and would surely incur consequences. But the lure of gold trumped peril and politics, and the reporters filed interesting stories that barely hinted at any existing or foreseen danger.[3]

Crawford could well have been in Dodge's camp as an interloper, variously observing the business at hand, prospecting some, penning stories, and all the while staying below the level of visibility. It was probably quite easy to hide in the bustle if he found that necessary, and one senses that he did. With the coming and going of supply wagons from Fort Laramie and the relatively separate commotions in teamster and army camps, the hubbub was constant. Even so, uninvited civilians were seen as trespassers. A quip from Crawford later that he was among those expelled from the Black Hills, likely by Crook, suggests his own sense of the tenuousness of his visit.[4]

Crawford wrote two letters from the 1875 expedition. Crawford signed both letters "Ned". How he chose that pseudonym is unknown, and how it should be concluded that Ned is Jack Crawford is a matter of circumstantial evidence. To be sure, these letters from 1875 are delightfully literate and exhibit the same style and flair evident in Crawford's personally signed correspondence with the *Bee* a few months later. The *Bee* itself tipped the Crawford connection when he passed back through Omaha at the close of his initial Black Hills sojourn. The paper's 7 October 1875 personals column observed that Crawford had been, "for a time, traveling correspondent of the *Bee*." In 1875, the *Bee* had carried no other on-the-scene reporting from the Black Hills. Moreover, the likelihood of any other *Bee* correspondent lacing one of his letters with inconsequential poetry, as did NED and as would Jack in 1876, almost certainly lifts the veil.

In 1875, Crawford did not yet see news value in the commonplace of staging areas, trails, and associates, matters he would report on much more thoroughly when returning to the gulches in 1876. Instead, the news that *Bee* subscribers most wished to read had to do with gold, and on this matter Crawford was effusive. Two kinds of gold were to be found in the placer diggings, he told readers, flake and shot, and the farther north in the Black Hills one went, the coarser the gold. While it was not yet fair to judge the richness of the gold in the Black Hills, Crawford remarked in his second letter of 6 August with what would become his characteristic candor and reserve, gold had been found in many of the creeks prospected thus far, with the largest nugget yet seen worth "90 cts." At that time, the United States Treasury fixed the price of gold at $20.67 per troy ounce, but in the gulches, it typically varied in worth from $18.25 to $20 per troy ounce.[5] In 1876, Crawford repeatedly noted the worth of gold at $20 per ounce, and at that value, the 90¢ nugget weighed slightly less than one pennyweight, or about one-twentieth troy ounce. Remarkable nuggets and hefty daily cleanups from rockers and sluices would soon become commonplace news in the *Bee*, and other nuggets would dwarf this small one, but it was a start. In the end, of course, Jack Crawford's Black Hills stories then and to come were all about gold and rumors of gold.

[*Omaha Daily Bee*, 5 July 1875]

THE BLACK HILLS

(Special Correspondence of the BEE)

BLACK HILLS EXPEDITION,
CUSTER'S GULCH, FRENCH CREEK,
CAMP HARNEY, D. T., June 28, 1875.

EDITOR BEE:

Your correspondent would have written to you ere this, but as nothing of interest pertaining to the gold excitement happened till we reached the above camp, this first letter was delayed till I could take in the whole situation.

Camp Harney, where we are located, is situated in Custer's Gulch, on French Creek, about nine miles south of Harney's Peak, and at the stockade built by Gordon's party last winter, and 32 miles, a little north of east, of Camp Jenney, our first resting place, situated on the east fork of Beaver Creek. The composition of the expedition, as you are aware, was as follows: Col. R. I. Dodge, of the 23d Infantry, who is well known to the readers of the BEE, and therefore to the Omaha public generally, is Commander; Lt. M. C. Foot, of the 9th Infantry, Adjutant; Lt. J. G. Bourke, of 3d Cavalry, who, last Thursday with a detachment under Lt. R. A. Whitman, returned to Omaha via Fort Laramie and Cheyenne, is A. D. C [aide-de-camp].

The material wants of the inner man of the expedition (if 550 souls can be called one man) have been well considered and carefully provided for by Lt. J. F. Trout, whom grasshoppered Nebraska will not soon forget because of his efforts to ameliorate the sufferings of the thousands in the rural districts of your suffering State.

This gentleman accompanies the expedition as acting assistant quartermaster and assistant commissary sergeant. The bodily ailments are under the supervision of Drs. [George P.] Jacquette and Laine. Among the military officers who compose the escort are Maj. Burt, Capt. [Samuel] Munson, Capt. [Edward J.] Spaulding, Capt. [William] Hawley, Capt. [Gerald] Russell, Capt. [Henry W. Wessells] Wessell, Lieut. [Albert] King, Lieut. [Christopher T.] Hall, Lieut. [Joseph] Lawson, Lieut. [John H.] Coale, Lieut. [James E. H.] Foster, Lieut. [Frederick W.] Kingsbury, Lieut. [Charles] Morton and Lieut. [Hayden] DeLany. There were six companies of cavalry and two of infantry. Lieut. [Louis A.] Craig, who accompanied the expedition to Camp Jenney, returned to Fort Laramie to proceed to Arizona, in which territory he is now stationed.

You will remember the expedition left Fort Laramie on the 24th ultimo, and on the 25th took up its line of march to the Hills. The general direction of the route was northerly, crossing the streams known as the Raw Hide, Niobrara, Old Woman's Fork, South Cheyenne, Beaver and the east fork of the Beaver, situated in the southwestern portion of the Black Hills, and on whose banks our first permanent camp was located, and which we reached after a march of nine days' duration. Work was commenced at once by the construction of two redoubts on buttes commanding the camp and a commissary store-house, located in the centre of the command.

On June 5th Major Burt, with Co. "H," and Captain Munson, with Co. "C," 9th Infantry, returned to Fort Laramie with the train, to obtain 60 days' supplies for the whole command, and on the 9th, Col. Dodge, with an escort of three companies of cavalry, accompanied by Prof. Jenney and party, started for the north boundary of Harney's Peak. They moved up the east fork of Beaver creek to the north, following the trail used by the Indians in their journeys to and from the region known as the Big Horn and Powder rivers country. Leaving this trail, in sight of Inyan Kara [a distinctive Black Hills mountain peak], they struck off to the north and east, coming upon the divide which separates the waters of the north and south forks of the Big Cheyenne, and after traversing a deep ravine came upon Custer's trail and into Floral Valley, during a rain and snow storm, encountered the second day out.

The line of march was taken up from this point to the divide, situated southeast of Floral Valley Camp, and was extended over the divide down the valley drained by a stream named Castle Creek, so called by General Custer, on his expedition to the Hills last summer. A camp was made near the confluence of Castle and Rapid creeks, and four miles further on.

The panning out of color, in the last named stream, was the occasion of Prof. Jenney remaining there for three days, while Colonel Dodge, with two companies, pushed forward to the present camp, passing through Custer's Park and Custer's Gulch to the stockade. Prof. Jenney followed after the three days' examination of Rapid Creek.

Immediately after the arrival of the command under Col. Dodge prospecting commenced, and everywhere that earth was panned, color was found.

It was discovered that several miles up the gulch and on French Creek, that mining parties had staked claims. No fewer than four different companies had been formed, numbering in all twenty-four men. On the arrival of the military, these at once put themselves in an attitude of defense, but on being informed that it was not the intention of the military to molest or interfere with them, they came out from behind the rocks in which they had ensconced themselves. They stated, on being questioned, that they had been in the Hills a number of weeks, the latest arrivals having left Fort Laramie on the heel of the expedition, and reaching the gulch a few days previous to our entrance. From them were obtained numerous specimens of dust, some of which doubtless you have already seen, and a sample of which I will send you. The particles of gold panned out in the gulch indicate that there are two kinds to be found in the placer diggings, namely flake and shot gold. The former, that is the flake, occurs in the more immediate vicinity of Camp Harney, while the latter, the shot gold, has been panned out in the diggings higher up.

With the caution of a scientist, Prof. Jenney is inclined to view the field as containing diggings, which on the whole, would not pay sufficient to warrant prospecting by the ordinary miner.

The miners, on the contrary, take a view of an entirely different nature. Those who have been here for six weeks claim that each additional day has given them proof undoubted of the wealth of the country.

To fortify this position they cite the fact of their sending men, money and mules to Fort Laramie, Red Cloud Agency and Sidney for supplies to aid in prosecuting their labors in developing their claims. As a further proof of this I may state that on last Saturday 34 miners were added to the number already on the ground.

This company left Fort Laramie last Monday (21st) with six wagons loaded with a plentiful supply of provisions and mining implements with which to carry forward their work. This makes probably about 100 miners scattered throughout various portions of the Hills. Meantime, as may be imagined, everything is at a stand still in view of the suspension of negotiations for the purchase of this vast and valuable country.

The rapid impressions here given would utterly fail to convey anything like an accurate conception of the events and incidents of the journey from our starting point to the present camp.

I can only refer briefly to observations made along the route. While the culmination of our discoveries has been keyed in the finding of gold, my remarks would be crude and imperfect if they concluded at this stage. The Hills have well earned their name from the dark green forests with which they are clothed. From the moment of sighting them until we penetrated to the granite peaks that skirt this side of the Hills, the views have been as changing as those of a panorama, and as rugged and grand as ever inspired artist's brush or poet's pen. In the vicinity of Camp Jenney, buttes or hills, as they are known throughout Dakota and Wyoming, frowned above us by the thousand feet; valleys with wandering streams, streaking the low lands with silver waters, verdant banks bordering the streams, while to the north the hillocks grow into knolls of white gypsum that were miles in extent. The pine forests, however, held themselves aloof from us until the command came upon Custer's trail, and we struck the land of granite and gold.

The pine trees scattered throughout Custer's Park and Gulch are, in themselves, a mine of wealth. My observation has been that they will average in diameter from 16 to 22 inches, and yield a timber not inferior for building purposes to that of the Michigan and Wisconsin forests.

There are also groves of oak, patches of elm, strips of a species of box elder, some little cottonwood, any quantity of white birch, and other arborial growths, companions of these. Here we found the old time gooseberries large enough to be tempting; strawberry vines covered with blossoms; blackberries here and there; wild cherries, enough to start a pectoral factory; and wild plums in abundance.

The land in the little valleys has a rich alluvial soil, several feet in thickness, and is covered with a heavy grass that makes excellent grazing.

French Creek, which rises in the hills to the west of us, and pursues its course down the gulch through our camp and past the stockade, is fed by numerous lesser streams, springing out of the hills, and perennially flowing toward the Big Cheyenne.

Within a circle of a quarter of a mile we are treated to four different kinds of water,—the creek, with its source among the distant hills, a fine spring oozing from a gravelly bed, and an iron and sulphur spring, in close proximity to each other.

At present engineering and geological parties have gone out from camp—the one to the south under Dr. V[alentine] T. McGillicuddy, the other to the south under Prof. W. P. Jenney.

It is anticipated that the present camp will be broken about July 15th or 20th, and the expedition will take up its line of march for Bear Lodge by way of Castle Creek, Floral Valley, Inyan Kara, and thence north to the peak named. Here the next permanent camp will be located, about September 1st, and the country examined as this has been and will be before our departure.

The hills on the north will be circled, the streams explored, and the valleys prospected all the way round, touching Bear Butte, and coming down on the eastern side between the hills and the foot hills to their extreme southeastern limit. The exploration of the Hills accomplished, it is Prof. Jenney's intention to proceed to the White Earth Creek country, reported by Prof. [Othniel C.] Marsh to contain vast fossil deposits. The programme will take in the carrying out until the middle of October, at which time, we will again seek civilization and join as heartily as the boys do now about their camp-fires in singing the ditty to the tune of "When Johnny comes marching home":

When Jenney's work in the Hills is done,
  Hurrah! Hurrah!
When Jenney's work in the Hills is done,
  Hurrah! Says I!
When Jenney's work in the Hills is done,
We'll send his bones to Washington,
And we'll all feel gay
When Walter comes marching home.

NED.

[*Omaha Daily Bee*, 19 August 1875]

THE BLACK HILLS GOLD REGION

(Special Correspondence of the Bee)

BLACK HILLS EXPEDITION,

Camp Crook, on Rapid Creek, D.T.

August 6, 1875.

There has been a great deal of work done since the command arrived at Camp Harney on French Creek. The work for which Prof. Jenney came to the Hills has progressed with great rapidity and has met with a most desirable success. Prospect holes were sunk at many points along French Creek, and colors were found in all. The largest nugget that I have seen taken from there was by a miner named Shaw, about six miles above the stockade, weighing 90 cts. The soldiers, for several days, were very busy panning out gold, but soldier-fashion, being tired of work, they quit, only to start to life again, by one more industrious than the rest, finding a very nice color and showing it. Thus time passed in the camp while Prof. Jenney and his party were kept continually in the mountains, mapping, taking astronomical and geographical surveys, and at the same time stereoscopic views, the latter part of the work devolving upon Mr. [A. Guerin] Guevin, of St. Louis. Whatever is said concerning the mineral value of the Hills, the half cannot be written of the beauty of them. Whichever way you turn, at every step you take, new scenes meet the eye, presenting a beautiful, yes grand, panorama; here a high, bald peak towering up towards heaven, while from its base a velvety lawn slopes gracefully down to the rolling stream, while again we have a long, high ridge rising abruptly from the bank of the creek, and upon whose sides the lofty pine with its shady foliage forms a picture which must be seen to be appreciated. Beautiful tracts of prairie land lay along the streams in intervals, some extending for one and two miles in length, which from these, entrance is had to small gulches, rich in grazing, and enabling us to herd 1,000 head of stock for four weeks within a radius of three miles without in the least running them down, but on the contrary, enabling them all, when leaving there, to appear in a most desirable condition. The grazing in these gulches and along the creek could not be bettered in the country, and lucky indeed is he who, when this country shall have been opened to the public, can obtain one of the numerous situations described above.

As to the vegetation of the country, although this is probably rather early to say anything about it, lettuce, peas and a few other early vegetables were raised by a miner about five miles above the stockade, and who reached the Hills early in the spring.

Parties were continually arriving and it is estimated that nearly a thousand miners were in the Hills at one time, but I think from careful inquiry, and from casual remarks gleaned at different intervals, that 500 would cover the whole number.

These men are scattered throughout the Hills, and there are so many crevices, which form a natural seclusion from observation, that it would be very hard to [find] one twenty-fifth part of them [were] they disposed to conceal themselves. Mining operations on this creek were in full blast, when a report was circulated that General Crook, with two companies of cavalry, was on his way to the Hills for the purpose of removing all miners from the same, and then there was a scrambling. Provisions, wagons, and a great many other goods were cashed (buried) and each sought his hole, while the stream presented a deserted look.

Finding it to be a false alarm, one by one they crawled from their hiding places, and everything "went merry as a marriage bell," till the report came in from Spring Creek, about twenty-four miles north of Camp Harney, that Prof. Jenney had found richer diggings, and again French Creek seemed deserted, and all wished to locate on that newly found grounds. Prof. Jenney had already established a camp there with an escort of two companies of infantry. On the 19th of July Col. Dodge, with two companies of cavalry, left Camp Harney, and passing by where the infantry are stationed, cut over the country to the present camp. On the 25th of the month the remainder of the command, under Captain Hawley, followed.

The country through which we passed was more broken than that heretofore experienced by the command, and the scenery accordingly more grand. Cathedral-like cliffs, at intervals along the road, rise in their grandeur and recall the stories of ruins of olden times as reported by eastern travelers, and making them seem more natural by the striking resemblance to the pictures which are handed down to us as representatives of the same. Canyons, which on first entering would seem to have no outlet, presenting to the view nothing but high walls; but on pushing our way through with many crooks and turns, opened out to beautiful valleys, rich with grass knee deep. Would that I had the gift to write the lines that should be written on

From Camp Harney on French Creek, Lieutenant Colonel Richard Dodge's troops supported a second mineral survey in 1875 that confirmed the presence of gold in the Black Hills in paying quantities. *Albert Guerin photograph. J. Leonard Jennewein Collection, Dakota Wesleyan University Archives, Mitchell, S.Dak.*

the beauties of the Hills. Words cannot describe them, and the best idea of them, next to seeing, can be obtained from the photographer, who will probably have enough views to satisfy those who may wish them, and they will all more than satisfy the most fastidious. After traveling about four miles over hills and through rich and fertile valleys, we struck a large tract of open prairie. It consisted of rolling ground, and the soil was very dark, while on every side could be seen croppings of iron ore in all conceivable shapes. A very fine collection of curiosities could be made in this country.

Stones of all colors and formation can be found; among the most prominent are the white and rose quartz, which are found in large quantities; on French Creek garnets are also plenty, while here and there can be found petrified wood. On leaving the high prairie land we followed down a long dry gulch leading to Rapid Creek, on which is our present camp. On every side could be seen the blazed trees, while others were fallen, some shattered to pieces with the force of lightning.

Thunder showers are plentifully strewn in in our campaign, and we are often invited to a shower bath which, although inexpensive, are sometimes decidedly unpleasant. The gold digging on this creek has not been carried on so extensively as at the other two mentioned above. What has been found is of a coarser quality, and the facts seem to be that the farther north you get, the coarser the gold. It would be hardly fair to judge of the richness of gold in the Hills, but it is the fact that *gold has been found* on all the creeks that have, thus far, been prospected.

On Castle Creek, a tributary of Rapid, 15 miles north, gold has been found of still coarser quality. The general direction of the gold-bearing section of the hills seems to be N. N. W. by S. S. E, and extends as far as now known, over a territory of from 35 to 40 miles in length, and from east to west, from the backbone of the hills (whence flow the network of streams to the Cheyenne), to the foot hills.

Quartz leads are found in great numbers, but the value of them cannot be determined until they have been assayed, but they have a good look, while in come specimens traces of gold is found.

On Wednesday, July 27th, General Crook, with Colonel [Major Thaddeus H.] Stanton, paymaster, Captain Pollock, Captain Mix, Major [Second Lieutenant Charles] Morton, and several other army officers and a party of citizens, arrived in camp and created quite a stir. On Friday part of the party started on a hunt, and on the first day killed sixteen deer, one elk, and one mountain sheep; on the second day the result of their labor was ten deer. The spoils were divided among the troops and teamsters.

The most interesting item in regard to General Crook's coming out here is, how did the miners receive him? I have already stated that they had one scare, which having blown over, every miner, setting it down in his own mind as such, resumed work. The general's advent was so sudden and unexpected that it caught them napping. Everything was abandoned, and the men flew to the hills. Incidents are cited of some preparing to defend themselves against the troops,

PROCLAMATION!!!

WHEREAS the President of the United States has directed that no miners, or other unauthorized citizens, be allowed to remain in the Indian reservation of the Black Hills, or in the unceded territory to the west, until some new treaty arrangements have been made with the Indians:

And WHEREAS, by the same authority, the undersigned is directed to occupy said reservation and territory with troops, and to remove all miners and other unauthorized citizens, who may be now, or may hereafter come into this country in violation of the treaty obligations:—

Therefore, the undersigned hereby requires every miner and other unauthorized citizen to leave the territory known as the Black Hills, the Powder river, and Big Horn country by and before the 15th day of August next.

He hopes that the good sense and law abiding disposition of the miners will prompt them to obey this order without compelling a resort to force.

It is suggested that the miners, now in the hills, assemble at the military post about to be established at Camp Harney, near the stockade on French creek, on or before the 10th day of August.

That they, then and there hold a meeting, and take such steps as may seem best to them, by organization and drafting of proper resolutions, to secure to each, when this country shall have been opened, the benefit of his discoveries and the labor he has expended.

(Signed) GEORGE CROOK,

Brigadier General, U. S. A,
Com'g Dep't of the Platte.

Camp Crook, D. T.,
July 29, 1875.

In 1875, General Crook plastered copies of this 8 x 10-inch proclamation throughout the Black Hills placer diggings, serving notice that miners and other unauthorized citizens must leave the Hills before 15 August 1875. Crook's eviction largely failed, and the gold rush continued apace. *Paul L. Hedren*

not wishing to share the fate of some who were caught on their way to the Hills. After a short parley and being assured that the intention of the troops was not to arrest them, they came out from their hiding-places and commenced operations again. On the 29th of July the general issued a proclamation ordering miners and all other unauthorized citizens to leave the Hills by the 15th of August, and advised them to hold a meeting about the 10th to consult and organize, and to pass such resolutions as would secure for them the benefits of their discoveries.

The miners all seemed to think very favorably of General Crook's plan and speak very highly of the courteous and gentlemanly manner in which he treated them.

In case more miners should come in, a temporary post has been established at the stockade with troops sufficient to make it very disagreeable, if not dangerous, for a miner to be seen.

The wagon train goes in tomorrow to obtain another month's rations, which will run us until the 15th of October. On the 8th instant Col. Dodge and staff, with two companies of cavalry, will leave here for Camp Harney, to attend the meeting of miners on the 10th, and to prevent any disturbance if such a thing should threaten.

The weather here is delightfully comfortable, and while you are probably weltering in the hot rays of an August sun, we are enjoying the delicious breezes from the mountain peaks, and sleep very comfortably under four or five blankets. More anon.

NED.

2

ON THE TRAIL TO CUSTER CITY, JANUARY–FEBRUARY 1876

For reasons never explained, Jack Crawford abandoned Dodge's Black Hills expedition about a month before the survey concluded. His second letter from the Hills was dated 6 August 1875 and helps frame his length of stay. He may simply have traveled to Fort Laramie in mid-August with one of the supply trains and continued on to Cheyenne, where he connected with an east-bound Union Pacific train for Omaha. Or, just as likely, he may have departed with General Crook in mid-August, counted among the several hundred miners willingly and calmly escorted from the Black Hills at the conclusion of the general's visit. In Crawford's unpublished Black Hills reminiscence, he noted that he had been "twice captured by the troops and removed from the Black Hills."[1] That detail does not particularly square with the sense of openness and purpose one senses in his 1875 letters, or the simple and frank manner in which the *Bee* spoke of their "correspondent in the Hills." Then again, perhaps he really was an interloper with no established cover.

In a certain way, of course, removal by the army was something of a badge of honor or measure of credibility among the early Black Hillers, even if only once and with Crook. Neither records at Fort Laramie nor the Cheyenne or Sidney newspapers noted Crawford's passing south, suggesting that he had done little as yet to elevate his visibility.

But that was about to change. A bit of Crawford doggerel, a three-stanza poem titled "Under the Sod," about a cowboy burial on the plains, appeared in the *Bee* on 18 September 1875 and helps date his travel from the Hills. The ditty was signed simply "J.W.C."

On 7 October, a brief item in the *Bee* recorded that Crawford passed through Omaha. The item gave him the title "Captain" for the first time. Crawford's use of this honorific military title has confounded his biographers ever since. An early writer suggested that his adoption of the sobriquet somehow dated or derived from the time of his discharge from the Forty-eighth Pennsylvania Volunteers at the close of the Civil War, and that perhaps it was an entitlement emanating from his having been wounded. But Crawford was a mere teenage private at the time, and enlisted men, wounded or not, received no such recognition beyond the imaginary. Others have suggested that Crawford earned the title because he headed the Black Hills Rangers, but that was an affiliation yet to come, and he was never in command.[2] Another writer supposed that, during Crawford's days as a civilian scout consorting with the regular army during the Indian wars, he "thought of himself as 'Captain,' and . . . he was immensely pleased with his association with commissioned officers."[3] That line of reasoning is partly accurate, but the sequencing is wrong. While Crawford's connections to the Indian wars were yet to come, by 1875, he had been exposed to and almost surely befriended a number of commissioned army officers, starting with Captain Andrew Burt of the Dodge Expedition.

Yet another writer suggested in 1886 that Crawford gained the title of Captain Jack because of "his devotion and loyalty to the principles of justice, patriotism, and humanity."[4] This explanation, too, may have been part of the story, but by 1875 Crawford had not yet developed much of a public character that exuded those qualities, and this conclusion, like others, seems premature. Almost surely what was occurring, however, was the careful honing of Crawford's self-image and the budding of a public persona, instilled by exposure to men like Buffalo Bill, Texas Jack, Wild Bill, and California Joe and officers like Burt, Dodge, and Crook. The adoption of a military title was but one facet of this transformation, and when Crawford was next seen in Omaha, in late December 1875 before embarking again for the Black Hills, his makeover was virtually complete in appearance, dress, and title. Crawford now sported an ornamented, broadcollared shirt, beaded gaiters, knee-length fringed-leather coat, broad-brimmed hat, shoulder-length hair, and dapper mustache and goatee, all marking the character elements of a plainsman, at least as Cody, Omohundro, and Hickok led audiences to perceive them. And he was no longer Ned or merely J. W. C., but "Captain Jack Crawford," and he had set out to become the "Poet Scout of the Black Hills."[5]

Crawford had gone east in October 1875 to Indianapolis, said the *Bee*, to go into business, the nature of which was both undisclosed and apparently short-lived. By 27 December, he had returned to Omaha and was organizing his return to the Black Hills, again as a paid correspondent for the newspaper. Crawford was actually one of two reporters the paper engaged to cover the gold rush. John Harwood Pierce, writing as "Ranger," was then embarking on the Union Pacific Railroad for cities like North Platte, Sidney, Cheyenne, and Laramie as a "special telegraphic correspondent." Pierce's lengthy reports focused on the bustle in those communities, especially as linked to the gold rush, and featured the prominent citizens encountered along the way and the coming and going of Hillers. Dispatched to Omaha by telegraph, Pierce's stories had a distinct immediacy about them. Crawford, meanwhile, was bound straight for the central Black Hills and filed his letters by mail, usually via Sidney and occasionally Cheyenne, from where they traveled to Omaha by rail. The vagaries of mail service from the Black Hills at a time when delivery contracts and routes were not yet established caused Crawford's correspondence to lag far behind Pierce's.[6]

Crawford reached the Black Hills by way of the so-called Sidney route, meaning that he traveled from Omaha to Sidney on the Union Pacific Railroad and then journeyed overland from Sidney to Custer City. The route north as far as Red Cloud Agency, 120 miles distant on the White River, was "a good government road," having served since 1874 as a regular avenue from the railroad to the Red Cloud and Spotted Tail Indian agencies and Camps Robinson and Sheridan, all in far northwestern Nebraska in the Pine Ridge country.[7] As yet, no bridge spanned the North Platte River on this road, and Crawford's crossing in January, slogging through water and ice as he relates in his letter of the seventh, was memorable. The route from Red Cloud to Custer City was less well defined but generally aligned straight north from the agency to a passageway into the Hills at Buffalo Gap. The road then followed Beaver Creek northwestward to near Point of Rocks and turned directly north to Custer City.[8]

Editor Rosewater of the *Bee* coyly noted in his paper that every road west of the Missouri River lead directly to the Black Hills and that every town in Nebraska and Wyoming was the best outfitting and starting point for the diggings. Rosewater declared that the *Bee* would not disparage any locality. But the paper's Nebraska biases were evident all along, and Crawford, doubtless with Rosewater's quiet encouragement, proved a tireless advocate for the Sidney route, reminding readers repeatedly that it was variously seventy, eighty, or ninety miles shorter than the always more popular Cheyenne route, supposedly less troubled by Indians and road agents, and better watered, grassed, and wooded. His facts were skewed greatly, particularly early on. The Sidney route was perhaps a dozen miles shorter at best, and partisans in Cheyenne offered comparable claims for their road, rightly boasting that Fort Laramie and its nearby iron bridge across the North Platte River helped make that road both safe and practical. Until mid-1876, Fort Laramie possessed the only bridge spanning the North Platte. Throughout the rush, neither Sidney nor Cheyenne conceded any quality or attribute to the other routes, and both roads were in fact heavily used, especially after the so-called Clarke bridge on the Sidney route opened in June. A small complement of troops constructed and occupied a blockhouse on the river's north bank at that crossing to guard the new bridge and trail.[9]

While Crawford paused in Sidney to arrange his travel north, sample the local entertainment, and gossip with and about the locals, he also wrangled an additional reporting assignment from Joseph B. Gossage, editor of the *Sidney Telegraph*. In the months ahead, Captain Jack's by-line appeared occasionally in that newspaper, too, and his letters never exactly duplicated the reports he provided the *Bee*. The first one, written on 23 January, appeared in the *Telegraph* on 12 February. Crawford's acquaintance with Gossage and the *Telegraph* would bring him additional attention.

During Crawford's brief time in Sidney, he had learned of the death of a man he identified only as Carrol. Crawford speculated in his 23 January letter that his killer, Harveson, would most certainly be acquitted. John Carrol was a soldier in Company C, Third Cavalry, stationed at nearby Sidney Barracks. His killer was William B. Habison, proprietor of the Cosmopolitan Saloon, a "low den and dance house" located just south of the Sidney railroad depot. In a row on Christmas night 1875, Habison struck Carrol on the head with a pistol, the hammer fracturing his skill. He died two days later. A friendly Sidney jury did indeed acquit Habison, and the story had a strange ending. An army surgeon removed a portion of Carrol's skull for evidence in the Habison trial. The skull specimen was then forwarded to the Army Medical Museum in Washington, D.C., and exhibited at the Centennial Exhibition in Philadelphia, a perfect specimen, so the surgeon deemed, of a "punctured fracture." Doubtless, Carrol's skull fragment survives in Washington to this day.[10]

Along the way north, Crawford befriended an array of individuals who would figure repeatedly in his letters. Zeb or Zebedee Swearington, a name Crawford repeatedly misspelled and whom some have mistakenly confused with saloon keeper Al Swearingen (who will appear later in Crawford's letters), was a Black Hills pioneer and tireless promoter most recently from Sioux City and the California gold country. Swearington claimed to have made his way to the Hills with, or shortly after, the arrival of the first Gordon party in late 1874 and to have been among those expelled by the army. He also claimed to have been with the second Gordon party, which the army intercepted north of the Niobrara River in May 1875, but he still found his way into the Hills and was actively prospecting when the Dodge Expedition arrived, only to be expelled again, this time by Crook. On that occasion, Swearington supposedly took with him some fifteen ounces of placer gold to show in Washington, D. C., and later crossed paths with Crawford in Indianapolis. Swearington was Crawford's guide from Sidney northward in January.[11]

Other new Crawford acquaintances included John W. Dear, a licensed Indian trader at Red Cloud Agency,[12] from which point Crawford wrote on 13 January. While the miners, all still illegal, had reason to fear the Indians, they had no trouble with the Lakotas from either the Red Cloud or Spotted Tail agency, although Crawford's letters foreshadow the trouble to come. Crawford even encountered the famous Spotted Tail for whom the latter agency was named. In his first letter to the *Sidney Telegraph*, written on 23 January, Crawford introduced Ed Current, a genial prospector who opened his cabin to Jack when he arrived in Custer City. Crawford's long letter published in the *Bee* on 26 February briefly mentioned Judge William L. Kuykendall, a lawyer and Custer City organizer who would later preside at the Hickok murder trial in Deadwood (Kuykendall was another name that Crawford repeatedly misspelled). In the same letter, the *Bee* correspondent mentioned Richard "Banjo Dick" Brown, who would become one of his closest Black Hills friends. Brown was a traveling musician who already enjoyed a certain acclaim in the West and who had most recently entertained barroom and theater audiences in Denver and Cheyenne. Brown is best remembered as the composer of the iconic ballad "The Black Hills," sung throughout the Black Hills diggings and the American West and remembered ever after by the even more apt title "The Dreary Black Hills."

In two of his early letters, Crawford also obliquely mentioned another Black Hills character who was already of note in some circles, although apparently not his, or so he led his readers to believe. Three miles west of Custer City, up French Creek, was Calamity Bar, a mining prospect providing a good yield and named, Crawford acknowledged in his *Bee* letter published on 19 February, for Calamity Jane, "a woman who accompanied the soldiers last summer." Martha "Calamity Jane" Canary had, indeed, been in the Hills in 1875, lurking among the teamsters of the Dodge-Jenney Expedition. Her presence was widely known among the expedition's officers and civilians, who made light of it. Certainly Crawford could well have encountered her then. In a remembrance of Canary written in 1904, Crawford purported that he, as an assistant marshal in Custer City, had arrested her there in 1876 for intoxication and disorderly conduct.[13] Crawford is puzzlingly silent about such doings in his correspondence, though he did sign several of his Black Hills letters with a twist to his name, "Calamity Jack."

During the time that Crawford was wending his way to the gold fields, the *Omaha Daily Bee* featured a steady flow of other Black Hills news. On 9 January 1876, Rosewater interviewed Captain Edwin Pollock, whom Crook had charged in Custer City with the task of denying access to the diggings; Pollock had been recalled from that duty in November. Despite the onset of winter, work in the gulches continued, Pollock acknowledged, though miners could only work half days and had to allow water to accumulate in the other half. All the creeks showed good gold prospects, he declared, and in his opinion, the best way to the Black Hills was by way of Fort Laramie and its new iron bridge across the North Platte. A week later, the

Edward Rosewater owned and edited the *Omaha Bee,* the city's leading newspaper in the nineteenth century. Rosewater tirelessly promoted the Black Hills gold country and dispatched a succession of field reporters to cover the rush, beginning with Jack Crawford. *Nebraska State Historical Society, RG2411-PH-0-4772-3*

Bee reproduced an interview with Professor Walter Jenney that had first appeared in the *Chicago Inter-Ocean*. Jenney's calculated reticence over the worth of the Black Hills gold country apparent in his official reports had now become unabashed enthusiasm, especially as he kept learning of impressive gold discoveries in the gulches, including nuggets worth twenty-one dollars and twenty-seven dollars that were supposedly the largest gold pieces yet recovered.[14] In a *Bee* editorial, Rosewater crowed that the ever cautious Jenney had now become "unreserved in his conclusions about the mineral wealth of the Black Hills."[15]

Reports of other gold recoveries continued to provide headlines. On 11 February, the *Bee* reprinted a Black Hills "Letter from an Old Montanian" that reported plentiful game, a pleasant winter thus far, and good recoveries of gold: $1.25 per pan—three pans in succession—and an instance of $28.75 in one pan.[16] By 7 February, Crawford, too, was heralding phenomenal gold recoveries, including instances of a single pan yielding $34 because of the recovery of a single nugget valued at more than thirty dollars. He, however, cautioned against too-great enthusiasm. Experienced practical miners generally understood that over time, stream gravels agitated in periods of high water, that placer gold had a way of progressively drifting downstream and migrating to bedrock, and that gold collected in the natural riffles of bedrock seams. These miners knew that the fine gold characterizing the French Creek placers had drifted considerably from its sources, while evidence of coarser gold suggested a nearness to sources. Bedrock enrichments were known as pay streaks, and almost surely placer recoveries as astounding as $28.75 and $34 to the pan were uniquely coming from these endlessly sought-for and exceedingly rare phenomenon. But experienced miners also understood that the theories of gold movement in streambeds were merely that, and that only physically demanding and tiresome work yielded rewards.[17] As Captain Jack cautioned, not everyone would reap a reward.

[*Omaha Daily Bee*, 6 January 1876]

ON TO THE BLACK HILLS.

(Correspondence of the BEE.)

SIDNEY, NEB., Jan 4.

EDITOR BEE:

We are now packing our teams, and will start to-morrow morning about 8 o'clock for the Hills. There are ten men in the party ready to go to-morrow, while the balance will wait for the next outfit. We are all stopping at the American House, and Messrs. Williams & Co., the proprietors, are doing all they can to make us comfortable; we are sorry that we must so soon leave his table and the delicious buffalo steaks.

There are plenty of teams on their way here from Spotted Tail, and those wishing to come this way will find ample accommodations and good outfits. Our party bought their own teams, which are oxen, as we can make beef of them when we get to the Hills if necessary. Good ox teams can be bought here for from $65 to $100, and wagons for about the same. Mr. Geo. W. Dudley furnishes flour, bacon, etc., as cheap as it can be bought in Omaha at retail, and Mr. H. Behan furnishes good ponies for saddle business for from $30 to $80. In fact whole outfits can be purchased very cheap, as the business men offer good inducements to Black Hillers.

There will be three teams of oxen and six horses in our party, and as your humble servant has a good horse, purchased from Mr. Behan, antelope are likely to suffer, as we will have ample time to hunt on the way. Sidney is lively at present. Billy Harveson's Varieties are crowded nightly with a mixed audience of soldiers and citizens. Ben Brown, formerly with Robinson's minstrels, is stage manager, and is a fine performer. Billy Brace is a young comedian of much promise, and is a great favorite among the boys.

Shooting is on the decline since the death of Carrol. Harveson is under $5,000 bail to appear at the next term of court. He had over $50,000 on his bond, and has the sympathy of nearly everybody, and it is asserted by nearly every one that he will be acquitted.

Buffalo meat is plenty, and jack rabbits are found five miles from here in great numbers.

I will now close, as we have little time to load up and get ready. Will write you from Red Cloud, which is 120 miles from here. Oh! ye gods; think of it,

Twenty miles a day,
On beans and hay,
And oxen for to drive.

JACK.

P.S. Mr. Z. Swaringer is our guide, and Mr. William McCue has charge of the party and we are second in command.

J.

[*Omaha Daily Bee*, 15 January 1876]

ON TO THE BLACK HILLS.

(Correspondence of the BEE.)

NORTH BANK OF PLATTE,

January 7, 1876.

In my last letter I stated that we were about leaving Sidney for the Hills. Mr. Smiley, with three others, started with the wagon and made thirty miles from 10 A.M. on Wednesday till 11 P.M. Had to make the time on account of not being able to find water. We, on horseback, did not start till 10 a.m. yesterday, and came up with the team and outfit at 10 p. m., having made forty-five miles. Last night was pretty cold, and we all bunked together and slept very comfortable; but this morning came the tug of war. The river was frozen over, yet not hard enough to bear, and we had to cut the ice over half a mile across the Platte. We unloaded part of our stuff, and started with about half of it. We got into the river and hauled the wagon across on the ice, nearly half way, where we again unloaded, and making a sled out of the front board of our wagon, we hauled our flour, twenty hundred, to a sand bar. We each worked hard, and waded into the water knee deep, and after getting across every man was wet and cold, but we managed to make a good fire, dry our socks, and get away with a good supper of venison, pork and coffee. And now while I am writing on the north bank of the Platte, sitting beside the camp-fire while the boys are packing the wagon, I feel just as comfortable as if I was in the office of the BEE. Chimney Rock is plainly visible from here standing like a smokestack on a point of bluff, which looks like a huge hay-stack about ten miles distant. Court House Rock is on the other side of the river due south and is an ornament to the plain. It can be seen for twenty miles very distinctly.

We are now 75 miles from Red Cloud and 165 miles from the Hills. We expect twenty miles per day from now on. Mr. Wm. McCue, who is our main stay, and a good fellow, makes things lively. He is always cheerful and the first to lend a hand in an emergency. Reports reached here to-day of shooting at Red Cloud, but anything definite could not be ascertained.

It is now growing late so I will have to close, as we will be turning in for the night. I will write you again either from Red Cloud or Custar City if we keep our hair.

SNAKE CREEK, Jan. 10th.

Have not met the stage yet—expect to meet it to-day.

Camped night before last at Red Willow about 6 p. m. A snow and wind storm came up and blew almost a hurrican[e]. It cleared up yesterday and we hauled out about noon; arrived here on Snake Creek about 7 p. m. We are now about 47 miles from Red Cloud. The roads are now in excellent condition and there is not two inches of snow anywhere we have yet seen. We have met several Squaw men [slang: white men married to Indian women] to-day, and they say we will encounter no difficulty and will be well treated by them. We will go through the old Spotted Tail agency, thereby avoiding both Spotted Tail and Red Cloud—although we fear no opposition from either the Indians or agents.

To-night we make a dry camp, as it is thirty-seven miles to the next water. Will write as soon as I get another opportunity.

CAPT. JACK.

[*Omaha Daily Bee*, 24 January 1876]

ON TO THE BLACK HILLS.

(Correspondence of the BEE.)

SIOUX RESERVATION, BET.
SPOTTED TAIL & RED CLOUD,
January 13, 1876.

Last night we camped two miles from Red Cloud, and Mr. Swaringen and myself started after supper for the agency, where we arrived about 10 o'clock at night, and if you ever saw two hungry men enjoy themselves, you can imagine how we went for the delicacies of the season which Mr. J. W. Dear served up to us in style; and if ever there lived a whole-souled, jovial good fellow, Mr. Dear is one of them. After partaking of the good things, Mr. Dear introduced us to Dr. Palmer, physician at the agency, we were very soon engaged in conversation regarding the Hills.

Reports were circulated to the effect that the present agent, Mr. [James S.] Hastings, was opposed to miners entering the Hills. Mr. Dear and the Doctor informs us such is not the case. Mr. Hastings has never been opposed to any one so far, nor does he intend to interfere. A party of 20 left Red Cloud day before yesterday, and joined a party at Spotted Tail. Twenty wagons left there a few days ago, and yesterday Mess'rs [Pat] Murphy and [Tom Monahan] Monaghan shipped a saw mill from Spotted Tail. We expect to overtake them in two days from now. We are right in among the Indians, seventeen miles from Spotted Tail, and seven miles from Crow Butte, near White Clay river; the reds are friendly and show no ill will. Of course we keep at a proper distance and carry no whiskey, and if all parties coming into the Hills would refuse to give the Indians liquor there would be no trouble; besides they fear their supplies being stopped should they interfere. There are now about forty teams on their way to Sidney from Red Cloud and Spotted Tail, and there will be ample means for freighting from there in two weeks. The weather is beautiful, and no snow so far to speak of, and parties who just come out report no snow on the eastern slopes of the Hills; they say there are at least 1,000 miners in the Hills now, and 300 in Custer City.

Some horses were stolen early this week from the Cheyennes, and they caught the thief, who proved to be a white man, and instead of shooting him as was thought, they stripped him of his shoes, pants, coat, vest, and hat, and whipped him; then let him go, telling him if he could make the agency in safety he might go. He was brought into Red Cloud by Sitting Bull of the Sioux, and the agent and commanding officers here, after consulting together, found that although there was proof positive against him, yet the laws conflicted in such a way that they were compelled to let him go, giving him a few hours to leave this country.

A herder, whose name I had not time to learn, was shot on last Monday by his comrade herder, named Jerry Eagan, who was drunk. The young man was shot through the lungs, but last night there were hopes of his recovery. Eagan has fled.

"Sitting Bull," of Red Cloud agency (not of the north), informed us of the death of a brave named Spotted Wolf, by the accidental discharge of his gun. His squaw immediately sharpened her knife and stabbed herself several times in the breast, which caused her death. Spotted Wolf was one of their great braves.

A party of seventy were met by some miners last week on their way to the Hills. They came from Laramie, and had about twenty-two teams.

January 14th, 1876.

To-day we made 16 miles over good road, from last nights camp. When we woke up this morning our cattle were all gone, and we had quite a scare; but we mounted our ponies, took our rifles, and found them about two miles from the camp all right.

After we crossed Ash Creek to-day we met old Spotted Tail and a squaw. He said "How, How," and "where you go?" We answered to Spotted Tail:—"we are yet on the road." He struck his breast with his fist and exclaimed: "*Me, me, that me*," and rode on very dignified.

One of the Cheyennes yesterday wanted to trade Smiley a pair of dirty socks for a six-shooter, but John told him, "I've whacked bulls across the plains before, and Injun can't fool me."

We will camp near Spotted Tail to-morrow evening, and from there we expect to make the Hills in five days.

The weather this week has been too warm to have an overcoat on, on horseback, and the nights are not very cold.

Mr. Swaringen will carry this to Spotted Tail to-morrow, as he knows the road. I would have gone, but Mr. S—, who is our guide, will not allow us to leave the train without a strong guard, or at least a well armed few. The Indians fear the miners, as they say they are bad men to fight and all carry the quick-speaking guns; but we have not had a night watch on since we came among them, and we have been assured that no stealing or interference will be indulged in by the Indians. This, I expect, will be the last letter before I reach Custar City, when I will tell you just how she is, and, as there is an artist with us, will send some sketches.

CAPT. JACK.

[*Sidney Telegraph*, 12 February 1876]

LAND OF GOLD!

Custer City, Jan. 23d, 1876.

Editor Telegraph:—

After a long and rather tedious journey, we arrived in Custer last evening. The reason of our being so long on the road was on account of our having cattle. We left Sidney on the 6th and arrived here on the 22d. We had beautiful weather until we reached the Cheyenne river, except a slight snow storm at Red Willow. After [illegible] experienced two severe snow storms with cold weather and a stiff northwester, and had some difficulty in finding our road through the snow drifts, although there was not more than four inches of snow until we reached the foot-hills, where we had from six to eight inches, which is (we are told) the first snow of note which they have had in the Hills.

New discoveries have been made north of here, which it is ascertained, surpasses all others in the Hills. There is quite a stampede just now in that direction. There are now, it is estimated, 1000 miners in the Hills. There is over 300 here, and about forty houses built and over sixty in progress, some of which is near completion. Custer City is destined to be the city of the Black Hills, and there has been many business men here, some of whom have located and returned for their goods.

There is four stores now here, and four saloons. Flour is $12 per hundred and bacon 30 cents per pound. A saw mill arrived here last week from Spotted Tail and will be in operation by the first of February.

There has been much jumping claims and loss, and old pioneers who had been the first in the Hills, and who went east on business, return to find their claims occupied and their houses taken and sold. For instance, Mr. Swaringen, who was one of the first in the Hills, and came back with our party last eve., rode up to his house expecting to find it occupied by the man whom he left in it and in charge of his effects. He was not a little surprised to find it occupied by strangers. The man, it seems, left for a few days, and on his return the house was occupied by a party who afterwards sold it for $135. Mr. S. was angry and asked for an explanation and was told that the trustees had given it to those parties as they claimed. It was not on his, Mr. Swaringen's, lot. Whether Swaringen can get any redress or not is yet to be seen. I am personally acquainted with Swaringen, and I can safely say that no man in this country has done more for its advancement than he has. I met him last month in Indianapolis and during his interviews with editors and reporters there, in Cincinnati, Chicago and other cities, I know that he has used every effort and explanation to advance the country and tell of its wealth and other resources and he is in my estimation, and in the estimation of every honest, square upright thinking miner, the last man who should be swindled or made to suffer.

The game is plenty and most of the boys are living high, on venison, mountain sheep and jack rabbits.

Ed. Current is one of your model men, he is a little fellow, and yet he has got a heart like an ox. That is, it's a big one. When our party arrived here last evening, Ed. saw us standing out in the cold, and said to the boys: "Come in my cabin, it is big enough for all; and eat till your heart's are contented and your bellies are full," and didn't we though? We made a side of venison look like a frame house struck with lightning. Long live Current, say we. Now for a line of machine poetry to Ed., to be handed down to posterity. Let me see, I believe one verse will suffice, so I will try an

ACROSTIC.

Edward, old boy, we wish you well—
Could we wish a dear friend more?
U in X L N C X L,
Regailing us from out your store.
Remember you! could we forget?
Especially since we shared your mess—
Not much, we'll think of you, you bet,
Till fortune crowns you with success.

And fortune will surely favor the brave, and when I say brave, I mean just what I say. To-day, hearing that a party with an ox-team were in the foot-hills, and unable to get through, he yoked up his team in a light sled, strapped on his blankets and mounting his pony, started to the rescue.

With his feet tied up in a gunny-sack,
And his gun upon his shoulder;

Said he, I'll bring a black-tail back—
Ed. C you are a soldier.

And now since I have started on a poetical strain, why should I stop thusly? Nay, rather let this soul-inspiring *current* flow on. And now for a few verses to the boys in the Hills, and then to bed, as my candle is like to-night, it is near the end of the week.

TO THE MINERS IN CUSTER.
I'm with you once again, pards,
And you bet, I'm going to stay;
But tell me, how have you made it go,
While I have been away.
Good, well I'm glad to hear it,
And so she pans-out well;
So its time that unless you try it,
You can't most always tell.

And Custer looms up lovely—
A hundred houses or more
Are built, or under head-way,
There will soon be twenty score.
And the season has been a fair one,
So you find its not a sell;
But without the pick and shovel,
You can't most always tell.

You bands of hardy miners—
There's danger boys, that's true—
But I'll bet my bottom dollar,
You'll paddle your own canoe.
And if the noble Red Cloud,
Should want a taste of hell;
Let him bring his braves to Custer,
But you can't most always tell.

And so the diggings are rich boys?
I hear it from every man,
You have found it the place,
Just fifteen cents to the pan.

Now that isn't very slow, pards,
Thank fortune, all is well;
But its just as I laid before men,
You can't most always tell.

Now Calamity bar is a good one,
Yes, Calamity, that's its name;
And it must be a great calamity,
If its like old Calamity Jane.
But remember boys when I left you,
I had a cabin and lot as well;
But some rooster jumped and sold it,
But you can't most always tell.

No matter, there's logs on the mountain,
And plenty of room in Custer;
I'll stick up another shanty,
And build it myself or bust her.
Let friendship still unite us,
And peace among us dwell;
Perhaps *Old Red Cloud will fight us*,
But you can't most always tell.

Calamity Jack.

[*Omaha Daily Bee*, 7 February 1876]

IN THE BLACK HILLS.

Custer City, Jan. 25.

After a long and tedious journey we arrived here on Saturday evening, the 22d. We left Sidney on the 5th, making the trip—with cattle teams—in seventeen days. We had beautiful weather until we struck the Cheyenne river, with the exception of a slight wind and snow storm at Red Willow camp, after crossing the Platte. After crossing the Cheyenne at Burnt Wood creek we encountered a severe snow storm, which laid us up for one day, and were joined there by another outfit, from Spotted Tail, among whom was Geary Shaw, a hotel keeper, and Joe Garner, a scout and trapper. Being thus reinforced, we started on next day, and, it being very cold and the snow drifting, we experienced much difficulty in reaching Buffalo Gap, in the foot hills; where we camped in good shelter, amid plenty of timber, and made our camp merry with story-telling, singing, etc.

We also had quite a lively hunt after some mountain sheep, but they were too cunning for us and made good their escape. Joe, however, made the wool fly from one of them, but they are harder to kill than a cat, and unless you give them a death wound, you are sure to lose them.

Next morning we started for Custer, and arrived here at sunset. We were surprised, on arriving at the summit of the hill when Custer City burst upon our gaze, to see quite a town. There are forty houses completed, and over sixty in process of erection, and 134 lots taken up in all. The city is one mile square, and is beautifully situated in a native park, surrounded by fine forests of white pine.

Water has been found twenty feet from the surface in Custer City, and we have a large well in the centre of town which supplies all, miners and stock.

A saw mill from Spotted Tail arrived here last week, and found water to-day in a large well they have been digging, and will be ready for operation in eight days. Lumber will not be over $35 per thousand, of this I was assured by Mr. Murphy, one of the proprietors.

There are some houses nearly finished now, two stories high, of hewed lumber, which look as neat as any cut lumber. There are four stores and four saloons in operation. Flour is worth $12 per 100 pound, and bacon 30 cents per pound. Many business men from Cheyenne and other points have been here, located and returned for goods, while their houses are being built.

Carpenters will now be in demand and will command from four to six dollars per day.

The miners are building their own cabins. Stock is living well right in the City and growing fat on bunch grass.

New parties who arrived here this winter made new laws, and many of the old pioneers will find on their return that their mining claims and town lots have been jumped and are being built upon.

There has been considerable wrangling but no fighting. The town is made up of a majority of peace-abiding citizens, and gamblers are unknown. Roughs and sharpers will have a hard road to travel if they come here expecting to reap a rich harvest, other than by the sweat of their brow; the miners say they will have no foolishness, and woe be to the wretches who may be deserving of their vengeance.

Miner's claims are 350 feet wide, reaching from bank to bank across the gulch, and town lots are 50 feet front by 150 back, which is according to the present law, and unless another and stronger party come in and overrule said law, it will stand. But the northern stampede will no doubt detract from this place sufficient to enable the present situation to hold the majority.

Miners from the north, this side of the Big Horn, who have just arrived, report new discoveries far surpassing any yet made, and there were thirty miners started for there yesterday and to-day on a prospecting tour.

The new discoveries are over eighty miles from here.

No regular mail has yet been put in operation. The pony mail to Spotted Tail made but one trip, and was then abandoned, for what reason we cannot say.

Mr. Z. Swaringer, one of the first pioneers in the Hills, and who accompanied our party, found his house and lot in possession of other parties on his return here, and loses considerable thereby. His claim on Calamity Bar, however, was held by his partners, and he has taken another lot and will commence building at once. We will commence on our frame to-morrow. For the present we find a warm corner in Ed. Current's cabin, which was formerly Capt. Pollock's headquarters. Ed. is a whole-souled pioneer, and gave us a hearty "How, how."

Mr. P. J. ["Pete"] Keefer, recorder of city lots, is a gentleman of intelligence and very obliging. He very kindly furnished us his records for examination, and you can rely on the truth of these statements regarding the city. He also furnished us most of the material for this letter, and has our thanks for the same.

There is but one woman in the Hills, and she is a grass widow, her husband having been scared off by some misdemeanor. She has two children, and the miners are building her a good house. We helped to-day to put up some of the logs. She will make a good living by washing and ironing.

Red Cloud has gone north with several hundred of his braves, and this party from Spotted Tail say that he asserted he would die on the war path with his braves, rather than stay at the agency and starve to death. The miners here are not the least uneasy, as they have full confidence in themselves to repel him and his whole band. Old Sitting Bull of the north, it is said, will co-operate with him, and, if so, you can rest assured we will have lively times on the border.

Sickness, with the exception of slight colds, is unknown here, and consumptives who came here seemingly on their last legs during the last summer are lusty and healthy, and are working at mining, building, etc. This would make a delightful summer resort, and if some enterprising eastern or western man will come here and build a good hotel, his fortune will be made.

There is excellent hunting, and the streams are well supplied with fish. The boys are tired of venison and jack-rabbits. Such food is hanging up in every cabin, and nearly every miner is a good hunter.

After I have built my cabin and prospected some, I will give you another letter.

CAPT. JACK.

[*Omaha Daily Bee*, 19 February 1876]

CUSTER CITY.

(Special Correspondence of the BEE.)

CUSTER CITY, Feb. 5.

As a party of four men start for Cheyenne to-morrow, I thought I would write a few lines. Have just finished washing the dishes, after eating a hearty supper and doing a good day's work on the cabin. There is not much news since my last letter; yet there are some things worthy of note. A party arrived here last evening from the Old Woman's Fork, 85 miles from here on the Cheyenne road, who report that a party of fifty Indians ran off six horses belonging to their outfit, and they are here in search of horses or cattle to help them in. It seems that the Indians have been raiding on other parties as well. As they had about thirty head of stock with them, they made no attempt to molest the people, but rode off as fast as they could go. There were only seven in the party of whites, and they could not follow them up.

We tried to organize a party to follow them and cut them off, but could not raise horses enough that would stand such a long ride. All the stock that is here now has been worked almost off their feet, and more than half of them have come here within this month. Parties coming in should organize in parties of not less than fifty, and after passing the agencies and for forty miles before arriving here, should keep a vigilant night watch, or travel nights and lay over all day.

There is a new town being built twelve miles from here, on Spring creek. There are ten buildings completed and many commenced.

The lots are 100 by 150. To-morrow evening a meeting is called for the purpose of cutting the lots down to 50x150—same as here. There are many from here going over to locate a lot and build a cabin on it, which will hold it; and should Spring creek prove good, or, better than this, they can sell out and go there. In either case, they will have their choice.

Miners from Dead Wood, 85 miles north, still keep coming in and report diggings there very fine from top clear down to bed-rock, and many have sold their lots here and started for the new discoveries.

We rode out yesterday in company with Mr. Current, for the purpose of locating a ranch, and found that every desirable spot within a radius of five miles had been located, and some of the locations have cabins already built upon them. We returned without locating, but not without some game. The unerring rifle of Current brought down a fine white-tail deer, while I shot the head off of a prairie chicken. There were nine deers brought in on Saturday evening, and were sold at from $3 to $5 each.

A wagon load of goods from Fort Laramie arrived here on Friday, and the proprietor told us this evening that he has sold more than two thirds of it already.

A variety theatre was finished to-day, and it is said the performers are now on the road from Cheyenne.

There is no lack of building.

The weather to-day was quite cold, and the sound of the axe could be heard all around.

Mr. Charles Swarthouse, an estimable old gentleman and an experienced miner, is lying very ill in his cabin. Mr. Current is doing all he can for his comfort, and Pete Keefer, city recorder, who is some on doctoring, is attending to him. Mr. Swarthouse is nearly sixty years of age. His sickness is caused by a severe cold, and fears are entertained that it may result in pleurisy. Mr. S. is, I believe, the only sick man in the Hills, with the exception of some parties who froze their feet north of here.

Mr. Keefer amputated three fingers for a German who had his hands frozen some time ago, and this man is now doing well.

The saw-mills will commence to cut lumber in three days. There are two more mills on their way in, and also a planing-mill.

It is rumored here that there are seven companies of soldiers on their way in, but there is no credence given to the report.

There have been several horses missing here lately, but as no Indians have been seen here, they cannot be credited with their disappearance. There are so many miners going north, and those who have no horses must find something to ride; so no doubt if there are any parties stealing they are those who have no horses and no money to buy them.

A Mr. Rodabank came in to-day from Utah and is now in this cabin. He says that there were hundreds in Utah preparing to come to the Hills, and many would start in a few days. There will undoubtedly be a great rush here in the spring. Mr. R. came here to prospect for *quartz*, and he says there will be plenty of capital here in the spring.

A party just left here to bring in those whose horses were stolen by the Indians, and they are to receive $115 for their services. A meeting was called last night by a few discontented beings for the purpose of altering and amending the present city laws and electing new trustees. In fact, to upset all the present city government; but they were far in the minority and were beaten by a vote of over two-thirds.

A little shooting was indulged in a few evenings ago, but the parties were drunk, and if repeated they will swing or be ordered to take a walk.

There are now 100 houses built and nearly 400 lots on which are foundations, and people are arriving daily. A beautiful site for a public park was surveyed and laid out yesterday. Also one square for a court house; also a beautiful hill site, similar to Omaha's Capitol hill, for a high school.

Everybody is busy; weather fine; snow nearly all gone and sunshine instead.

Calamity Bar is a fine mining claim about 3 miles from Custer on this gulch. We visited it yesterday and there is considerable work done on it. They have found from 5 cents to 15 cents to the pan. Calamity Bar derived its name from a woman who accompanied the soldiers last summer. They called her *Calamity Jane*.

CAPTAIN JACK.

[*Omaha Daily Bee*, 26 February 1876]

THE GOLD FIELDS.

(Special Correspondence of the BEE.)

CUSTER CITY, Feb. 5.

The dead have come to life again,
And Smiley lives and smiles;
McHugh, well and happy too—
From home six hundred miles.
And Jack, alas, is living yet,
To bore you with his rhymes,
And he intends to live, you bet,
To be as old as Grimes.

And such is the case, Dame Rumor to the contrary notwithstanding.

Mr. Saunders and others arrived here this afternoon from Cheyenne, and Mr. McHugh, Smiley and myself were not a little surprised to learn that we were all, or part of us, *dead*. Now, if such is the case, we are not sensible of the fact; besides, you never saw as healthy a party of beef-eaters since you crossed the Missouri.

McHugh, Smiley, Stokes and myself have been building cabins and helping each other. I have got a cabin of my own, and am now writing in it, while Smiley is using his left (and the only hand that is *left*) at the same business. We have each located lots in the central part of the city, and there is *lots* more on the outskirts.

We have a physician here now—Dr. James Lehan [Lehane]—who was formerly with the Jenny expedition. Dr. Lehan is a graduate of the Apothecary Hall, Dublin, Ireland, and seems quite intelligent and well read. Business is dull, however, in his line. He has but one patient—Mr. Swarthouse—who is in this cabin and is very low. Pneumonia is what the Doctor is treating him for, and doubts are entertained of his recovery. Should we lose Mr. Swarthouse we would lose one of our best and most respected comrades. He is one of the board of trustees, and a very intelligent one. We will sit up with him to-night, and will, as we have heretofore, do all we can to restore him to health.

Mr. Sanders and party will record lots and lay foundations thereon on Monday in Custer, after which they will leave for Spring Creek, where they have and intend locating mining claims. The party are all in good spirits, excepting now and then a cuss word about the Cheyenne road *twenty one days' travel with horse teams,* when they expected to make it in ten or twelve. They had to carry wood and water nearly one-third of the way.

Dick Brown, the great banjo player and favorite of the Pacific slope, is in Custer, and is one of the pioneers of the country. Dick has a fine ranche adjoining town and two good mining claims, and is working every day with his axe and saw, building, etc. Although he left an engagement at $60 per week at Cheyenne, when he came here, he says he thinks he can do better in the Hills, and has bid farewell to the stage. We wish Dick success, as he is a gentleman of the first water. Nearly every evening, "Home, Sweet Home," and variations, "Last Rose of Summer," and variations, and "The Days of '49," are played for our benefit, and we all enjoy music so much when played by so excellent a hand.

New discoveries are still being made north of here, and specimens are being brought in every few days; very good quartz is also found, and many will realize fortune in the next few years.

Sunday Night.

Have just returned from Harney's Peak, about 12 miles distant from here, northeast. The day being clear we could see for over one hundred miles out into the open prairie, and, then turning round, the hills and valleys resembled a round basin or large park. Nearly all the snow had disappeared, and the cattle were feeding on the luxuriant bunch grass, to be found in every gulch and hill side. We brought some quartz with us which we found within a few miles of Harney's Peak, which our most expert miners—Messrs. Current, Keefer, Barker, and Sanders—pronounce the best that they have yet seen for silver-bearing, and believe it will go over $2,000 to the ton. Will send some out with Mr. McHugh in a few days to be assayed. Every day some miners bring in specimens, and there are now bushels of quartz in the city, but the facilities for sending it out are so poor that there is not much done with it, although many of the miners make their own assays, and keep it to themselves.

A petition containing over one hundred names was handed to us this evening to be sent to the postmaster general asking for a mail route and postoffice to be established here. We will obtain about two or three hundred signers and then forward to the postmaster general at Washington through our worthy citizen, Judge Kuykendale, who got up the petition. It is essentially necessary to have a mail route established here at once, as the facilities for getting mail at present are very poor, and many letters are delayed and some lost.

There were fifty men arrivals this day, some from Sidney and part from Cheyenne.

Captain John A. Byers arrived here this evening, having walked all the way from Jefferson, 12 miles this side of Sioux City, 495 miles. He was accompanied by a boy named Charley Holt, 18 years old. From the mouth of the Whetstone to Spotted Tail they made 280 miles in 9 days. When within 20 miles of Spotted Tail the boy said:

"Captain, if we do not meet some one with grub before to-morrow we may say our prayers."

They had lived on parched coffee for four days. Byers, looking back, saw four Indians riding at full speed towards them, and remarked:

"Charley, you won't have to wait until to-morrow; you can commence your prayers now."

The Indians rode up within hailing distance, and proved to be a part of the war party of Sioux who had been fighting the Snakes. They coveted a scarf and some other little things belonging to the captain and boy. After showing by signs that they had nothing to eat, the Indians cooked them some antelope and gave them enough to carry them to the agency. At the agency they were told that had the Indians met them 20 or 30 miles further from the agency they would have lifted their hair. At Spotted Tail the boy would go no farther as he was played out and afraid of the snow and the Indians. But Byers started for Custer City and made the trip (100 miles) in five days, through the snow. While I write, he is enjoying a good comfortable nap by our fireside on the floor, and now and then a word is muttered about "Charley," or "courage boy," imagining, no doubt, he is still toiling on his weary way. Old trappers and hunters who met Mr. Byers at the agency said they would not undertake such a trip for all the wealth in the Hills. All the fire arms he had was a navy revolver. Byers was during the war a captain of the 1st Virginia cavalry, is 36 years of age, and stands six feet high in his stocking feet. He is looked upon here by old miners and pioneers as a man of great bravery and endurance, and his looks would certainly indicate that he is a very determined man. He is the only man known of that has yet attempted to reach the Black Hills alone, and without knowing the country.

MONDAY, Feb 7th, 1876.

Parties who came in to-day brought Omaha papers of January 25th. A correspondent from Laramie to the *Herald* gets a little off in his letter to that paper, wherein he states that flour is hard to get at $22 per cwt. This is false; flour is selling for $12 *per 100 pounds*, and we saw 8 sacks, of 100 pounds each, sell, last week, for $8 a sack. Bacon is 30 cents, and we bought first-class ranch butter to-night from Judge Kuykendale, for 60 cents per pound. Provisions are no higher here than in Cheyenne and Sidney, only the cost of freight is added. Another statement regarding $34 to the pan, of gold. Such may have been the case, as in one instance where a man found a nugget weighing over $30, but people must not understand by that that every pan contains that amount. There are parties now north of here taking out a dollar an hour; but their facilities are good, they have plenty of water, and are an organized company. No doubt in the spring, when men can work steadily all day long, there will be two dollars an hour taken out to the man; but these are shallow diggings, and only from three to five feet to bed rock. Parties coming here will have to work hard to get gold. It is wrong to report these things and influence people to come to this country who expect to pick up gold by the shovelful. There are good $10 diggings in the Hills, and plenty of them; but no such panning as forty, fifty or one hundred cents to the pan; five to seven cents will pay over $10, if the diggings are not too deep.

More anon.

CALAMITY JACK.

[*Sidney Telegraph*, 4 March 1876]

BLACK HILLS!

The following letter was received by Mr. J. W. Dear, of Red Cloud, and handed to us for publication.

CUSTER CITY, Feb. 7th, 1876.

Friend Dear:—

I suppose the parties going out will give you all the news. Yet, I feel duty bound to say a few words. We are progressing splendidly.

Nearly 100 houses are completed and nearly 100 more commenced and under way. I believe if you had a branch store here you could do well. There are now nine places of business here, and they are all doing well. Flour $12; bacon 30 cts; canned tomatoes 40; sugar 30; butter 50 to 65; whiskey, *very* [illegible] 25 cents per dose; tea $1 to $2; &c. [illegible] proportion. There was [illegible] this will be a large town in one year, and a good business place. I believe it will be to the Hills, what Denver is to Colorado. The supply depot of the country.

New discoveries are being made north of here, which I think will prove a good thing, as the diggings are shallow and easily worked. I think you will have a great deal of travel via Red Cloud.

Mr. Sanders and party arrived here day before yesterday, from Cheyenne. The party are all in good spirits, excepting now and then a cuss word about the Cheyenne road TWENTY-ONE DAYS' TRAVEL WITH HORSE TEAMS, when they expected to make it in ten or twelve. They had to carry wood and water nearly one-third of the way.

I have been writing up the route ever since I left Sidney, although some of the Cheyenne people reported our outfit all frozen to death. Yet, we live to tell of the pleasant trip, the fine natural road. Although Swaringen took us to old Spotted Tail, 40 miles out of our way. Yet, we reached the Hills, with our bull team, in 17 days from Sidney, and three days we never turned a wheel, and you bet I am telling the people of it, not only in Omaha, but in other eastern papers.

I have a petition signed by nearly two hundred asking the Postmaster General for a post office and mail route from Cheyenne. It was handed to me to-day by the city recorder, and also petitioning for your humble servant as P. M. So mote it be.

A Capt. John A. Byers arrived here this evening, having walked from Jefferson, Dakota, 495 miles, and from Spotted Tail here in five days. Respectfully,

J. W. CRAWFORD.

3

CUSTER CITY, FEBRUARY–MARCH 1876

Captain Jack quickly settled into a routine of writing once or twice a week to the *Bee*. News about gold in late winter was scarce, as snows and cold often kept claim holders and prospectors from the diggings and off the sidehills, but he still found plenty to write about, even though issues with mail plagued him in his attempt to get the news out. He and other Black Hillers worked to better the mail service, but the situation would not improve until well into 1877 when formal mail contracts were awarded to the Cheyenne and Black Hills stage line. Mail was just one of the issues that needed resolution in this extralegal settlement.

Crawford had arrived in Custer City when that hamlet was barely more than a cluster of log cabins, many of which Pollock's infantry had occupied or constructed the previous summer and fall. At its inception, Custer City had been called Stonewall, or Stonewall City, at the insistence of southerners who sought to honor Confederate Lieutenant General Thomas "Stonewall" Jackson. General Crook had a hand in renaming the town Custer, or Custer City, a matter the assembled miners had voted upon the previous August before departing the Hills with the general. The prospectors and miners coming into the Hills in the winter of 1875–1876 quickly claimed the army cabins after the troops departed, and Crawford himself occupied Pollock's headquarters cabin. Miners took over the Gordon Stockade some three and a

This photograph of the interior of the Gordon Stockade shows troops from Dodge's expedition in residence in the summer of 1875. The soldiers brought along a twelve-pounder mountain howitzer mounted on a unique wide-axle prairie carriage. The stockade was continually occupied throughout the gold rush. *Albert Guerin photograph. J. Leonard Jennewein Collection, Dakota Wesleyan University Archives, Mitchell, S.Dak.*

half miles down the valley as well.[1] For the next few months, Custer City was the foremost community in the Black Hills, and the steady stream of arriving businessmen, sawmills, stagecoaches, professionals, and ne'er-do-wells was common chatter in Crawford's letters.

Crawford also reported on the seemingly common disputes between cabin and lot owners and jumpers and squatters. Property disagreements arose for several reasons. When Crook had traveled through the diggings in 1875 to corral and evict miners, some had

The Flick-Pollock-Crawford-Flick cabin survives today in downtown Custer as one of the more fascinating, if nearly unheralded, witnesses of the earliest days of the Black Hills gold rush. *Paul L. Hedren*

already established cabins in the Custer City locale, and in departing with Crook, these owners presumed a right to retake possession of their property when the Black Hills opened. In other instances, businessmen and promoters temporarily abandoned their cabins to return to places like Cheyenne or Omaha to resupply, intending to return in due course, and often leaving the care of their property in the hands of a friend or partner, sometimes unsuccessfully. For the oncoming and unaware, the availability of abandoned cabins proved an opportunity worth seizing but often led to quarreling and legal disputes when original owners returned.

One of the more interesting early squatter disputes involved Crawford himself. Returning to Custer City in 1876, he had claimed Pollock's abandoned headquarters and would use the cabin for nearly four months before its rightful owner, Doctor D. W. Flick, returned with his wife. Flick had departed with Crook during the exodus of miners, his cabin then only partially finished. Captain Pollock's troops completed the building and occupied it as their military headquarters that fall. Crawford appropriated the cabin in late January and, later still, returning from one of his many explorations in the Hills, unceremoniously entered what he thought was his own cabin and found Flick awaiting. Crawford presumed that he, not Flick, had been jumped. Flick explained himself, but the conversation grew heated. Captain Jack withdrew but immediately engaged a lawyer, who brought an action against Flick for a supposed unlawful entry. Justice E. P. Keiffer (P. J. "Pete" Keefer in the letters) and a jury of five miners eventually heard the case and, duly sensitive to property title issues, found for Flick. Crawford did not relate this incident to his *Bee* or *Telegraph* readers, but he did rather casually report Flick's arrival in town with a shipment of freight in a 9 April letter to the *Telegraph*.[2]

Establishing a provisional government became pressing business for Custer City's citizens during these winter months, and Crawford returned to the topic several times in his letters. Ownership disputes were but one matter vexing residents. Equally problematic was the anticipated arrival that spring of, as Crawford put it, "a class of lawless, bad men, whose mission to the Hills was not to work hard and honest for a living, but . . . to prey upon the community, and rob, steal, and . . . kill." To prepare, the residents wanted "laws and officers of law, to put a curb on such individuals," Crawford declared on 9 February. The organization of society to prevent and control crime and regulate the ownership of claims had been a recognized activity in American mining camps since the time of the California gold rush, and it spoke to America's pioneering instinct for spontaneous organization and self-government. In due course, a committee was drawn from Custer City's leading citizens that included Judge Kuykendall and Captain Jack, and over the course of several meetings and weeks, it drafted ordinances and nominated candidates for justices, marshal, and other city officials. Crawford declined a nomination for marshal. In short order, elections occurred, ordinances were adopted, and officials selected.[3]

In addition to the class of troublemakers feared that spring, Crawford told of the legal chaos that a devious lawyer from Omaha rained on Custer City. Isaac Hascall, or "Hascall the rascal," appeared in several of Crawford's letters, always working, it seemed, to disrupt community affairs in every imaginable way, including challenging the citizens' law-making authority. Finally, the irate citizens drove him from the Black Hills, perhaps back to Omaha, Crawford speculated, or maybe to Yankton, where, no doubt, he would continue his boorish scheming.[4]

Crawford also made the acquaintance of saloon-keeper Ellis Alfred "Al" Swearingen, though one senses that no particular friendship or bond formed between the two men, perhaps because Crawford had forsworn alcohol. Originally from Iowa, thirty-year-old Swearingen opened a hurdy-gurdy in Custer City in March in what was then the largest building yet constructed in town. Built of logs and floored throughout, Swearingen's dance hall and saloon featured a long bar on one side, a dance floor on the other, candle and oil lamp illumination throughout, and fourteen rooms or cribs in the back where his girls "slept." Harry "Sam" Young remembered that Swearingen brought fourteen women with him from Cheyenne; Crawford mentioned only four.[5] Captain Jack's description of the hall, called Swannger's in his 27 March *Bee* letter, is deliciously circumspect but also a rather revealing look at a hurdy-gurdy, that unsavory dance, gambling, and entertainment enterprise that was a standard feature in virtually every western mining and trail town. Swearingen's establishment also frequently doubled as a meeting hall for Custer City residents, a point noted often in Crawford's letters.

As opportunity and the weather allowed, Crawford ranged beyond the immediacy of Custer City to explore the French and Spring creek diggings, and he invariably found them paying well. Claims had to be "represented" every week, he reported on 27 March, meaning that miners had to show regular active labor on their claims in order to maintain title. In late February, Crawford had ventured down French Creek some twelve miles, where he chanced upon "three colored men" making good prospects and showing pieces of gold weighing up to $1.10. "Quartz is all the rage now," he wrote on 1 March, and miners were showing fine specimens. In the natural progression of prospecting in the Black Hills or in any mining region, prospectors invariably turned their attention from auriferous gravels to the hard-rock slopes lining the gulches, from whence placer gold had eroded over the millennia. Visible gold in white quartz and gray schist and granite, qualities particularly inherent in Deadwood

Gulch, spurred hard-rock prospecting and mining in the northern Hills. But such mining was time-consuming work and demanded resources normally beyond the means of working stiffs in the placer diggings. Before Crawford departed the Black Hills in early summer, he explored several early hard-rock claims in Deadwood Gulch and later did what he could to encourage outside investment in the mines. His efforts seemed unsuccessful, but in time hard rock-mining indeed became "all the rage" in the Black Hills.[6]

Crawford also found an abandoned military camp from the year before when Captain John Mix and Company M, Second Cavalry, ventured into the Hills from Fort Laramie to track trespassing miners. Mix's movement had occurred at that time when soldiers still regularly patrolled the Black Hills searching for and evicting miners.[7] The cavalry campsite was a littered mess but also filled with interesting curiosities, including a board tacked to a tree upon which "Some Boys in Blue" had scratched a short poem. Because Crawford had an appreciation for poetry, he documented the instance carefully in his 1 March letter to the *Bee*. The ten-line ditty, titled "Our Sentiments," captured the soldiers' candor about their predicament, the miners they encountered, the Indians impeding the way, and the apparent likelihood of an all-out Indian war erupting over the Black Hills and its precious gold. The little poem closed with the astonishingly pithy line, "So let the reds and miners fight." War and rumors of war were thus in the air. In the same letter, Crawford also referenced the fact that Brigadier General George Crook had taken the field against the Sioux in early February.

One of Crawford's steady companions in the late-winter was Charles R. Whitehead, a thirty-three-year-old newspaperman from Kansas City who arrived in Custer on 29 February. A veteran reporter who had earlier worked in Denver, Whitehead now corresponded for the *Kansas City Times*. Crawford's March letters to the *Bee* recounted several of their explorations together, including a nearly disastrous attempt at climbing Harney Peak, the highest mountain in the Black Hills. When a winter storm trapped them on the mountain and their horses wandered off in the middle of the night, the two penmen hastily abandoned camp but got separated as they chased their mounts. Their misadventure ended reasonably well, both reporters returning to Custer City cold, tired, but alive. When both men revisited what Whitehead called "Calamity Camp" some while later, they found it thoroughly ransacked, with all useful possessions missing and everything else burned. Crawford took the worst of it, losing an irreplaceable scrapbook containing, he said, over five hundred poems and valuable letters from soldiers and statesmen. The two men blamed Indians, and, as only he would do, Crawford wrote a poem about it for the *Bee* in his 21 March missive.

That Crawford dotted his *Bee* letters and filled assorted notebooks with poetry was more than a mere sidelight, though he claimed no particular forethought or intent in his embrace of poetry. As he explained in *The Poet Scout*, his first published anthology in 1879, his sketches and poems were "the unpolished and often impromptu offspring of my idle hours, wherein many past incidents of an adventurous life reproduced themselves in memory, and took the shape of verse."[8] Certainly Captain Jack played to his audience. During this time period, most Americans lingered over the pages of newspapers and magazines, where verse was a regular feature.[9] In his Black Hills letters, Crawford's poems were mostly simple embellishments and easily forgotten. But some were republished later in one or another of his anthologies, and he usually included headnotes that explained the circumstances or inspiration for the respective verse. Many of those headnotes add substantially to our understanding of Crawford's adventures in the Black Hills, as do many of the collected poems themselves.

As always, in addition to Crawford's dispatches, the *Omaha Daily Bee* featured other news from the Black Hills nearly every day. Especially important in March were stories about the supposed commencement of scheduled stage service between Cheyenne and Custer City and the efforts the Union Pacific (UP) Railroad was making to cooperate with the stage company in providing an inexpensive, reliable through-connection from Omaha to Custer City via Cheyenne. The UP already offered Black Hillers special rates: to Sidney, twenty-one dollars first class and thirteen dollars third class, and to Cheyenne, twenty-five dollars first class and fifteen dollars third class. On a combined through-ticket, the stage fare from Cheyenne to Custer added twenty dollars to first-class fare and ten dollars to a third-class ticket. The *Bee* was also quick to notice that the Omaha brothers John and Gilbert Collins had just opened a new hotel at Fort Laramie called The Rustic, built specifically to accommodate Black Hills travelers. John Collins was Fort Laramie's post trader and stocked all manner of provisions, hardware, and mining equipment.[10] But promoting stage travel and actually providing regularly scheduled service were different matters, as Crawford noted in his 21 March letter. Although a Cheyenne stage arrived in Custer City on 20 March, two horses were killed in the experiment, and regular service was still weeks away. "Until the regular line starts running and gets here we will not believe," Crawford complained dryly. Only in mid-April did the eagerly welcomed coaches appear in Custer on a predictable schedule.[11]

News of gold continued to provide good reading in the *Bee*, including a curious note on 25 February that Omaha jeweler John Baumer had manufactured to order an 18-carat-gold eagle's claw clasping a Black Hills nugget. Less out of the ordinary were reports like that from Samuel Minard, just in from the Hills, who called on the *Bee* office and showed fine samples of gold dust that had averaged three dollars to four dollars to the pan. The *Bee's* reporter in Cheyenne, who signed himself "Ranger," also forwarded news received from parties extolling prospects in the Deadwood country. Miners there could be expected to average eight dollars per day in what were described as shallow diggings with little stripping necessary. Ranger also reported that Spring and Rapid creeks had been worked all winter, but the diggings were deep and that Calamity Bar, three miles above Custer, would soon be yielding from six to eight dollars a day. Most miners, he observed, were longing for spring.[12]

[*Omaha Daily Bee*, 23 February 1876]

THE LAND OF GOLD.

(Special Correspondence of the BEE.)

CUSTER CITY, D. T.,

Feb. 9th, 1876.

As Mr. Wm. McHugh will leave here on Friday for Omaha, I will send a few lines by him direct to the BEE.

Every day brings additional reinforcements of citizens and miners, who are locating as soon as they arrive.

Messrs. J. C. Sanders and Bowten, proprietors of the saw mill, now five days' distant from here, report that last evening, after passing a large party of miners who were coming in, some of whom had been in the Hills last summer, they heard reports of over fifty shots fired, and between that a party of Indians attempted to run off their stock, but met with a warm reception, as there was a large party, well disciplined and thoroughly armed.

A difficulty arose this evening between two miners, who claimed the same lot. One of the miners, Mr. Taylor, formerly from Omaha, has occupied and lived in a double cabin built by the soldiers. Said cabin is partly on his lot, which has been recorded in accordance with law, but since the city has been surveyed it seems that Taylor's cabin is partly on an alley, and another party put his four logs on the lot and claimed it. This afternoon Mr. Harlow hauled some logs on the lot for the purpose of building thereon, as he had refused to abide by the decision of the trustees, to whom all such matters has been referred. Harlow used some strong language, and Taylor struck him down. Harlow then told Taylor that he (Taylor) could whip him with his fist, but challenged him to step ten paces with seven-shooters, and immediately started for his shooter. Taylor, in the meantime, entered his cabin, loaded his needle gun and awaited the return of Harlow, who appeared soon and ordered Taylor to open the door and come out. Taylor opened the door, and, with rifle in hand, told Harlow to keep away or he would use the needle, not being an expert with the navy [revolver]. We and some others, however, prevailed upon Mr. Harlow to desist from the use of his weapons and leave the matter to a committee of arbitration, and after a meeting of the miners and citizens to-night, Harlow again pulled his shooter on Taylor, but Taylor was quick and caught the weapon, and Harlow was finally persuaded not to use it.

A meeting was called this evening of the miners and citizens of this city and gulch. Mr. P. J. Keefer was elected president, and J. W. Crawford secretary. Judge Kuekendall was then called upon to state the object of the meeting. His statement was to the following effect:

That as hundreds of honest, hardworking men had come to this country for the purpose of obtaining an honest livelihood, and that hundreds would follow, and with the coming spring would come a class of lawless, bad men, whose mission to the Hills was not to work hard and honest for a living, but by every unfair means to prey upon the community, and rob, steal, and, if need be to accomplish their designs, kill; therefore we want laws and officers of law, to put a curb on such individuals and be prepared to treat them as they deserve.

On motion of Judge Kuekendall, a committee of six was appointed to draft resolutions and devise means whereby proper laws can be made to govern this city and surrounding country.

P. J. Keefer, president of the meeting, appointed the following committee: Judge Kuekendall, Judge Bob Tate, J. W. Crawford, S. R. Shanklin, Mr. Annely and Mr. Smith.

A Mr. Boltz represented that he had cached some goods back at the Old Woman's Fork, and that a party now on the way in had raised said goods and broken open the trunks, etc., taking their contents. A committee of twenty men were appointed to meet said team and investigate the matter, and if said goods were found with this party to have them restored to the owner. This party who represented to have lost said goods is the same whose horses were stolen by Indians, of which I informed you in a former letter. We have been informed that since the meeting this evening that said party are innocent.

After the meeting the committee on laws, etc., met at the house of P. J. Keefer, city recorder, and to-morrow evening, at which time we meet again, will report about as follows:

That two police justices and a marshal be elected according to the laws governing city elections; that the trustees make a city ordinance and appoint as many special police as they deem sufficient to assist the officers in doing their duty. Preamble and resolutions will also be introduced in the report, and in a short time we will have our city in such shape that ruffians and black-legs, who may come here thinking to run the concern, will find a set of men determined and fearless, who will deal out to them justice as it should be in such cases. As this is only Tuesday, and I have all day to-morrow and to-morrow evening to finish, I will go to bed, as it is late.

THURSDAY, Noon—Feb. 10.

Considerable wrangling to-day regarding Harlom Falon. Pistols were drawn, but by parties who had no intention of using them.

Saw mill is at work, and is turning out lumber very fast, and it is being used up just as fast as it can be sawed. There are now nearly 500 lots taken, and about 200 buildings nearly completed.

This evening the adjourned meeting convened at Swaringen's hall at 7 p. m., and the committee on organization handed in their report, which is as follows:

REPORT

Report of committee on organization of a government for the preservation of law and order, and the preservation and protection of life and property in Custer City, Dakota territory, as reported at an adjourned meeting held for the purpose, at Swaringen's Hall, in said city, on February 10th, A.D. 1876:

Mr. Chairman:

We, the undersigned, your committee appointed for the purpose above set forth, beg leave to report the following preamble and resolutions:

WHEREAS, Law and order should reign in every community, to the end that every person therein may be secure in the enjoyment of life, liberty and property, and be protected therein; and

WHEREAS, In view of the great influx of population that is expected to enter this place at an early day, many of whom no doubt will be of the lawless class, it is necessary that all law-abiding citizens should be a unit in the support of law and order; and,

WHEREAS, At present there is no law that can be applied to the situation of affairs, and, from present appearances, there will be none for some time to come, therefore be it

Resolved, That it is the sense of this meeting (composed of a large majority of the citizens of Custer City), that a provisional government should be instituted at once for the purpose herein before set forth, to be and remain in force until properly-constituted authorities shall be ready to assume control; and be it further

Resolved, That in addition to the present powers vested in the trustees of Custer City, power is hereby granted them to make or pass, change, alter or amend any existing laws or ordinances now in force, or that may hereafter be passed or adopted; and be it further

Resolved, That for the purpose of carrying into effect and enforcing all of said laws and ordinances two police justices and one city marshal be elected at an election hereby ordered to be held on the 14th day of February, [1876], at the city recorder's office, and that the returns thereof shall be made to the trustees aforesaid by the judges and clerks of such election, immediately after the same; and that said trustees shall then canvass the vote and declare the persons having the greatest number of votes elected to said offices; be it further

Resolved, That in addition to the powers hereinbefore granted, the police justice, when elected, shall have jurisdiction in all cases arising under the laws of Dakota, as provided therein, except that their decisions or judgments shall be final until otherwise changed; and the city marshal, when elected, shall be ex-officio constable, and shall be vested with full power to execute all warrants, subpoenas, summons, and other process of law issued by either of said justices under the ordinances of said city, and in all cases wherein they have jurisdiction as above granted, also to make arrests on sight in all such cases where personally cognizant that a crime or offense has been committed; and be it further

Resolved, That the trustees shall have power at any regular meeting to remove either of said justices, or said marshal, for corruption, malfeasance in office, inconsistency, or when it shall appear that the best interests of said city shall demand it; such vacancies shall be filled by an election to be held for the purpose; and be it further

Resolved, That we agree to assist and sustain the provisional government hereby instituted, to the end that law and order may prevail, and that the name of Custer City may not become a by-word among the people of our country.

In addition to the foregoing preamble and resolutions, we, your committee, would also recommend that they be adopted unanimously.

Custer City, D. T., Feb. 10, '76.

ROBERT TATE,

J. W. CRAWFORD,

S. R. SHANKLAND,

D. K. SNIVELY,
H. S. SCHMIDT,
Committee.

On motion of Mr. Tailor the above was adopted as read, and the following nominations made for justices: H. S. Schmidt, P. J. Keefer, present city recorder, Mr. De Line.

On motion nominations for justices closed, and were opened for marshal, and the following were nominated: J. W. Crawford, who declined, Wm. Thompson, Wm. A. D. Frass, John Barrows [Burrows].

On motion closed.

On motion, the time for holding the election to be from 9 a. m. till 6 p. m. After which the meeting adjourned.

Last night's meeting had the effect to alarm some sneak thieves who had stolen some goods, which they returned to-day. We have good men in nomination, and we intend to assist, all in our power, to preserve good order.

The shooting, back on the Cheyenne road, yesterday, was only a party of 16 practicing.

Mr. Wm. McHugh will carry this to the office of the BEE. He will leave here to-morrow forenoon. Bill is one of the boys, and you can rely on anything he tells you regarding this country. Mc. has made a host of friends here, and when he returns with his goods he will certainly receive a goodly share of the patronage.

And now, good night, and may peace and quiet reign. We feel all right; will scribble soon again, and tell you all the news in simpleness and truth. No one has got the blues, and we are a happy youth, you bet.

CALAMITY JACK.

[*Omaha Daily Bee*, 26 February 1876]

CUSTER CITY.

(Correspondence of the BEE.)

CUSTER CITY, Feb. 17, 1876.

I am just about starting north on a hunt and prospecting tour, and as Judge Kirkendall is going to Cheyenne to-morrow, will write a few lines.

Well, election is over. P. J. Keefer and H. S. Smith were elected justices, and John Burrows city marshal. The whole number of votes polled was 332, of which Mr. Keefer, the favorite candidate, received 325. The fight was principally between Burrows and Trask, who were close all through. Burrows received 179 and Trask 150.

A young man by the name of Relgner, from Omaha, thirty years old, died last night or early this morning. He ate a hearty supper last night and worked yesterday, and did not complain. A post mortem examination will be held. This is the first natural death which has occurred in the Hills since it has been inhabited by whites.

Dr. Robinson and a party arrived here the latter part of last week and are busy locating and preparing to build. There are nearly 600 lots located now, and the recorder is busy all the time, only when he sleeps, recording.

Will write you from Hills City and Spring Creek as soon as we get over and look around. Our object is prospecting for quartz.

CALAMITY JACK.

[*Omaha Daily Bee*, 7 March 1876]

THE LAND OF GOLD.

(Special Correspondence of the BEE.)

CUSTER CITY, Feb. 23, 1876.

I have just returned from prospecting and hunting on Spring creek and Newton fork. We started from here on the 16th. The same day I sent a letter to the BEE. On our way to Spring creek, about two miles north of Custer, we found a fine lead [lode] of mica, or isinglass, which we think is good; will enclose some specimens which we took from the surface with a pick. It is strangely formed and runs in all directions through the rock; it is in great white quartz rock, and the rock must be blasted from around it before it can be gotten out in large pieces, although we got pieces as clear as crystal without a flaw, which squared 4x5 inches. We have taken up the lead and intend to prospect it soon. We sent specimens to some gentlemen in Chicago, whom we met when there, and with whom we have since corresponded. They will send a man here soon who understands working it.

A young man named Taylor and your correspondent also found a fine quartz lead, which has prospected well. After we had the quartz tested, three other men took an extension on our claim. We took up

Captain Jack, seated with his back to the white tent, poses with Deadwood-bound Hillers along Spring Creek in early June 1876. This photograph is one of two taken by D. S. Mitchell that featured Crawford as a central character. Jack served as Mitchell's guide during his initial travels through the Black Hills. *Robert Kolbe*

3,000 feet, all the law allows us. If the quartz prospects as well down, and it generally does better, we have all we want.

Well, on Wednesday evening, the same day we left Custer, we struck camp about 4 p. m., on Current's discovery, on Spring creek. Mr. Current was with the party. After striking camp your correspondent staked out a claim, and after a little singing and story telling, turned into our tent for the night.

THURSDAY, 17TH.

While the other boys worked in the gulch, Mr. Current and myself tackled a high bar, Current on the side of one bar, and I sank prospect hole between two bars. The hole was eight feet long by three feet wide, and rather hard to dig, but gold was the object, and hope made our task easy, although an occasional blister told how our hands were affected. At dinner time we had the sweet satisfaction of standing shoulder deep in the hole, and on our way to dinner we brought a pan of gravel with us and found four colors, which means four small pieces of gold, as large as pin-heads. This was indeed gratifying. After dinner, four of us (the whole party) started to build a cabin, and by 5 p. m. we had finished, excepting the roof. The weather was beautiful and snow all gone.

FRIDAY, 18TH.

Another fine day; finished cabin, and into the prospect hole once more; sunk her 12 feet by 6 p. m., and threw out all the dirt with a short-handled shovel. At this depth struck a large white quartz rock; thought it was bed rock, but it was not; back ached and we were glad we could go no farther. About 30 teams passed us going north.

SATURDAY, 19TH.

Tackled rock in hole, and got it on end; not yet on bed rock; prospected and got about 6 cents to the pan, and quit. Current suggested, "Jack, let's go out and get a deer, our fresh meat is getting short." Started towards Harney Peak, over mountains, down gulches, and finally struck Crawford's gulch. Here we shot a fine black tail deer, and Mr. Current, after fastening it on his poney, started back up the gulch along the base of Harney's Peak, and said he, "Jack, you strike southwest and meet me near Grizzly Grange." I started out, rifle in hand, and putting spurs to my Arabian, was soon watching for another buck, but old "Sol" was sinking in the west, and I had to make haste to reach the appointed grange. When arriving there, it was dusk, and what was my surprise, when I found that Current was not there, although he had three miles of a cut-off to get there. I sat down and waited; then I hollered; then I saw a wolf, and shot my rifle off, and yet no response from Current. I think, however, I missed the wolf, as he scampered off very leisurely, occasionally looking back, as much as to say "try again," and although he was 500 yards off, I fixed my sights and blazed away. He again started off, but this time on three legs. I hit him in the front fore leg, but it was too dark to see him after he got further up the mountain. In the meantime Current had nearly arrived at camp, having purposely left me to find my way, and when 9 p. m. arrived and no word from me, he remarked to the boys, "Well, if Jack lays out to-night, it will be an item for the Bee." But although I confess I was lost, I managed to climb a high mountain, leading my pony, and from its summit I beheld a fire.

A beacon light to guide my footsteps
  Through the hills so rich with gold,
And it was a welcome beacon,
  For the night was growing cold.

So I came down the opposite side from which I went up, and on approaching the fire, which was on Spring Gulch, I saw a solitary individual with long hair and whiskers, and a dog, which reminded me somewhat of Rip Van Winkle and his dog Snyder. I approached him and found he had camped for the night, and upon enquiring where I was, he replied, in broken English, "Vell, I guess you vos in der Black Hill."

I answered, "I know that, my friend; but what gulch is this?"

The man informed me that he "vos a shtranger in dis coundry, und don't know; but," said he, "I guess you is aboud twelf miles from Cusder Cidy." Finally he told me that there was a party camped two miles down, with a big tent. "Now, pard," said I, "you've hit me; put it there!" and after giving Dutchy a good hand-shake I started out and had no trouble in finding camp, where I arrived almost frozen. All the welcome I received was a laugh at my expense, so I warmed at our big camp fire, and laughed myself; yet, had I slept out without even an overcoat and only my saddle blanket, I think I would scarcely have relished the joke so well. However, after a good round of venison and some fresh bread and coffee, I felt all right and believed I could whip my weight in wildcats, "Ranger" included, by Jove!

SUNDAY, 20TH.

We broke camp and moved to Newton's Fork, a gulch not before prospected. I hunted across the mountain with Current, while the team went round, and shot some chickens and squirrels.

MONDAY, 21ST.

Sunk hole on bed of creek at head of gulch; water sinks above and raises to surface below; went down to bed rock and only got small prospects. While at work M. P. Cody, an old mountaineer and experienced miner, dropped into camp, took off his coat and went to work prospecting with us. He said he was well pleased with the country, and never saw better indications of gold. We found several quartz leads on the mountains near us and brought some home with us to prospect.

TUESDAY MORNING.

Broke camp again and started for Custer; came across a hunting party who had killed twenty-four deer in five days; four men stopped for dinner at DeVoe's cabin; five men digging ditch to carry water over to our post; and work progressing finely; everyone in good spirits and prospects good.

Arriving at Custer we learned that 100 head of stock were run off on the night before on Spring Creek; a large party out after them; think it was the Indians who did it; ten head were stolen on Dead Wood last week. Fears are entertained of Indian raids, as soon as the snow is entirely off, in the north.

A notice was posted this morning, Feb. 24th, calling for a meeting on the 26th of citizens and miners for the purpose of organizing a company for the protection of life and property from Indians.

Mr. Franklin, owner of claim No. 7, above ours, panned out forty cents to one pan yesterday, and averaged ten cents to the pan, on this (French creek), two miles above Custer.

Three hundred houses are up and being finished.

Mr. T. Hooper, of Cheyenne, formerly city recorder of this place, is preparing a sketch of Custer City as she now is, especially for the BEE, and will send it by the next person going out. Mr. Hooper is a good artist, and will do it justice.

There are at least 600 lots taken up at present, and some lots are being bought and sold for from $300 to $500.

Provisions are reasonable.

Messrs. Ward & Co.'s saw mill will commence to saw lumber next week. The present party sell exclusively for cash, and ask $40 per M, but Messrs Ward & Co. will sell for $35, and on time and good security.

As the mail is about leaving, I must close for the present.

JACK.

[*Omaha Daily Bee*, 27 March 1876]

CUSTER CITY.

CUSTER CITY, March 1.

EDITOR BEE:

I have just returned from another prospect down French creek, twelve miles from Custer City. W. H. Wood, recorder of the lower district, accompanied us. The scenery is grand from Custer all the way to Glen Wallace. Glens and mountains, beautiful pineries, timber from six inches to two feet and a half through, and hay from one to three feet are all along the creek. Glen Wallace is a grand and pretty spot; it is where the road comes into Spring creek, which Captain Mix took last summer when he brought the miners out.

There are many strange devices carved on the trees by soldiers—crosses, spears, initials of persons, number of regiment and letter of company. On one board nailed to a tree were these lines:

OUR SENTIMENTS.

We soldiers have got the blues—
Cause—the d—d infernal Sioux;
We know the miner boys are bricks,
But we obey Commander Mix.
We know the time is not afar
When we will see an Indian war;
We know our efforts are as vain
As to make this creek run up again;
We know the miners, too, are right.
So let the reds and miners fight.

SOME BOYS IN BLUE.

Besides these verses we found many other strange sayings, such as soldiers will think or write as they pass along on a campaign.

We found four men prospecting nearly as far down as Glenn Wallace, and about three miles above them were three colored men, who were taking out good prospects. One piece of gold we saw weighed $1.10, and other pieces as much as 30 and 50 cents.

The Indians, it was reported to us, were down the creek, and we made it our business to scout around considerable, for the purpose of finding some signs, but nary a sign did we see, although we expect to hear of them every day. There has been considerable stock run off already, and now that Gen. Crook is after them, we may expect some bold raids from the north.

Property is still on the advance here. There are hundreds waiting for places to put their goods in, and the streets are covered with teams, and almost every other lot is occupied by a tent, wherein people are living, waiting till their houses are built.

Mr. Thompson is putting up a building and has it nearly completed, 40x60, in which there are twenty-four rooms up stairs.

There is still a noticeable increase of building all over town.

Mr. Charles Whitehead, special correspondent of the Kansas City *Times*, arrived here yesterday, and is one of the boys. He has had much experience in western life, and he looks hearty; he took a little tramp to-day as far as the stockade, and he is delighted with the country beyond anything he ever expected. In fact he acknowledged that he was considerably prejudiced against the country, but this evening he told us he would never live anywhere else. He is going back to Kansas City for his wife and family in a short time. He said if there was no gold in the country, it was good enough; but he has seen the gold, and has himself taken it out, as we did. He will write a long descriptive letter to-night.

Mr. Thomas Hooper has finished a sketch of Custer, and will forward with this letter; will want 500 copies here as soon as you get it lithographed. We have orders for 200. You will see Custer City as it now is with Harney's Peak and other mountains in the distance.

Mr. W. H. Wood will leave here on next Saturday, for Omaha, with several specimens of gold and silver [ore] to be assayed. He will take some from our lode, which you will please have assayed and let me know the result through Mr. Wood.

Quartz is all the rage now, and miners are out prospecting and bringing in fine specimens.

Mail matter is lying at Red Cloud by the bushel. Postmasters send it there, we suppose, to get rid of it. There is so much of it at the agency now that parties coming in that way will not carry it on account of its weight. We hope soon to have a mail route, and get our papers regularly.

Ward's saw-mill will belch in about three days, and then we will have plenty of lumber. Messrs. Ward & Co. are fine men, and will have more orders than they can attend to as soon as they are ready.

We expect a BEE press in every day; there is nothing more needful. More anon.

CAPTAIN JACK.

[*Omaha Daily Bee*, 18 March 1876]

THE GOLD FIELDS.

(Special Correspondence of the BEE.)

CUSTER CITY, March 8.

We start to-morrow for the summit of Harney's Peak, in company with Mr. Whitehead, correspondent of the Kansas City *Times*, and will give you a poetical and prosaic description of the Hills from that point.

This evening a gentleman by the name of Allen delivered a lecture for the benefit or entertainment of the miners, his subject being the Black Hills. The lecturer is a fair orator, though somewhat bombastic, and not a little "off." The lecture was rather dry and the subject displayed poor taste in selection, inasmuch as he alluded to the Black Hills and their richness, though he only arrived in Custer City three days ago from Cheyenne. Most of his hearers have been here nearly all winter, and have learned more than he could tell them in a week. He also spoke about Nebraska, and the sufferers, and said that she looked to the Black Hills to be lifted out of her poverty. We did not remain to hear him finish, as we had other business to attend to. Judge Dougherty followed Mr. Allen, and it is said that his remarks were more timely and of more general interest. The judge seems well pleased with our new government, and although he is one of the old "Stonewall Jackson" men who first laid out and organized the town, he says he won't squeal.

Fritz Drongmond [Drogmund], formerly of Elkhorn station, was arrested this morning by the United States marshal from Yankton, for selling liquor on the Indian reservation without a license. Rumsellers will please make a note of this. Fritz is now on his way to Yankton, and leaves a young wife and pretty babe, and the finest hotel building in the city unfinished—two stories high and containing 24 rooms. As soon as the marshal arrives at Yankton, and after turning Fritz over to the proper authorities, he will return with warrants for ten or twelve other gentlemen in the hardware business, and will have force enough to take them all with him, unless they depart for fields more appropriate and pastures new. Selling liquor on the Indian reservation (and let it be remembered that this is still part of it until treated for, or until the red man is removed) is a penitentiary offense, and those who sell, do it at a great risk.

Mr. Wm Gay, whom I mentioned in my last letter, has been in my cabin this evening, and the following is our conversation:

Jack—"Bill, when did you go out of the Hills?"

Bill—"I left next day after your arrival, which was January 23d."

Jack—"How much gold did you take out with you?"

Bill—"I had $120 when I left Custer, after coming from White Wood, and brought it all to Spotted Tail with me.

Jack—"How long did it take you to get that out?"

Bill—"Well, there were five of us. We lived on meat straight for twenty days, and, when we got to work, one cooked, one hunted, and three men sluiced that out in fifteen hours, and we did not work very hard either?"

Jack—What did you do with the gold?"

Bill—"Well, I gave away considerable at the agency, and sold some there, and gave the balance, $86, to A. J. Feay, the sutler at Camp Sheridan."

Jack—"How is it we heard nothing of your gold through the papers?"

Bill—"Well, I asked Feay why he did not report it to the Omaha Bee, and he said he did not want Omaha to know anything about it."

Jack—"What was his reason?"

Bill—"Damn-fi-know."

Jack—"You are satisfied, then, that there is gold in paying quantities on White and Dead Wood."

Bill—"Yes, I should say I was. I wouldn't go to all this expense if I didn't," referring to the provisions he went out for.

There was much more said during our intercourse, during which Mr. Gay said that the people only laughed at him when he told of the richness of the country. "But," said he, "She's there, pard, and we have got it."

Mr. Charles Jacobs just came in this evening. He showed your correspondent $2.80, which he is willing to swear he panned out in two pans. Another man panned out $7.20 in three pans, and he says two other men took out $13.60 in six pans, before he left, last Thursday. A man by the name of Aleck McBeth, and a boy, went to work on a claim twelve miles from the foot hills. McBeth was shot at and wounded in the thigh by three Indians, who fired upon them. He got behind a tree and let drive at them, and they retreated. A party of seventy men started out after them, and made a camp at "Fort Speagle," (a German's ranche). The proprietor thought they came to jump him, and he threatened to shoot the whole outfit. Scouts had been sent out, but had not returned when Mr. Jacobs left. Two more Indians were seen to-day eight miles from here, and were shot at. No one hurt.

A party of high-toned roosters, oily tongued speculators, and men of means, arrived here to-day from Rapid City—that is Upper Rapid. There are two Rapid City's and neither are building up very rapidly. It seems this party came from Yankton to Rapid and organized or established a town site in Lower Rapid; but the people agreed to disagree, and the majority moved rapidly up to another place, laid out a town, built some cabins, and called it Upper Rapid. This, of course, has been done very rapidly. This high-toned party I speak of are not like the hardy miner, who comes here to earn his fortune (if the old dame favors him), but a party who, it seems, came here for the purpose of speculating. They had with them a fine surveyor, a secretary of some high official. The United States marshal, who, of course, had to make his expenses, took Mr. Drougmond out for selling liquor, and others. This party intend to show the eastern people *gold* found in and around Rapid City, so they will say. They will also pronounce this part of the country a fraud, and try to induce people not to come by way of Cheyenne or Sidney, as their route, the Missouri river via old Ft. Pierre, is the only route—the nearest and the best. Now the eastern people will just swallow about one dose of their medicine and then vomit. No doubt they will advertise extensively and offer big inducements, but if the miners and others wish to keep their hair let them come by Sidney or Cheyenne, for just as sure as a dead Indian is a good Indian, there will be war in the north, and no end of scalping, just as soon as Sitting Bull and Little Bad Man are pursued by Gen. Crook. Besides, this same party goes from Rapid City to Custer; thence to Spotted Tail; thence to Sidney; there leave their teams, and take train for Yankton, intending to come back the same way. Oh! consistency, thou art a jewel.

CAPT. JACK.

[*Omaha Daily Bee*, 20 March 1876]

THE LAND OF GOLD.

(Correspondence of the BEE.)

CUSTER CITY, March 10.

In my last letter I told you I was about to start for Harney's Peak, and so we did yesterday—Mr. Whitehead and myself—having four days' rations, our blankets strapped on our ponies, and a delightful morning. We started up the Laughing Water, due north, for four miles, then northeast between two mountains of solid rock. I will not attempt a description of the scenery, for no pen can describe it.

Parks almost as green as in summer, natural amphitheatres surrounded by walls of granite, and stately trees, from one to three feet through, and a natural arch of willows growing on each side of the creek for miles. In one of those little Eden's we camped for dinner, and let our ponies feed on the luxuriant grass. Whitehead baked the slap-jacks (pancakes), while I cooked the bacon and boiled the coffee, after which, spreading our buffalo robe on Nature's table, we sat down to a good square meal. After dinner I remarked to Charley that it was not worth while to wash the dishes. "No," said he, "just wipe the frying pan with some bunch grass, and that will do till supper. After packing and being ready, Charley bade your correspondent mount a rock, (if we could climb) and find out which way we could get out of the park best. We climbed the rock about forty feet, then mounting a tree which grew in a ledge climbed that, swinging onto another ledge, and finally reached the top, nearly two hundred feet from the ground. Yet it seemed as if I had not left the ground when I looked around at those gigantic rocks still hundreds of feet above, and all around me. I saw the gap, however, and we left our camping ground and traveled on foot up the mountain, leading our ponies. I might here mention that a snow storm, which seemed almost to darken the sky, came on while preparing dinner, but the clouds soon passed away, and the snow, which was something like small hailstones, but soft, came tumbling down, seemingly dancing in the sunshine, while we sat in our shirt sleeves enjoying our meal and the scene. Nearly an hour was occupied in ascending the mountain, and when on its summit, we both sat down to rest and again feast upon nature's grandeur. Full forty miles northeast could be seen around the mountain tops, we being above them. They looked like the domes of grand buildings, all thrown in together. Harney's

Peak, still far above us, southeast, looked somewhat gloomy as it reared its head toward the sky; and then looking back over the country through which we had traveled, Charley said: "Jack, they talk about their Switzerland, the Yosemite Valley, and scenes in Africa. I have seen them all, but this is grander than all I have ever beheld." Said he: "I fear that people will think—I am sure they will—in fact, we are drawing it too strong, but pshaw, no man can begin to give an outline description of it;" and then he would wish that he had some of his friends here from Kansas City to enjoy it.

After putting up our field glasses, with our *little hatchets* we blazed a tree right on the top of this mountain, next in height to Harney's, and named it *Bee Mount*, under which we scribbled these lines:

TO BEE MOUNT.

The busy Bee will toil all day
To fill his little locker;
The miners, by the first of May,
With sluice and pan and rocker,
Will toil till shades of evening fall,
And *gold* will be their pay,
But we would freely give it all
For this grand scene to-day.
J. W. C. (Capt. Jack.)
Charley Whitehead.

MARCH 8th, 1876.

A large ravine divided Bee Mount from the Peak, and down we went, intending to cross the creek, camp at the base of Harney, and ascend early this morning.

But,

The best laid plans of Mice and Men,
Gang aft aglee,
With us it was the same just then,
As you shall see.

On reaching the foot of the mountain we entered a grove of trees—tall hemlock—and coming into a pretty spot, concluded to camp alongside of the creek, as there was good grass for our ponies and so many dry sticks and twigs that the red skins would find some trouble in getting close to us. We had scarcely removed our blankets and saddles when snow again commenced falling, this time faster and thicker than before. We found a splendid shelter, however. Eight trees, from one to two feet through, stood in a circle and formed one of the prettiest natural bowers we ever saw, and all came together at the top, making it look like an Indian tepee on the ground. After removing the dry sticks, leaves, etc., we found moss from three to four inches deep, and as soft as feathers. We took our lariat rope, and running it across from tree to tree formed a roof, which we covered with boughs, and setting some between each of the trees soon had a comfortable house, with a bright camp fire and a natural chimney 100 feet high. Charley advised us to tie our ponies, but I told him mine would not leave where I was, and the trees being so dense we feared they would get tangled, so we let them loose, for which we had cause afterwards to regret. After our ponies seemed contented and browsing, we prepared supper, Charley mixing the slap-jacks, while I baked them; he buttering them while hot. After supper we felt so tired we concluded we would not do any writing, except making some notes. After incidents, Charley told quite a detailed history of his life, which was very interesting, and we in return related part of ours, after which we retired for the night. By this time the snow had fallen nearly four inches deep.

And,

With the beautiful snow above us,
    And beneath us the moss-covered sod,
To dream of the dear ones who love us,
    And watched by the angels of God.

Our dreams, however, were of short duration, for about one o'clock in the morning, Charley nudged me with his elbow, and jumping up, I soon had my rifle ready for use. Twigs cracked promiscuously, and as soon as our eyes were open, we knew that the Indians would not make such a racket. We were soon satisfied as to the cause; Charley's pony passed by the tent, and I spoke to him. He paid no attention to me, except to whinner, and went on. My mare had gone ahead—I could see that,—and the thought struck me at once that they were making for Custer City, either the snowstorm or something else having scared them. Charley, having a pair of overshoes handy, jumped into them, and followed the ponies for a short distance, but returned, not being able to see the trail. Then my boots were frozen, it having turned cold, and by the time I got them thawed out and on the ponies' trail, they had a good start. I went after them, however clambering up the hill, and when on its summit near the trees which we inscribed, we found that the ponies had gone on down; still we followed on the trail the ponies being scarcely visible at times, and before we thought of returning had got six miles from camp. We held a council then, and wondered which would be best—to go back to camp or go on to Custer, for there is where our ponies were going, and we concluded to "go on to Custer or bust," as the boys said, when going to Pikes Peak. We had neither rifle or revolver, nothing but a jack-knife, and even forgot our gloves; but on we went, falling down every hundred yards or so, bare hands into the snow; finally we put our hands in our pockets; next time we fell, in trying to get our hands out, and while rolling down hill in the snow, we ripped our pants, the buckle on the back being open, all the way down to the seat. This made the atmosphere effectively cool, and the rapid inflation of that garment reminded us of balloon days in Omaha. The cold gas, however, caused us to make a little better headway to Custer. Unfortunately we soon lost the trail; but believing the ponies would go right to town we did not care to keep it, but hurried on making a cut-off occasionally. We arrived at Custer at 5 a.m., cold, tired and sleepy; cooked some grub, and lay down by the fire to take a nap and caught a bad cold; up at 6:30, and started to hunt for another poney with which to find my own; could not catch any in Smiley's herd, so I went back home, one and a half miles, for rope; made a lasso, and roped a stallion, belonging to Mr. S. K. Current, on the jump; rode back to meet Charley or find the horses and take them back, and was surprised to see him coming down the Laughing Water, 2 miles above Custer, on his own poney, having found him about a mile above. Charley's condition was indeed pitiful—his moustache white with ice, and his hair silvered with frost. He told me that he walked till within one half mile of where we met him, and, said he, "I am so still and lame that I could not have walked one-half mile further." I gave my gun to a miner, who was coming in, to carry for me, and as soon as I saw the poney I mounted him and made him [Charley] go into a cabin near by and warm, till I went up for my Arabian, which I found feeding with some other cattle, and then came back and made Charley mount my saddled stallion, while I took it bare-back the rest of the way home, and, ye Gods! how that horse did *cut up*.

His back-bone was sharp as a razor,
  Right back from his mane to his tail,
And, by the great Nebuchadnezer,
  I'd sooner be rode on a rail.

Well, Charley imagined all sorts of things about "we'uns;" he thought we were captured by reds or engulfed in a snow-drift, or something equally horrible. He cooked a big breakfast for us this morning, and said he did not sleep a wink all night, but kept up a big fire as a beacon light to guide us back to our haven of shelter and safety. He left everything but my cartridge belt, knife and rifle, so we must return to-morrow or next day for them.

The snow is about five inches deep, and the weather is rather cold, but the sky is beautifully clear and bright.

Several gamblers left here to-day disgruntled. They said they came here to gamble (they ought to have said steal), and would do nothing else; but there is no mining going yet around Custer, nor will there be any money taken out till May 1st.

We hope all the gamblers will give Custer a wide birth. They are not wanted here, and we can get along without them. One thing is certain: the citizens of Custer City are good, law-abiding citizens, most of them poor and honest, and will stand no nonsense from rowdies, gamblers, or red skins, and the first party who will be guilty of a misdemeanor will suffer just as sure as there's a God. There is no doubt but what Custer will be peopled with a progressive class of citizens. True, there are a few sore-heads here, who wanted the whole city to themselves—in fact, one of them did fence in a whole block; and because the trustees took it away from him, he's kicking; and since the arrival of Hascall, the rascal, there has been more dissatisfaction than we have had since the city was organized. The idea of that cheeky individual entering a trustee meeting, and because some of this jumping element were with him, take the power of settling adverse claims out of their hands. There is, however, another and better element at work, and the right will prevail.

As this letter is mailed snow to the extent of eight inches covers the ground, and it still is falling.

CAPT. JACK.

[*Omaha Daily Bee*, 20 March 1876]

A SHOOTING SCRAPE AT CUSTER CITY.

(Special to the BEE.)

CUSTER CITY, March 16.

Alexander Shaw was shot through the head last evening by his partner, named Milligan, while the latter was under the influence of liquor. Shaw still lives, but will die to-day. The jury acquitted Milligan, as it was proven an accident, but he was fined twenty-five dollars and costs for shooting in the city limits. Snow six inches deep. The storm is over, and though cold, the sun shines brightly.

CAPT. JACK.

[*Omaha Daily Bee*, 1 April 1876]

CUSTER CITY.

(Special Correspondence of the BEE.)

CUSTER CITY, March 21.

Another snow storm has come and gone, and to-day the sun shines in his usual splendor. Everybody seems busy, doing something, the most exciting part of the last week's programme being jumping lots. Many have built cabins six and seven feet high, leaving them so, and believing them safe, but they are far from it. The trustees passed a resolution giving such parties as wished to put board or shingle roofs on their buildings until April 15th, provided such buildings were eight feet high, with a door cut in. There have been some 40 or 50 lots and buildings already jumped, and every day adds more to the number that is jumpable.

Mr. Chas. Whitehead and your correspondent started for the foot of Harney's Peak on the 13th, to bring home our effects left there when our Bronchos left us, and our surprise may be imagined when on reaching our old camp (which Charles since named "Calamity Camp") to find that all was gone except a field glass (which we borrowed), a navy revolver and a pair of spurs. These Mr. Whitehead put under some dried brush, and at the roots of the trees, the snow afterwards covering them up; but the thieves, (reds or whites we cannot say, as the snow drifted too much to distinguish the trail,) after taking two buffalo robes, two pair of blankets, two good saddles and four days' rations, set fire to the camp, and hence the glass and revolver were totally ruined. We believe that it was the work of Indians, as we found a camp fire still smouldering one mile northeast of the Peak. We had brought nothing with us save enough bread and bacon for a lunch, and could not follow the trail. We left Custer about 9 a. m., without bridles or saddles, and with simply a blanket thrown across the backs of our bronchos; and to say that those horses "cut up," would be drawing it exceedingly mild. We care not for the pecuniary loss we sustained, nor does Mr. Whitehead; but one article we can never replace—our old scrap-book, which your correspondent valued very much, and which was in our saddle-bag. It contained over 500 poems, etc., of our own composition, some of them composed toward the close of the late war, when we had to employ another to write down the words, as we were then unable to do so; verses composed during our boyhood, replete with reminiscences and sweet recollections of by-gone days. We also lost valuable letters from soldiers and statesmen, which were highly prized.

But never more my eyes shall feast
   On those plain lines so dear, so free;
Those simple verses of the heart,
   Oh, red skin give them back to me.
In solitude and lonely hours,
   How oft have I scanned each line,
Until I saw fair blooming flowers
   And thanked kind heaven those lines were mine.

And must I lose them now, alas!
   I know not, think not, where to look;
And while my heart is sad, indeed,
   I can but say, farewell old book;
Farewell, companion of my soul,
   No other book your tale can tell,
No other lines my heart console;
   Old book of yore, farewell, farewell!

Reports from the north say that a fight between the Indians and miners had taken place, in which thirty of the Indians were killed and one white man. It seems that about three weeks ago, the Indians run off a lot of stock; at the same time they shot a miner in the thigh. A party of 70 miners started out after them, having six experienced scouts with them. The scouts found the Indians in camp, and the miners surprising them, killing 30, while only one white man was killed on the side of the miners. We have reason to believe this is true, as we are well acquainted with some of the party who were on their trail; and we know that they were well posted and determined men.

It is thought now that General Crook has gone north after the warriors, and that they will strike for the Hills for the purpose of evading the military and plundering the miners.

The first omnibus arrived in Custer on last Saturday, loaded with passengers from Cheyenne. Immediately after its arrival Mr. P. McKay, Tom Hooper, John Burrows, Dr. Beamis, and several other gentlemen jumped in and ordered the driver to give them a whirl around the block just to commemorate the arrival of the first 'bus into Custer. After an hour's drive, most of which time they were *standing still* singing lines and passing the bottle, they left the bus and went to the house of Mr. Moody to celebrate his birthday, while mirth was monarch of the town. Next morning Mrs. Peterson, the better half owner of said 'bus, brought in a little bill of twenty-five dollars, *just to celebrate the first 'bus bill, you know*. It was cheerfully paid by the gentlemen, however, and Mrs. P. departed. Last evening her husband, Mr. P, dragged her out of their rented cabin by the hair of the head, and gave her a bad looking head and face. She retaliated, afterward, with frying pans, etc., which she flung at his head. It seems the twenty-five dollars was enough to set both on a spree, even if "benzine" is twenty-five cents per drink.

Since the arrival of Hascall, the rascal, in Custer we have had no peace. Before he arrived here there were no law suits—all matters regarding rights to lots were left with the board of trustees to decide, but he (Hascall) went into their meeting as counsel for John P. Harlow against John Taylor, and by his bombastic, prepared oration, and with the consent of the president, who should have kicked him out, made the trustees, composed of 12 citizens, believe that they were not capable of deciding such cases, and therefore it was thrown into court, and since then the justices and lawyers are reaping a rich harvest. Most of it, however, is what the miners call jaw-bone, or bed-rock pay—wait till you get it.

Hascall is credited with being the principal framer of a new organic act, presented to the people on the eve of March 17th. Although Judge [J. W.] Lytle shoulders a large part of it, and worked hard for its adoption, Mr. Charles Whitehead of the Kansas City *Times*, took up the matter, section by section, and showed the people that the law was a trap which they themselves would spring if they voted for them, and after reading our original provisional law, he was vociferous applauded, and the proposed laws overthrown. A committee of 12 men was then appointed to frame laws which would in no way conflict with our present provisional government, unless it was deemed for the best interests of the people. The laws proposed are forwarded in the original manuscript.

Hascall left here a day or two before the meeting, and various reports are afloat regarding his movements. Some say he went to Omaha; others that he left for the purpose of going to Yankton to secure an office by appointment, or do some scheming. No matter where he goes, however, he will be better thought of to stay away from here. Let no man come here and attempt to plot against the people to enhance himself; it won't go. The people are capable of making their own laws, and have agreed to stand by the provisional government until such times as the legally constituted authority takes control, which will be as soon as the government opens the Hills by treaty or other means.

An election will be held on next Saturday, on which occasion there will be elected one city clerk, one city surveyor, one recorder, one appellate judge, city treasurer, one assessor; also 12 trustees, whose president will be ex-officio mayor. We are not as yet acquainted with the nature of the new amendment, which the committee will present. If, however, they conflict with the old laws, the people will get up and buck against them. But if they are favorable to the people they will be adopted by them.

Why does not some of your enterprising young Omaha lawyers make a trip out here? There is room for millions more. There are only seven professors here now. Judge Hascall has laid the foundation for law suits for twenty years to come.

There is no prospecting being done at present. People are kept too busy building just now to save their lots from the jumpers.

There is no press in the Hills as yet, but soon will be. Mr. Whitehead, of the Kansas City *Times*, who is interested in the Evening *News*, of that city, will return with a press in April.

Another saw mill will be in this week. Parties are now hauling logs and laying the foundation. Messrs. Ward & Parshal are doing an extensive business in that line, and sell their lumber for $35 per 1000 feet.

The Spotted Tail Saw Mill Company charged $50 for lumber until Ward came in; yet they had the assurance to ask the city for several lots gratis for a lumber yard, because they were first here. But the city could not see it that way.

Messrs. [H. E.] Brown & [Frank] Yates arrived here yesterday with the first stage, making the trip from Cheyenne via Red Cloud in five days, and killing two horses by the experiment. They say their line will start April 1st, but we are getting tired here listening to reports, and until the regular line starts running and gets here we will not believe. We were promised a regular line by February 15th from Red Cloud. Mr. Dear informs us by letter that his stages are now running from Sidney and will leave for the Hills forthwith. Good 'nuf.

CAPT. JACK.

[*Omaha Daily Bee*, 11 April 1876]

CUSTER CITY.

(Special Correspondence of the BEE.)

CUSTER CITY, March 27.

Since my last letter hundreds of miners have arrived in Custer from the East and West. Also professional gentlemen, doctors, lawyers and business men of almost every description.

Claim jumping has been the order of the day, but some of the jumpers have at last run against the right party. A man by the name of A. R. Lasher, secured four poles about ten feet long and two to four inches thick, and with a notice which read thusly: "I claim this lot for building purposes," and put them on Mr. Wm. McHugh's lot for a foundation. This lot is in the best part of the city, and next to the corner of Crook and Sixth street. A certain John A. Smiley had charge of said lot, and had complied with the law. A cabin was up on the back of the lot, holding it until Mr. McHugh would arrive with his goods preparatory to building a large business house. About an hour after this lot was claimed by this jumper, John Smiley was informed of the fact. He immediately repaired to his cabin, and securing his shooting-irons went in search of the jumper. In the mean time he had thrown away the fishing poles which staked and claimed the lot, and attracted quite a crowd by his energetic actions. To say that John was mad would be drawing it mild, and had he seen the man placing his poles on the lot he would have shot him without a moment's hesitation. After an hour's search Smiley found his man in a store, and calmly remarked, "Are you the man who jumped my lot?" "I don't know; I put my poles and notice on a lot which I was told was jumpable." "Well, look ye here," said John, "if ever I catch you on that there lot, d—n you, I'll kill you! My name is John A. Smiley, and I've been on the plains and fighting jumpers for twenty years." The gentleman had very little to say, except that he would institute a law suit. "No," said John, "you come on there again, and you'll never attend another law suit." The lot has not been jumped since, and the jumpers now are asking a great many questions regarding the characters of the men whose lots are jumpable.

Swannger's Hall, or Hurdey Gurdey house, as it is termed, is open and in full blast for some time back. On the opening night the hall presented a peculiar appearance. On entering the first thing we met was the bar to the left, running back about fifteen feet; on the right was the fire-place, where pine knots were blazing; and still farther to the right a lot of bedding, buffalo robes, &c.; next, to the right, came two horses eating some corn, while in the other half of the building was a floor on which were four fairy-like forms gliding around in the gay quadrille, while four of the hardy miner boys, whose heavy boots sounded like so many trip-hammers in a foundry, were handling the girls as they would flowers in the spring time—they looked so delicate, you know. Four candles illuminated the room, but these have since been replaced by lamps and oil; a complete floor has been laid, and it costs those who wish to indulge in a dance the sum of fifty cents for each set, to be paid at the bar after the dance is over, for which he receives a cigar or drink, and his girl, or the young lady he danced with, also receives a treat.

Another mass meeting was held on the 22d to hear report of committee of twelve who were appointed to draft laws for the government of Custer City. Said committee were instructed to draft laws which would in no wise conflict with the present laws; and the committee, of which Dr. J[oseph] G. Bemis was chairman, carried out their instructions faithfully and well, with the exception of the last section, which read in the latter part: "Also, that all *pre-existing* laws *be and are hereby repealed*." Your correspondent objected to this, and with the assistance of Hon. P. McKay and others, we amended the section so as to not interfere with existing laws which found an existence at the ballot box but a few weeks ago. All officers elected by ballot we retained in office until January 1st, 1877. A new board of twelve trustees will be elected on next Saturday, when the new laws, or, rather, amendments to the old, will also be voted upon. There will also be elected one city treasurer, city attorney, surveyor, superior judge, coroner, assessor, and two justices of the peace.

Dr. A. S. Pendery and E. Archer, both from Omaha, arrived here all O. K., and are delighted with the country. They say they had a very fair trip, but considerable snow. The doctor *froze* the point of his *nose*, which I will *disclose*, and it's red as a *rose*. He'll be mad I suppose, as he said to me, "Jack, you needn't say anything about the *nose*," but I suppose everybody *nose* it by this time.

Well, Dr. P. and Mr. Archer are gentlemen of character and will make good citizens. The doctor will have his drug store up in a few days, and intends to remain here.

I am meeting people from all parts of the country, who enquire for me every day, and their first salutation generally is, "Jack, how are you? We have read your letters; is the country as good as you say?" And I always answer, "Well, you can look around for a few days, and satisfy yourselves." And I have seen but very few dissatisfied. Enterprise district, of which Mr. Wood is recorder, was thrown open, or will be on the 29th of this month, and each claim must be represented one day out of every six.

JACK.

[*Omaha Daily Bee*, 12 April 1876]

CUSTER CITY.

(Special Correspondence of the BEE.)

CUSTER CITY, March 28.

It has been snowing here almost continually every day for a week, and the sun melts it just as fast, and although it is snowing now very fast, there is scarcely any on the ground.

The total vote cast at the city election to-day was 552, and owing to the inclemency of the weather and the fact that many refused to vote because the candidates were unknown to them, they having so lately arrived. It is estimated that not more than a two-thirds vote was polled. Besides there are many miners down the gulch as far as 12 miles and up 6 or 8 miles, working their claims, who did not come to town.

The judges and clerks are now counting the votes, and they will in all probability be busy all night, as there are nineteen offices to be filled. Hence, nineteen names on each ticket and all written, besides there was any amount of scratching done.

THIS LITTLE WORLD OF OURS

And so it is a little world,
  Surrounded by the plain—
A world of wealth as yet untold,
  And yet of worldly fame;
And mountains towering to the sky,
  Where rests the snowy showers,
Will bloom with roses by and by
  In this little world of ours.

Let poets write of fairy lands,
  Or fables old and gray;
I'll soar around these snow-clad,
  And from them take my lay,
And when the grass from out the sod
  Is peeping with the flowers,
I'll sit and gaze from Harney's peak
  On this little world of ours.

The humblest miner passing by,
  With buckskin on his back,
Will whistle, with a twinkling eye,
  God bless you, old boy Jack.
And this is good enough for me;
  I bless these happy hours,
That fill my soul with joy and glee,
  In this little world of ours.

That settles it. Good night.

SUNDAY MORNING.

And still the votes are not counted. Those candidates who had much opposition are anxiously waiting for the verdict, and the barrooms are being well patronized. A game of faro is going on in the saloon of one of our candidates for treasurer, and numerous small games of poker and freeze-out are being indulged in by the small-fry gamblers who came here with scarce enough cash for a stake, but who expected to find plenty of dust among the miners. *But they didn't.*

A terrific snow storm is prevailing, with a cold northeaster blowing quite a gale, and the stock can be seen huddled around on the sheltered sides of the cabins with a hump on their backs. Poor animals! They will suffer terribly unless this snow ceases and goes off. I paid 12 cents per pound for corn to-day to feed my pony, and it is scarce even at that. Corn can be sold here at 7 cents per pound, and a good profit made on it then; if some party would ship a few carloads in at once it would sell rapidly. If the snow does not go off soon, and corn still remains at such high figures, one-half of our stock will surely die of starvation.

Later.—The counting of votes is completed, after nineteen hours of unceasing work by the judges and clerks of election, and the following are elected:

Total number of votes cast, 552. For Organic Act, 288; against, 24.

Trustees. J. G. Bemis, 517; S. R. Shankland, 495; Jack Crawford, 438; Chas. Miller, 387; D. K. Snively, 387; C. Caldwell, 357; G. E. Thornton, 348; J. W. Rodabank, 344; J. W. Grant, 308; A. A. Abbey, 293; O. B. Jacobs, 288; J. Shondy, 280.

Judge of Superior Court—T. E. Harvey, 486.

Justices of the Peace—Robt. Tale, 492; J. P. Harlow, 335.

City Attorney—A. B. Chalpine, 301.

City Treasurer—T. B. Moody, 221.

City Surveyor—A. J. Parshal, 469.

Coroner—J. Taylor, 261.

City Assessor—Charles Weston, 266.

The election of constables and clerk are of no effect, inasmuch as our present city marshal, J. H. Burrows, is compelled, according to the new laws, to appoint three deputies, whose fees shall be the same as the marshal's, when called upon.

Our present recorder and city clerk has been legally elected by ballot, and must, according to the new laws, continue therein for one year, ending January 1, 1877.

A party arrived here last week from Cheyenne with what was called a printing press, but when we went to look at the elephant it turned out to be only a mouse—a little square box full of type, a roller, and about six quires [twenty-four sheets] of paper. The party concluded they would go north and dig for gold, and left their baby with your correspondent to sell for $20. We are now using some of their paper to write our correspondence on, as ours has run out long since.

There has been a report here that Gen. Crook has made a big fight with the northern Sioux, and whipped them, and we hope it is so; and should he need recruits, we want to hear from him.

Persimon Bill, that renegade and horse thief, is now in the Hills. he traveled four days with a party on the way in from Ft. Laramie last week, and left them twenty miles from here, saying he would eat supper in Custer and then go to Rapid City. We are liable to hear of stock being run off now at any time. There is a big reward for this persimon, and he will be a fat oyster for our Marshal John if he gets him, and he'll get him, too, if he remains in these hills, for he is now on his trail.

JACK.

4

INDIANS, OUTLAWS, AND THE BLACK HILLS RANGERS, APRIL–MAY 1876

The pent-up tension in the Black Hills mining camps finally broke in April as winter gave way to spring and news from the gulches in the northern Hills grew increasingly inviting. Throughout the winter, tales of extraordinary recoveries in the north found their way to Custer City, Cheyenne, Omaha, and the nation. Jack Crawford had not yet traveled there to investigate those diggings, but in his 5 April letter, he included a long missive from William Gay, an acquaintance from the trail. Gay candidly reported severe weather but also good recoveries from Deadwood and Whitewood creeks, including pan yields of ten cents to twenty-five cents and as high as five dollars. Charley Whitehead of the *Kansas City Times* had not yet traveled north either, but he was also collecting glowing news from the Deadwood and Whitewood districts, including details gained from a man named George Mavor, who was in Custer buying supplies. According to Mavor, at least twelve hundred men were then located on Deadwood, Whitewood, and Iron creeks, all waiting and watching for their claims to thaw. "There is no humbug about the northern mines," he asserted. "I have seen men pan out gold by the aid of camp kettles filled with hot water, and make a dollar to the pan right along." Whitehead judged it to be true because, he said, "all the old miners who have arrived here have gone on to the new diggings." Indeed, the "stampede" to Deadwood was on.[1]

In June 1876, Custer City remained an important transportation and communications hub on the Sidney and Cheyenne trails connecting to the Union Pacific Railroad. By this time, however, the focus of the Black Hills gold rush had shifted from Custer City and French Creek in the central Hills to Whitewood and Deadwood creeks in the northern Hills. The wide valley that surrounded Custer City is evident in this photograph. *D. S. Mitchell photograph. Robert Kolbe*

In the weeks ahead, the rush to the northern Black Hills would almost empty Custer City of its residents and businesses as the promising news from the north countered a growing pessimism over the worth of the French Creek diggings. A letter printed in the *Bee* from a sour individual named G. R. "Bob" Armstrong, based in Hill City, appeared a few days after Whitehead's story and assailed the problems he saw with the Custer City locale and the manner in which news was being reported from there. Stories of Indian troubles, which saturated Crawford's April letters, made sensational news, Armstrong asserted, but he saw things differently. "We have no trouble with the Indians, except by their running off stock," he claimed. "At least, when stock is stolen, the Indians are accused of doing it; but most of the people here believe that white men are the guilty parties." Although Crawford was generous in his praise of Armstrong in his 5 April letter, Armstrong did not return the favor, declaring in a blistering tone that the "sensational reports of Indian raids and rich gold discoveries originate in the brains of the letter-writers at Custer City, where there is nothing to 'pan out' but town lots. The fact is," he wailed, "that Custer City—on French Creek—is in a locality where mining will not pay. . . . French Creek never did prospect well. Experienced miners do not tarry long at Custer; but newspaper correspondents do."[2]

Armstrong's criticism of the French Creek diggings could be misconstrued to suggest that little placer gold existed on French Creek, or that the placers were already worked out, but neither instance was true. Geography worked against easy placer mining on French Creek, where the valley for miles on either side of Custer City was wide, gently sloped, and contained limited water. Successful mining there required a maze of dams, drainage ditches, and diversionary channels. Such features, in evidence all along French Creek, required considerable labor that was usually beyond the capacity of single miners and small partnerships working only with pans, rockers, and sluices. From the start, army officer Richard Dodge had forecast that large investments in hydraulic equipment would be required to extract the gold, but it never materialized in the Custer locale, owing largely to the lure of other easier possibilities. North of Custer, such creeks as Spring, Castle, and Rapid were well watered, and the gold was much coarser than the common thin flakes found in French Creek. And the placer riches were even more encouraging farther north yet in Whitewood and Deadwood gulches.[3]

Captain Jack rebutted criticisms about the value of the French Creek claims, noting his veracity in his 9 April letter to the *Sidney Telegraph*. "I was sent here to write the truth," he said, "and as I expect to live and die in this country, and be one of its citizens, I wish no man to censure me for misrepresentation when I knew better." The truth about French Creek, however, was somewhere in between. There was gold in the creek—in marginally paying quantities. As one historian familiar with the Black Hills gold story put it, "For rich gold deposits, prospectors will destroy stream valleys, regardless of geography." French Creek and its valley were never thoroughly upturned, though evidence of placer mining is still plainly evident, especially in the upper valley beyond Bear Rock.[4]

Despite the comments from individuals like Armstrong, one gains the strong sense from Crawford's letters that problems with Indians did indeed exist and were becoming more frequent. Crawford's letter of 8 April reported casualties that Captain James Egan's company of the Second Cavalry had suffered in the 17 March fight on the Powder River in Montana in what proved to be an ominous opening to the Great Sioux War. Egan had visited Custer City often and was a favorite among the citizens. In subsequent letters, Crawford reported local horse raiding, the wounding and killing of herders, Indian scares, chases, face-to-face encounters, and named and unnamed fatalities, some with arrows sticking from them or having been scalped. In fact, by the spring of 1876, the southern Black Hills and the Sidney and Cheyenne roads had thoroughly erupted with Indian trouble, particularly as the army commenced large-scale campaigning farther west and north in Wyoming and Montana in an attempt to move the Lakotas and their Cheyenne allies onto the Great Sioux Reservation. Most everyone understood that this Indian war was rooted in the Black Hills gold rush and that the increasing movement of Oglala and Brulé Sioux from the White River agencies in Nebraska to the camps of Crazy Horse and Sitting Bull in the Powder and Yellowstone River country put Indians and Hillers on confrontational paths; no one was safe. Complaints were widespread, and territorial officials were raising alarms, but government protection was still almost nonexistent north of the North Platte River.[5]

Where they could, Hillers addressed protection matters themselves. In Crawford's *Bee* letters as early as 23 February, he reported the call for volunteers and subsequent formation of a local militia unit known variously as the Custer City Minute Men, Custer City Rangers, or Black Hills Rangers (they were all one and the same). The premise was sound. These citizens organized for their self-defense against Indians, whom they intended to pursue and chastise when opportunity presented itself; they might even offer services to General Crook if aid was needed in or near the Hills. Custer City's

Edward Wynkoop and Jack Crawford partnered in the formation of the Black Hills Rangers in 1876. Wynkoop served as the outfit's prime organizer and commander and Jack as one of its scouts. Here the two have reunited in Santa Fe in the mid-1880s. *Ben Wittick photograph. Palace of the Governors Photo Archives (NMHM/DCA), 15714*

militiamen, with Major Edward W. Wynkoop commanding and Crawford appointed chief of scouts, actually responded credibly to a number of local incidents, exploits carefully detailed in Crawford's *Bee* letters of 20, 24, and 29 April. But the militia was also severely handicapped by poorly over-wintered horse stock, which hindered any greater effectiveness until well into spring when the local meadows had greened and supplies of grain were received from the railheads. Crawford's pleadings to civic-minded Omahans on 15 April to send grain to help recover the stock are both wrenching and almost humorous. In the long run, the need for the Custer City militia would greatly diminish in mid-June 1876 when army camps were established on the Cheyenne Road in the Hat Creek Breaks and at the mouth of Red Canyon and cavalry from Fort Laramie, Camp Robinson, and Sidney Barracks began to patrol the roads with measured frequency. Before then, the need was acute.[6]

Edward Wynkoop, commander of the Rangers, was another Black Hiller with a long history and a surname that Crawford repeatedly corrupted in his *Bee* letters. A native Pennsylvanian like Crawford, Wynkoop had worked his way west during the Colorado gold rush. In Denver, Wynkoop helped organize two different militia companies, serving as an officer and helping to curb local lawlessness in each. At the outbreak of the Civil War, Wynkoop joined the First Colorado Volunteer Infantry and was promptly commissioned, rising to the rank of major; he commanded troops during the Union's repulse of the Confederate invasion of New Mexico in 1862. Subsequent assignments brought him into close contact with Colorado's Indians, and he became an outspoken advocate in their behalf. At the request of regular army officials, Wynkoop investigated the Sand Creek Massacre that occurred on 29 November 1864, perpetrated by the Third Colorado Cavalry, a federalized militia unit. Wynkoop soundly condemned its commander, John Chivington, whom he labeled as an "inhuman monster." His condemnation of Chivington and the Sand Creek affair made him no friends in Colorado, where the Indian slaughter was roundly applauded. Indian affairs kept Wynkoop on the plains until 1868, when he returned to Pennsylvania. But the Black Hills gold rush lured him west in the summer of 1875, and he was among Custer City's founders.[7]

Meanwhile, the blood of non-Indians and Indians continued to pour across the interior and margins of the Black Hills. Two especially egregious episodes in April on the Cheyenne Road ultimately triggered the deployment of regular army troops. The first occurred on 16 April when Charles Metz, his wife, and their cook and driver were murdered in Red Canyon, some thirty miles southwest of Custer City. The Metzes had just sold a profitable bakery in town and were returning to their home in Laramie City. The killings were inordinately vicious and Indians were blamed, although the white outlaw William F. "Persimmon Bill" Chambers was also implicated and had been seen loitering in Custer in the days before the Metzes departed. And then H. E. "Stuttering" Brown was murdered on 21 April between the Cheyenne River crossing and Hat Creek stage station. Again, the likely perpetrator was the outlaw Persimmon Bill. Brown had been superintendent of the Fort Laramie-Custer City leg of the Cheyenne and Black Hills Stage, Mail and Express Company.[8] Captain Jack and the Rangers investigated the Metz and Brown killings, and he reported both episodes for *Bee* readers. Brown was a well-respected former Omahan whose body was returned there for burial. The death of Brown "was a severe blow to us" and another setback to the start of stage service, Crawford lamented on 29 April.

Other killings occurred, too, singly and occasionally in twos and threes. When Indians were implicated, Crawford's descriptions of them were colored with the strong language of the day. He was an undeniable product of that time in America when the righteousness of Manifest Destiny, the nation's conviction that it was entitled to the lands of the frontier irrespective of any other claims or costs, went unquestioned and when Indians were seen only as interfering. In Crawford's view, the Sioux were always prowling for stock and plunder; they were skulkers, dusky devils, or murdering thieves. Crawford rather candidly acknowledged that white men squatting on an Indian reservation had no rights either, but he passed no judgment on the miners and left it to his readers to draw their own conclusions. That stance was way too calculated, but in Captain Jack's day, the view was clear and unchallenged.

While Crawford was capable of almost thoughtless ethnocentrism regarding the Indians of the White River country south of the Black Hills and the Sioux people generally, he could also rather warmly embrace Indians and mixed-bloods who posed him no threat or stood with him in the face of danger. Jules Semineau, or Seminole, was such an individual, whom Crawford regarded as a superb guide. He "never saw a better" one, Crawford said on 20 April. Semineau was a Cheyenne mixed-blood interpreter at the White River agencies and Fort Laramie, had witnessed and perhaps interpreted at the Fort Laramie Treaty negotiations in 1868, and in early 1876 frequented the Custer City locale, where he assisted the Black Hills Rangers on several of their outings.[9]

Crawford was equally emphatic about the difficulties inherent in finding gold, which required hard labor, experience, and a fair streak of luck, and woe to the "reckless rovers" expecting simply to pick it up. Crawford especially enjoyed exposing the pilgrims or "pea nutheads" who arrived with no sense of the hardships of the gulches, traveled alone, came with no money or provisions, and, especially, carried no rifles for self-defense. The object of Crawford's scorn in his *Bee* letter written on 5 April was a rather feckless young man claiming to be the son of Judge Peter C. Shannon of Yankton. Supposedly, the ill-prepared boy's father had sent him to the Black Hills for a practical education, but the young man was rapidly dissipating his prospects and, in doing so, made a fine example for Captain Jack. But more of the story appeared in the *Bee* on 24 April when one of Judge Shannon's friends in Yankton penned a correction, noting that the man in the Hills was not Shannon's son. The judge had sons, the writer offered, but the eldest was a mere nine and in school. "Set this matter right," the friend admonished.[10] The ultimate fate of the boy from the Hills is unknown, but Judge Shannon's name would resurface when he presided at the Yankton trial in December 1876 of Jack McCall for the murder of Wild Bill Hickok.[11]

Reports of gold dust, nuggets, and shipments continued to titillate readers of the *Bee* and other newspapers. Despite the shortcomings of the French Creek placers, Crawford reported active mining in the district in April and instances of $40 and $45 recovered from sluices in single days and a nugget worth $9.15 taken from Claim No. 67 below Custer City in early May. In a letter to his hometown newspaper, the *Faribault* (Minnesota) *Republican*, on 22 April, Custer City's mayor, Joseph Bemis, echoed Crawford's unbridled optimism. "The miners are bringing in their bottles and buckskin pouches well filled with the yellow, and from the expression of their faces one would think they had been brought up on laughing gas," Bemis wrote. "Improved claims are selling for two and three thousand dollars apiece, and everything is lovely except the accursed Indians."[12]

Recoveries on Rapid and Castle creeks north of Custer City were promising, too, including a single nugget worth $14 that Crawford himself found on Castle Creek.[13] Jack also had claims on French and Spring creeks. By way of relative comparison, in the California placer mines a few decades earlier, a claim had been considered productive at an ounce of dust (about fifteen dollars) a day. Anything less was regarded as "Chinaman's diggings" because only a frugal Asian could supposedly subsist on it, and subsistence costs in the California diggings were inordinately exorbitant.[14] At the end of April in the Black Hills, Crawford recorded gold shipments from Custer City of 47 ounces, 18 pennyweights and 15 ounces, 19 pennyweights. Of that placer shipment, Crawford noted that 4 ounces, 16 pennyweights were taken out within one-quarter mile above Custer. At the prevailing local gold value, the worth of the 47-ounce consignment was $958, while the Custer City recovery amounted to $96. Crawford did not provide any details explaining these shipments. If the $958 consignment was from an individual and collected in a relatively short working period, it would have been a noteworthy recovery. If it was production from a partnership of sorts and recovered over a longer period of time, the per-capita worth of the shipment would have been marginal. Crawford was unclear, but his imprecision served his purpose.

[*Omaha Daily Bee*, 15 April 1876]

THE NEW ELDORADO.

(Special Correspondence of the BEE.)

CUSTER CITY, April 5, 1876.

An hour ago I returned from Hill City and Newton's fork, on Spring Creek.

Hill City is situated close to the mouth of Newton's fork, and in a very pretty little park. It is about three-quarters of a mile long by about four or five hundred yards wide. There are now about 150 houses in the town, 100 of which are not yet completed, and although there is a saw-mill at the mouth of the fork, within three hundred yards of town, there are as yet but two frame buildings commenced. The town is owned by a company, and each locator must pay $5 per lot, besides recorder's fees. In the first place the company drew lots by lottery. The best lots on Main street (there are but two streets) were numbered and put into a hat, and each member of the company drew out a number, which was either one corner lot or two between the corners. This took away the best lots, and the company immediately built cabins and are holding them now at big prices. Time alone can tell whether they will sell or not. If, after mining has commenced, Spring creek shows a good pay streak on the bed rock, then Hill City will advance. If, on the contrary, Spring creek mining does not pay, she is now in her prime, because Rapid City will be the connecting link between Custer City, Deadwood and the north.

Messrs. Bowten & Berry are cutting a great quantity of lumber at their saw mill, and are selling at reasonable prices to the miners—*on bed rock*—that is, on time, until the miners get the money out of their claims. These gentlemen say they will give the miners who will develop the country all the lumber they want on time, but none to build houses on two-penny tape lots, and we say good enough; and may the miners get the stuff out and be *a Bowton* time to pay, so that these gentlemen may be *Berry* happy; d' ye see?

We met Mr. Wm. S. Lewis at Hill City last evening, about 6 p. m. He had just come in from Rapid City, 15 miles east of north from Hill. He informed us of an Indian raid which took place on last Wednesday. The following are the particulars: On Tuesday night three men were camped near Rapid City under an overhanging rock or bluff, and about 9 p.m. one of their number, who was sitting back from the fire under this bluff, stepped out to put on some more wood, when

Hill City, located on Spring Creek, boomed briefly and then busted as the focus of the gold rush shifted to the northern diggings. *D. S. Mitchell photograph. Robert Kolbe*

he was fired upon from the bluff above and instantly killed. The Indians shouted down to the other two, one of whom was asleep, wrapped up in his blankets, until the shot was fired, and in good English said, "Come out, we've got one of you and we'll have the rest." The two men got up and ran along the bluff, and the Indians fired at them, wounding one through the arm, but the other escaped unhurt. The red devils immediately came down and took the scalp of the dead man, and stripped him of all his clothing. He was a Swede, from Nebraska, and his name was Charles Nelson. The other man's name Mr. Lewis had forgotten. After burrying Nelson, the morning following, Lewis and others went out to look around, and while fifty miners and citizens were standing on an eminence between the stock and city, two Indians rode up within a stone's throw and run off twenty-eight head of stock. Some fired at the Indians, while others stood looking on, and the Indians would throw themselves on the sides of their ponys to avoid being hit. Lewis and another man followed them across the creek, when the fire from the party behind became so hot that Lewis and his companion had to lay down to avoid being shot. Finally they all ran after the Indians, shooting and yelling, but the reds widened the gap in a short time, and the brave citizens of Upper Rapid City were lost without a hoof. There were only sixteen Indians all told. This is not the only instance. Stock is being run off every week from some part of the Hills. Only a week ago there were twenty-two horses stolen on the Cheyenne from a party coming into the Hills, and since then twenty-one mules were captured from freighters who were bringing goods to Judge Kuykendall; yet the people seem to care nothing about the matter. We tried every means in our power to organize a company to be ready at a moment's notice to jump into the saddle and chastise these murdering thieves; but the matter was dropped after the first excitement.

Last night we found shelter and a comfortable bunk, including the indelicaces of the season, at the little new log cabin of one of Omaha's good boys. His name is Bob Armstrong, and he treated us just as we would him or any one else from that section, excepting

That raw-boned snoozer, Hascall,
  Who tried to bust our laws,
Thank God the little rascal
  Is back in Omaha.
And yet he may not go there,
  But if he goes below,
You bet your bottom dollar,
  Old Nick won't have much show.

It seems that Bob was unfortunate enough to be in the party coming to the Hills with Hascall, and when Hascall arrived in Custer he secured comfortable lodgings for himself, and left Bob to camp out, in the coldest weather we had, for four days. Finally Bob broke camp and went to Hills City, where he has since located. He is in fine spirits, is fat and saucy, and is waiting with the others for the turn of the tide; and we hope that when his ship does come in she will be well laden with good things, for he deserves success. He is generous, shrewd and plucky, and they are all the attributes necessary to make a man.

After breakfasting with Bob this morning, we saddled our pony and in company with Brown—not Smith or Jones, but Capt. Brown, of the Hattie Howard, of Oswego, N. Y., and one of the boys, we started for our claims three miles above Hill City. Arriving there, we took off our outside clothing, rolled up our sleeves and pitched in to represent. We worked about half a day, and marking on our stake "represented" April 1, 1876, with our initials, we built a fire and smoked. About this time five of the boys from Custer came to our camp, accompanied by deputy Recorder Hiram Marble, and we thought we would get some grub from the party, but they expected to go back to a wagon after "representing," and get dinner, so Captain Brown started for Hill City, after giving us a pressing invite to join him, but we told him we had to write to the BEE to-night, and must go to Custer. We finally started for there, and about a mile above our claim we struck Keefer's ranch. His Pard, Joe, was in the cabin and about preparing dinner.

And now let me say a few words, I trust, of warning to such as contemplate a trip to the Hills. The country is flooded with reckless rovers, and much suffering will be the result. The miners who are here, as a general thing, have no more provisions than they need, and most of them have not enough to keep them until they open their claims, and hence cannot give it away to beggars.

Last Thursday a boy, who lives with his brother, came here from Yankton and was trying to sell his rifle, worth $35, for $15; finally pawned it for $10, and could not redeem it. He took his ten dollars, went to Al. Swaringen's dance house, got drunk, danced with the girls, and was jolly in his debauchery. Next morning he had no money, no rifle, and nothing to eat. On our way to Hill City we passed him going that way, with a single blanket rolled up in a bundle, carrying it in his hand. He claims to be the son of Judge Shannon, of Yankton, and said he was sent here by his father. Well, if the Judge sent him here to be tamed, he never struck a better school, and now his education commences, and if he left a good home and luxury he will find a great change here. I have repeatedly stated in my letters, and I will repeat, that no man should come to this country expecting to pick up gold as soon as he gets here. He has to work hard and long to get to the bed rock. There are ditches to dig, sluices to make, and, first of all, the pay streak to be found. A man may dig twenty prospect holes across his claim from 6 to 15 feet deep before he finds the pay, and sometimes may not find it at all. These are chances which every miner must run, and they are better able to take these chances than a pilgrim who never saw a mining camp.

Every man who comes here intending to stay should have three months' rations at least, and a hundred or two hundred dollars; many will come with one or two months' provisions, and work until it is gone and then have to desert their claims just at the time they are about to strike a streak. The country is not prospected, nor will it be for two years to come. It is true good pay diggings have been found, but the favorable news from one good mine will spread like wild-fire, and Dame Gossip and hearsay will make it 100 per cent better than it is in reality. We talked with a man yesterday at Hill City who has been making $5.00 per day washing out dirt, which he had to carry over two hundred yards to water. The gulch is a dry one and water cannot be got to it; where he gets his pay is on a high bar. But it requires work and experience to find these things. There will be eight sluices to work on this creek to-morrow, and it cost over $500 worth of labor to get them in operation. We hope that these remarks will suffice to warn parties from coming here who are not prepared for emergencies.

Mr. Archer, who arrived here with Dr. Pendery, started north this morning with a party of Montana boys, who had provisions for one year. These men, with the exception of Archer, are all old miners and understand the business. Each one had a pony for packing across the mountains, besides their wagon, which they will take as far as they can, and then pack to Deadwood and Whitewood.

There is another class of men arriving here every day. Ben. Carman, an old Forty-nine Sunney Boy, calls them "Pea nut Heads." As soon as they arrive they cuss the country and leave without even going out of town. Others leave because we have law and order here, and one man who accompanied the train with Dr. Bemis, our present mayor, heard there was law in Custer, and immediately on his arrival started back for Salt Lake.

The first fire in Custer broke out about 2 a. m. on last Friday morning in the saloon of John Dion, and the place, which was a frame structure, became enveloped in the flames, and also a coffee refreshment and bake stand next door. We went to work with our axes, and while some men scaled the adjoining buildings others carried water, barely saving them. At one time our axe went through a board and got fast, and, being rather warm, we done considerable squirming until we got it loose, to the great merriment of the boys, who shouted "stick to it Jack, if she takes yer hair;" but, fortunately, the back of our scalp still waves.

A party headed by Capt. A. P. Sanders, of Omaha, formerly with Prof. Jenney, started from here for a dry gulch 20 miles east of Harney's Peak on last Friday morning. The gulch is called "Rose-Bud," and derived its name from the fact that one of Jenney's party pulled up some briar roots and found a prospect under them in the soil. Capt. S. thinks there is a creek within a few miles of "Rose-Bud," which can be got in there, and if so, it will make a rich gulch. We intended going with the boys, but had to go to Spring Creek. We intend, however, to follow their trail tomorrow or next day if nothing turns up to prevent, and will let you know the result as soon as we return.

The weather has changed within the last few days, and spring is upon us with sunshine, and most of the snow has disappeared; and now, perhaps, you will allow a few verses of machine poetry:

SPRING IN THE BLACK HILLS

Beautiful Spring in the highlands of nature;
  Snow on the hill-tops and grass in the vale;
Sunshine is beaming on each living creature,
  And not e'en one sorrow our joys to assail.
The pine trees are bowing and bending before us,
  The miner is building his new cabin home,
The voice of the wind seems to whisper, while o'er us,
  "Angels watch o'er you, wherever you roam."

Beautiful Spring, you will loosen the fountains,
  Long sealed by the frost in the valleys and hills;
And down from the tops of the mightiest mountains
  Will dance little streamlets and murmuring rills.
Blessing will follow—we feel it, we believe it—
  If men will be faithful and work hand in hand.

Though many will tempt you, while working, to leave it;
  But don't you be fooled, boys, there's gold in this land.

Beautiful Spring, you will bring us sweet flowers;
  Thousands will gather from far o'er the land,
And many will revel in bliss in these bowers,
  Devouring the grandeur—for none is more grand.
Farmers will come with their plows and their harrows,
  The bright golden grain will be waving e'er long;
While civilization will bury the arrows—
  The red man is singing his death-warrant song.

These are our spring sentiments, and we feel just as we write in this instance.

Every one seems to have great confidence in the future growth of this country. I need not add or repeat that Custer is still progressing. Buildings are continually going up. There are three saw mills in full blast, cutting 25,000 feet at least per day; yet the demand far exceeds the supply. Two shingle machines will be in operation by Tuesday, and they have orders ahead for many weeks' cutting. There are also two shingle machines on the way in—one from Cheyenne and one from Yankton, so we are informed by parties coming in. We hope the parties will not come in in small bands, as spring will bring the grass, and with the grass will come the Indians in raiding bands. This they have promised they would do, and if men come in small parties they may expect attack from these dusky devils at any moment, while if the miners will come in companies of not less than one hundred they can "stand them off" with effect. A word to the wise is sufficient.

Provisions are on the rise. We have to pay 30 cents for sugar; bacon, 35; codfish, 25; potatoes, 12½, and corn 12 to 15 cents, just as the scarcity of the article regulates it. If there is no sugar in town except at one store, up goes the tariff, while if a load comes in and all the stores have got it, you can buy five pounds for one dollar. However, this will all be regulated as soon as we get our stores stocked and regular freighters running.

Gen. C. G. Campbell, from Yankton via Fort Pierre, arrived in Rapid City on the 28th, eight days from Fort Pierre, with 48 passengers and six coaches. He is now here with his coaches and stock, and will establish a stage line between this place, Hill City, Rapid City and Deadwood. His stock is in fine condition, and his coaches are of the best make for mountain use.

A party from Sidney arrived here to-day with mule teams, making the trip in 12 days. They report work progressing on the Platte river bridge, near Snyder's ranch, and think it will be completed before the high water comes. J. W. Dear's stages are expected from Red Cloud and Sidney about Wednesday with a great quantity of accumulated mail. We will be happy when they come, as we can get no late papers; all the papers sent us have been laying at Red Cloud for the past two months.

The cellar for a large brewery is being excavated, and the work of building will begin as soon as lumber can be secured.

MONDAY, April 3, 5 p. m.

Have just received a private letter from Mr. Wm. Gay, from Dead Wood, containing a specimen of quartz which contains free gold; will enclose letter and quartz as received. It will explain itself. Mr. Gay is a good man, and I believe him reliable.

> DEAD WOOD CREEK,
> LOST DISTRICT,
> March 31, 1876
> *J. W. Crawford (Capt Jack)*:
>
> DEAR SIR:—According to promise, I drop a line. I arrived here yesterday, and found everything all right. We had a very hard trip. The snow is about three feet deep and still snowing. There is quite a change here since I left. Instead of eighteen men there are several hundred. There has been a number of discoveries made since I left, both in placer and quartz. The weather has been so cold that prospecting has been very difficult, but wherever it has been tried they got good prospects. Prospects on Dead Wood and Whitewood are from 10 to 25 cents, and as high as $1.30 to the pan, while on some of the side gulches emptying into Dead Wood there has been as much as $5.00 to the pan. There have been a number of claims sold at prices varying from $500 to $4,000.
>
> When I got here the town sites I spoke to you about, had been taken up and all the lots taken; one is at the mouth of Whitewood, and is called Crook City; the other is a short dis-

These miners work sluice boxes in Deadwood Gulch in June 1876. The placer deposits in Deadwood and Whitewood gulches were among the richest in the Black Hills. *D. S. Mitchell photograph. Paul L. Hedren*

tance below the mouth of Deadwood, on Whitewood Creek, and is named Whitewood City. We are going to lay off a town here on Deadwood to be called Gay City. I will reserve a lot for you. Tell Curran that if he had come over with me, he could have had a chance to get a good claim on shares, but they are all taken now. Old Dan had sold his discovery claim before I got here. We have particularly developed some of the ledges we had staked, and two of them proved to be very good. I send you a specimen from the "Giant Lode," owned by Wm. Gay, A. H. Gay, M. J. Ingoldsby, E. D. Haggard, D. Muskles, and J. B. Pearson. We have another lode that we consider better, called the

"Blacktail," owned by the same parties. We propose to start on a prospecting expedition as soon as the snow leaves sufficiently, and if I find anything I will try and give you a show.

The Indians have made several attacks at the mouth of Whitewood, and have succeeded in running off about 100 head of horses. There has been two men wounded by them, but neither of them seriously. Last night they made an attack at the mouth of Bear-bute creek, and run off seven horses. We expect more trouble with them when the snow leaves, as they, we suppose, will come with more force. As yet none have been seen far in the Hills, as they cannot ride in. They have confined their operations to the foot-hills.

Let me know all the news, and whether the government intends to send troops to this part of the country.

My compliments to Mr. E. K. Curran.

Yours truly,

Wm. Gay,

Dead Wood Creek, B. H.

You will observe by this letter that the country north is not yet prospected. It is impossible to know what there is in that country until the snow is off the ground; besides it is dangerous for small parties to go out prospecting on account of the Indians; yet we are in hopes that a military post will be established here to operate between this place and Dead Wood.

James Van Daniker and party, from Omaha, arrived to-day. Jim has rented a fine building, 25x60 and two stories high, from E. K. Current & Co., for hotel purposes. It is situated on the corner of Crook and Sixth streets, on the Spring creek road, and is the best location in the city. If the hotel is conducted in a proper manner it will do a fine business.

Swaringer's dance hall has been enlarged, extending the whole length of the block. This was found necessary owing to the increase of business. The building will soon embrace the following apartments: 1st, bar and gambling room; 2d, hall and dance room; 3d, sleeping and dining rooms for the dance girls and boarders, while still further back will be the cooking and culinary department; and thus do we progress.

A city jail is in the course of construction and will soon be completed.

The plain, unvarnished truth,
  And facts that we may know,
And this is what the people want;
  If not, why tell me so.
All this I've tried to give,
  That *all* may understand;
I've gone into the prospect hole
  And told ye how she panned.

We tried to scale old Harney—
  The story has been told—
And did we say we made it?
  And there found lots of gold?
Not much—it was a failure;
  But was no fault of ours.
We'll go again with Charley
  When spring brings back the flowers.

My letter is getting too lengthy, so I will close, and follow this up with another in a few days, as we expect startling news from different quarters; and speaking of startling news reminds me that a gentleman interested here in business said to your correspondent this evening: "Jack, don't say anything about these Indian scares; it will injure the country." Now, in conclusion, I will say that I came here for the purpose of telling my employe[r] and the people all I knew or could find out truthfully; and when I hear of any scalping or horse-stealing I will let you know, for I want no man, woman or child to ever say that I kept back information that would have saved a single life. I think the people will give me credit for warning them of all dangers which I knew were to be encountered. My letters are neither flowery nor rhetorical, and I think there is no necessity for that.

CAPT. JACK.

[*Omaha Daily Bee*, 21 April 1876]

CUSTER CITY.

(Special Correspondence of the Bee.)

Custer City, April 8, 1876.

A report that Captain Eagan, of Gen. Crook's command, has had an encounter with the Indians in which he lost several men, has just come in from Red Cloud. The young bucks are reported to have left the agency, and there is little doubt but that they are prowling about the Hills in search of plunder.

A grand mass meeting will be held here this evening to devise measures for immediate organization for the protection of miners.

Gustave Natusch, formerly bookkeeper for the Omaha firm of Max Meyer & Co., has just opened a cigar and notion store in Custer City, and is doing well.

Will write more in detail about affairs in a day or two.

Capt. Jack.

[*Sidney Telegraph*, 22 April 1876]

LAND OF GOLD!

Custer City, D. T.,

April 9th, 1876.

Friend Gossage:

Your note, introducing Mr. Burgess, was received yesterday afternoon, and it is the first and only letter received from you since my arrival in Custer City. I have only received one bundle of papers, those containing my first letter, and but three papers containing my letters from the *Bee*. I notice in one of those that the editor omitted some of my letter regarding the Sidney route, that, however, was at the time the *Bee* was working up the Cheyenne supplement, besides it was a very severe criticism and condemnation of the Cheyenne schemers who reported that our party were frozen to death and lost, and I suppose rather severe. Nevertheless, without being prejudiced against Cheyenne, any statement by me regarding the superiority of the Sidney route over the Cheyenne cannot be contradicted. I know that Sidney is the route to Custer City.

Dr. Flick, who arrived here yesterday with Mr. McHugh, of Omaha, traveled over the route with 4,500 pounds of freight on each wagon, in ten days actual travel, and as this is their second trip over this route, we have every reason to believe them. The doctor also says that the distance from Sidney to Custer City, via Red Cloud, which is nearly due north, is, at the closest calculation, 182 miles, and we have traveled the same route and believe his calculations about correct; which makes the distance at least 75 or 80 miles nearer than Cheyenne, and by a much better road.

I am glad to learn from the doctor and party that your bridge across the Platte river is being so rapidly pushed forward to completion, and I am informed it will be finished by the first of May. Then surely you sleepy Sidneyites will awake to the sense of your duty, and tell the people of the United States who you are and what your facilities are. I have no interest in Sidney, but I have an interest in every man, woman or child who are en route or may come hereafter to this country.

I was sent here to write the truth, and as I expect to live and die in this country, and be one of its citizens, I wish no man to censure me for misrepresentation when I knew better. I have tried to tell the truth and will continue to try to do so. I have offered no inducements heretofore to parties to come into the Hills unless well prepared with arms, ammunition and provisions sufficient to last as least three months, as well as to have some ready cash.

There is gold here and in paying quantities, (for I have with my own hands helped to wash it out,) but it is not scattered promiscously all over the country. Men must come here and prospect for it. They must dig down into the gravel and touch the bed-rock to find the pay streaks. This grass-root gold is thin, to use a common expression, although gold has been found in the black soil; yet no man who ever saw a mining camp, will think for a moment that gold in paying quantities can be found in such a manner.

Well, old boy, our town is booming. She is a surprise to all new comers, especially those who left here as Mr. McHugh did, not two months ago. I tried to count the buildings last week, but that was impossible. I stood, or sat, rather, on a high mountain rock that overlooks the city.

There are now three saw mills here cutting all the lumber they can, one running night and day, and averaging over thirty thousand feet daily.

Now the question arises, are these people, most of whom are experienced miners, justified in making these outlays, having no title more than a squatters right on an Indian reservation, which is no right at all? I say are they justified in building a city which has now over 1,000 inhabitants and over 600 houses built or under headway? If there is no gold here, what are these men agoing to do with this property? I leave you, my friend, to draw your own conclusions.

I will write you a newsy letter in a week or so and let you know how things are in general.

Respectfully,

JACK.

[*Omaha Daily Bee*, 22 April 1876]

CUSTER CITY.

(Correspondence of the BEE.)

CUSTER CITY, April 15, 1876.

Your correspondent has but time for a short communication; but as this goes with the "Pony Express," we must particularly make a note of the fact. We have heard, ever since our arrival in the Hills, of mail stages starting from Cheyenne at different times. First we were informed, and by the newspapers, that a mail and passenger line of stages would start from Cheyenne on the 15th of March; next, on the 1st of April; and now, it is reported, on the 20th of April. We had engaged a man about the 1st of March to carry the mail between Custer and Red Cloud, but after securing two good ponies we saw a notice posted at the Recorder's office stating that Mr. James Roberts, of Custer City, had already started a messenger on that route; and after waiting for nearly two weeks patiently for the advertised messengers, we found that no such passenger had ever left Custer.

Finally, after waiting until this time for a line of stages, we have found a gentlemen enterprising enough to start a pony express. Judge Dougherty, of North Platte, and one of the old town pioneers, will start Charley Rivers (better known as Wild Charley) to Red Cloud with this letter and several hundred others. Charley is a good man, a scout and pioneer, and up to all the tricks of Indian deviltry, besides being conversant with their language. He said to us a few moments ago: "Pard, I'll be back in four days or lose my hair," and we have no doubt he will accomplish the trip in that time. Letters addressed via Red Cloud hereafter will get to Custer quicker than by any other address.

A large outfit from Sioux City, consisting of 164 men, arrived here yesterday afternoon—27 days making the trip. They are commanded by Tom Phillips, of Sioux City, and report a pleasant journey and no trouble with the red skins; nor will any large, well-armed and disciplined party have any trouble if they have an efficient commander, like Capt. Phillips. Indians don't hunt for or seek a fight with this kind of an outfit. They have two sets of blacksmith's outfits with them and men to use them. One house on wheels, which reminded of—and we thought at first it was, and wish it was,—a photograph establishment. Many of this party will locate in Custer, while others will seek their fortune in the north. They are pleased with and surprised at the growth of our magic Custer.

Reports of every description are floating all around us regarding Generals Crook and Custer. Some say Crook is captured, with his supplies; other say it is Custer. But we have too much faith in the ability of both of these veteran Indian fighters to give such reports credence. Old pioneers from Arizona say they know Gen. Crook too well for that, and we have some reason to know Custer, from experience, as a general, to be outflanked by Sitting Bull, or any other squatting set of crawling red devils on the continent. All *we* fear is that these two generals, in forming a junction in the north, will drive these reckless braves into our clutches, or rather that we will fall into their greasy grasp before we know it. Not that we are not masters of the situation, but we have not a horse that is fit for duty in case of an Indian raid, and should a few hundred Indians come into our city, run off part of our stock, and kill some of our citizens, we could not follow them.

To-morrow, however, we will organize a company of 150 or 200 men and make arrangements for self-defense, at least. If, after we are organized, we had enough grain to feed our horses thirty days, or until grass is good, we could then be prepared as we ought to be; but there is not ten bushels of grain in the city unless it came in within the last twenty-four hours. The last we bought our steed cost us fifteen cents per pound. This is more than we can stand, or any one else. If Omaha and Cheyenne would send us a contribution in grain sufficient to keep 100 head of stock, on six quarts per day, for three weeks, they would do the citizens of Custer a good turn, which would be appreciated and help them to protect themselves against Indians, as well as to follow and chastise them when we know of their whereabouts. Not only this, as soon as we organize, we propose to offer our services to Gen. Crook, or any other commander who may need our aid in or near the Hills. We would have no need of asking this was it in our power to secure it ourselves, but it is not, unless we would employ some teamsters here (which is hard to do) and that would occupy the time when grain will be most needed.

This matter has been talked over by the citizens generally, the want of grain being our greatest need; so if there can be arrangements made by some parties who deem this worthy of their attention, and by subscription or otherwise will send us a carload or so of grain, they will no doubt reap a benefit which is not now to be perceived. One thing we can see: there are thousands coming to the Hills, and all, or nearly all, come to Custer. If on the Cheyenne river, or anywhere in the foot hills, a party are attacked or their stock run off, at the first alarm we would be able, with corn-fed stock, to fly to their aid and perhaps recover thousands of dollars worth of stock, save life, and take any amount of scalps. The rest we leave with the people, and as this will appear in the Bee, thousands will read it, and the editor might suggest some worthy business man in Cheyenne with whom parties could communicate or send the staff of horse life. Do this, Mr. Editor, and oblige the "Custer City Rangers," that are to be after we have organized.

MAYOR'S CERTIFICATE

Custer City, April 15th '76.

Editor Bee:

Sir:—I have examined the foregoing statement of your correspondent, and endorse the same as being correct.

J. G. Bemis,
Mayor of Custer City.

Mayor Bemis has had over twenty years experience with the Indians, and writes understandingly when he endorses my statements, and I trust some action may be taken upon this matter by the people of Nebraska and Wyoming, and at once.

Mr. [W. A.] Laughlin is here with his press, but, being laid up with the rheumatism, has as yet, done nothing toward putting the thing in motion. Mr. B. F. Adams, one of our worthy citizens, has donated part of a lot, centrally located, to Mr. Laughlin for a building wherein to have his office. We hope soon to have a Black Hills paper in Custer City.

Mr. S. R. Shankland, on day before yesterday, surveyed out some lots on his ranch adjoining Custer on the east, and called it Shankland's addition. He has sold ten residence lots already at prices varying from thirty to fifty dollars. His addition is partly on top of a rolling hill, overlooking the city, and is a very beautiful location.

Old Billy Martin made a speech last evening to the Sioux City boys offering big inducements to them if they would come and locate on his ranch on Lower Rapid. The boys cheered the old man lustily, but told him that if he had no scalp to loose they had, and would prefer laying up in Custer for the present. The old man is nearly disgusted, inasmuch as he can't raise army enough to hold that ranch.

A party of explorers, headed by Cap. A. P. Sanders, of Omaha, started from here for Rosebud, 20 miles east of Harney's Peak. I believe I mentioned the fact in my last letter. We have heard nothing from them since they left. Gen. Campbell came in and since writing we learn that Campbell's party, on the evening before they reached Custer, met Sanders' party, and on taking their back trail to Custer, and shortly after meeting them, the trail of eleven Indians crossed Sanders' party's trail, and was fresh. That evening old Billy Martin, who came over with General Campbell, lost his mule and two horses, the Indians, rushing between the horses and the party, yelling and shooting, having no trouble in getting away with the three head. The balance of the horses were tied up to the wagons. The reason these facts were not reported in my last letter was because Martin and others interested in *dangerous property* denied that they ever saw an Indian or a sign of one; but we generally find these things out in time.

Three wagons from the Sioux City train have just started north. There are two cows yoked in the lead on the rear wagon, with a lame bull and a steer, and a dog behind.

Sanders and the boys have just returned; got good prospects and had a fight with the Indians; no one was hurt on their side. They have fine specimens of quartz and other minerals, which we have no time to have analyzed.

Bill McHugh has just got here from Omaha.

It is now 3 o'clock p. m., and Wild Charley awaits my letter. More anon.

CAPT. JACK.

[*Omaha Daily Bee*, 6 May 1876]

CUSTER CITY.

(Correspondence of the BEE.)

CUSTER CITY, April 20, 1876.

In my last letter I told you there was trouble brewing among the red skins, and now every day adds some new horror of Indian deviltry in the Hills. I have not slept five hours in the last forty-eight, and have just returned from an unsuccessful chase after the Indians, who came within half a mile of the city and ran off ten head of mules and horses.

Jule Seminole, a young half-breed, was immediately sent in advance to find the trail, and, in five minutes, he gave a whoop denoting he had found it, and I never saw a better guide.

We pressed the Indians pretty close, as they left seven head of stock on the road between Custer and Beaver, which is nearly fifty miles. One of the horses we rode home and led our other horse until within four miles of Custer, where we had to leave him. Jule's party crossed the trail of about thirty Indians, going north, up Beaver Creek, and we believe all this stealing and murder is committed by Sitting Bull's warriors, and that they are preparing for a big war. They are running all the stock north to be prepared for Crook on his return.

On our arrival at Brigham's ranch last evening we were horrified to learn that in Red Cannon, twenty miles from there, Mr. Charles Metz, a baker, and his wife had been murdered by the Indians, and the body of Mrs. Metz terribly mutilated. They also killed another man, named Lem Simpson, and wounded four more. The party were on their way to Cheyenne. They captured a colored woman—Mrs. Mosby, whose husband is here in Custer. He swears vengeance on the Sioux, and will go on the war path. There was another man killed last week and two wounded on the Cheyenne road; also, three wounded in Buffalo Gap, on the Spotted Tail and Red Cloud road, and one man missing, and every day will increase the number unless

The Beaver Creek locale south of Custer City and east of Point of Rocks, seen here in September 1876, was continually troubled by Indian raiders throughout the spring. Point of Rocks marked a critical turn on the Sidney Road as it neared Custer. *Stanley J. Morrow photograph. Montana Historical Society Research Center*

The infamous Metz Massacre occurred in this locale in Red Canyon, southwest of Custer City, in April 1876. D. S. Michell took this photograph in September 1876. *Jim Crain*

we get provisions for our horses and more arms. There is not one rifle in Custer to-day to every two men.

Thirty men went to Buffalo Gap yesterday, well armed and provisioned; also a team to haul their rations. The Major sent thirty more to Red Cannon this morning, but without horses.

And still the pilgrims continue to come in small parties of five to ten. Nine men came in last week with no fire-arms, save one old shot gun in the party, and many are going out again, just as they came, without grub, arms or money, begging their way. We met a man this a.m. on the way to Cheyenne alone, with nothing save a pair of blankets. He said he expected to fall in with some parties before he got to Cheyenne. Four miles from where we met this man, the Indians shot at a teamster yesterday who went out to meet Mr. Nealon, one of our party; yet for all this, men travel unarmed and alone.

Property is below par to-day in some portions of the city. Certain parties are scared and about to leave, are selling out for little or nothing, while others, who have an eye to business are gobbling it up.

Dr. A. S. Pendery will leave here to-morrow morning. He received a letter yesterday, dated March 9th, informing him of his wife's illness, and to come to Cincinnati at once. The Dr. has made many warm friends, and is leaving a good practice, but we hope for his speedy return, and the recovery of his wife to perfect health. The Dr. will carry this letter through, and unless he loses his hair, will no doubt present it to the BEE in person.

Mining commenced this week, and good pay is being found. I saw $40 taken out in one day by three men up the creek, and Mr. D. Olston has taken out $45 in one half day, sluicing, with three men. Mr. O. has worked hard on his claim, digging ditches, etc., all winter, and he deserves success.

Snow is still very deep in the north, but we are having beautiful warm weather here.

Provisions are scarce and high. Flour is $16 per hundred, corn meal is 30 cents per pound, and bacon 45 cents; and still the storekeepers are not happy.

The first ball was given by Mr. Felix at Roberts' new store, on last Saturday evening; and as it is the first ball in Custer, we must make a note of it. The room was tastefully decorated with evergreens, and the ladies' dressing-room was with BEE supplements, pictures, and white paper. There were one hundred persons at supper, which was furnished gratuitously by Felix, one of the best boys in Christendom; and pies, cakes, cold meats, bologna, tea and coffee, together with wine, cider, bottled ale and fresh milk, constituted part of the delicacies. It was in reality one of the finest suppers ever eaten in Custer. There were four sets on the floor, and we could have had ladies for five if we had had the room. There were twenty-two ladies in attendance, and one of your Omaha girls was undoubtedly the belle of the ball. Her dress was elegant and tastefully arranged, while her modest and lady-like manners elicited universal admiration. Miss Haserodt is the name of the lady, and she says she is not sick of the Hills, either.

Building is still advancing. McHugh's store is being pushed forward rapidly, while Van Daniker's & McGavock's is also going up fast.

A. G. Shaw has just completed a fine hotel, called the Custer House, and Mrs. Fritz Drogmond has almost completed the Metropolitan. Besides these there are 100 buildings worthy of note, stores, commission and auction houses.

One of Bill Gay's men just in from the north says they are paying $5 per day for laborers, and men are panning out $20 a day. About 50 men start out this morning, April 20, many of whom intend coming back after we have whipped the Indians. I must close, as the Dr. is waiting to go. He will give you further information, and I will write again in a day or two.

JACK.

[*Omaha Daily Bee*, 9 May 1876]

CUSTER CITY.

(Special Correspondence of the BEE.)

CUSTER CITY, April 24, 1876.

Your correspondent is about to start out with six scouts, to be gone ten days, and has been appointed chief of the scouts by the city and Major Winthrop, of the Rangers (not the BEE Rangers). It has been hot here for the last week and we have been very busy. We are now determined to find the haunts of these red devils and clean them out, if possible; also protect emigration as far as we possibly can with our present disadvantages in feed, etc.

Another fight occurred yesterday near or in Red Canon; five Indians are reported killed and one of our boys wounded in the arm.

Five Indians attacked a German named John Hanson, while riding toward town last Friday. John dismounted while they charged, and, taking the weather side of his horse, blazed away at them. The second shot brought one from his saddle. He was immediately lifted up by another, and the remainder separated, one following behind. John sent a shot under his arm while he was in the act of firing. The ball cut his coat and vest and horse's back, near the wethers; another shot hit the horse in the bowels near the flank, when he fell. John got down with him, still keeping him for a breastwork. About this time the remaining two turned their horses and left. It required over an hour for John to get to town and give the alarm, which was responded to by over fifty of the minute men on foot, and Major Wynkoop and your correspondent, with several others on horseback. We found the trail, but as the Indians had too much start, and with good horses, we knew that pursuit would be useless, as it has been heretofore with such stock as we had here. A stable and stockade is now being built near the center of the city, and several good horses will be fed for the use of our scouts. We have some good men, and as soon as we get a little grain into our stock we will be able to report progress. We have not heard of any party of over ten being attacked when well armed. Sitting Bull has sent word to the boys north that he would give them twenty-five days to leave the Hills, and some of us start today, but not for good. We wish to have an interview with some of his thieves, whom he has sent here to steal our stock and leave us a foot.

Henry Homan arrived here last week. He reports having had no trouble with the reds. He and his boys were fixed. He had with him Frank T. Smith, a young scout of metal, whom Mr. Homan speaks of in the highest terms. We have engaged Frank with our boys, and he leaves with your correspondent in an hour. We have also secured the services of Jule Seminole, a half-breed, known among the Cheyennes as Big White Man. I believe we spoke of him in our last letter. Sam Young and Little Buckskin Joe are also with us, and understand their "biz."

Henry Homan came through from Omaha in just 25 days, and tells me the route is all that could be desired. His party broke about sixty miles of road, making a good cut-off, and laid over five days on account of snow. From O'Neil City they traveled up the Niobrara to the ferry crossing, followed the divide between Niobrara and Kiapapau to the Randall road, thence to the head of the Big White Clay, which they followed to White Earth, and struck the government trail for Custer. Henry leaves for Sidney to-morrow with his teams for freight. Freight from Sidney is 4½ cents, and from Cheyenne 7 to 9 cents. The road is also nearly 90 miles shorter via Sidney.

Excuse brevity, as we must away. We have made arrangements with our city mayor, Dr. J. G. Bemis, to keep you posted in case we do not return, or if we are detained longer than expected.

No stages have yet arrived, and there is no mail route. The post-office is all over town. Why don't Uncle Sam give us a lift? If he does, we will help him lift some scalps this spring and summer.

Messrs. Newton and Turner, two of the best boys in Christendom, the former from Omaha and the latter Cheyenne, are doing the best business in the city—wholesale and retail liquor dealers, and have the best class of custom. Their receipts run over $150 per day. They just filled our pockets with cigars, for our boys presented us with a merschaum pipe and a pound of Bull tobacco, and if you don't think we are grateful you are off the track.

McHugh, McGavock and Van Daniker are the busyiest men in town and are good-sized carpenters. Their buildings are looming, and they propose to stay right here with us. You see they are composed of the right metal.

Mr. Sheldon arrived here with two large loads of goods on Friday; and while he was riding into town in front of his team, the alarm of Indians was given. Your correspondent was in his shirt sleeves, and seeing Mr. Sheldon on board a fine horse we rushed up to him and said: "Mister, can I have your horse to go after the reds?" His reply was, "Yes, by Jove, and all my mules; and here's as good a rifle as ever was cocked." We took the whole outfit, and pronounce Sheldon a brick. He will be successful; has the biggest stock of goods in the city; and is selling them reasonable. Horse is at the door, and for the present must let up.

CAPT. JACK.

[*Omaha Daily Bee*, 13 May 1876]

THE BLACK HILLS.

(Special Correspondence of the BEE.)

CUSTER CITY, April 29.

Another man by the name of Wood, who left here ten days ago, was discovered near Buffalo Gap this week with a bullet through his heart, an arrow sticking in him, and one lying by his side—his rashness caused his death. He was with a large party, and although they asked him to stay with them, he said he wished to make good time to Sioux City, and rode on. He was found in a ravine, 50 rods from the road. He had a horse valued at $250, which was a big inducement for a northern Sioux to get away with him.

Our scouts are now all in, but a party are preparing to go out to-night. We saw hundreds of Indian signs, and ran across four Indians driving seven or eight head of stock six miles south of Custer. There were but two of us together at the time. We fired on them. They were well mounted, returned one shot, and galloped off, leaving two of the stolen stock, which we sent to town the same evening.

We expect assistance from Gen. Crook soon, and believe there are troops now on the road to Custer. We are not sufficiently armed in this place; not one half of our people have rifles. Our company, commanded by Major Wynkook, will act with Crook if needed; also our scouts, and we are confident that with the miners now in the hills and the forces of Crook combined, we can whip the Sioux nation in 30 days.

The report of Brown being shot on the way out was a severe blow to us here, as it was said the stage company with whom he was connected will take off their line of fast freight. No stages have yet arrived yet. The Dougherty express has made two successful trips, bringing between 700 and 1,000 letters and papers from Red Cloud each time. It is a risky business, however, for a carrier, but in this country men can be found to undertake almost anything.

P. McGavock and Jim Van Daniker deserve especial mention. They commenced a building 25x60, two stories high, for hotel purposes, about the time [of] the big scare; yet they never relaxed their hold, but worked on with a determination to win, and they will surely be successful. Their hotel will be ready in a few days, and when the Omaha boys come here they will be well received and find good accommodations with Pat and Jim.

A party from Ft. Pierre, via the Missouri river, arrived here to-day. They report no trouble with the Indians.

Mr. Miller, who left here twelve days ago for Sidney, returned to-day with several wagon-loads of flour and feed. Flour immediately took a drop in price from $16 to $12 per hundred. Freight from Sidney is 4½ cents, and from six to eight days travel. We will be glad, as a people, when more provisions (such as bacon, sugar and flour) arrive from Sidney. Bacon is selling at 45@50c, and sugar at 45@50.

Mr. George Wolle, a particular personal friend of ours, came in day before yesterday from Sand creek with $200 in dust. He is buying provisions, and goes back to Sand creek to-morrow. He says he has got all he wants.

We have just returned from the office of the Cheyenne & Black Hills stage line and express, and we give below the result of our interview with Mr. George B. Monlon [Moulton], the agent for the company. We copy these figures—and figures don't lie:

Shipped to Cheyenne on the 26th inst—

47 ounces, 18 pennyweights, 9 grains; 31 ounces, 19 pennyweights, (consigned to L. Boorhees [Luke Voorhees], Cheyenne).

15 ounces, 19 pennyweights (consigned to Kurtz, Allen & Co., Cheyenne).

The above was brought to Mr. Moulton within three days, and without solicitation. Four ounces, 16 pennyweights and 8 grains of the above was French creek gold, taken out within one quarter of a mile of Custer City, above, and 23 ounces from Spring creek.

Mr. Moulton informs us that he could buy any quantity of gold if he wished to make a business of it. He is a man whose word can be relied on, and has had over sixteen years' experience in the mines, in nearly every gold and silver district in the world. He has more acquaintance, we believe, north of here, in Sand creek, Deadwood and Whitewood, and, in fact, every northern district, and every man with whom he has talked assures him that it is, in their opinion, a very rich country. Many of them assured him if he would buy their dust they would bring him from two to six pounds at a time; and we are still as firm as ever, and, in fact, doubly sure that the country is safe, reports of flying scudds [arrows that miss the mark] to the contrary notwithstanding, and we feel no small amount of pride in the fact that our predictions are panning out as we said they would as soon as spring would open.

Since our return from scouting we have been attending to two very sick men, one of whom was accidentally shot in the arm, the ball entering near the wrist and coming out above the muscle of the arm, and Jule, the half-breed. One of our scouts, is also very low with pneumonia. Drs. Bemis and Flick are attending them.

This evening a party of ten men, commanded by Lieut. Height, of the "Rangers," and guided by Frank Smith, better known as "Antelope Frank," started for Buffalo Gap to watch the movements of the Indians and report the same. Should there be a chance to encounter a party, and their force is not sufficient, Frank will bring us the news, and with a few more men well mounted we will hasten to the foot hills. Height is using every effort and encouraging all means of protection. We wish we could say the same of all the Omahosses. Time will work a mighty change, however, and when the spring time comes again, those men who are now protecting the country will be looked upon in a far different light.

Those children who are here to day,
  Who braved the winter's storm,
Who came from home so far away,
  Our country they adorn.
And mothers, too, so young and fair,
  Nor have they been afraid,
Nor did they wish to leave like some,
  Who laugh at our stockade.

For them we build a safe retreat,
  And if our scouts should say
Old Red Cloud, or some other beat,
  Is coming in this way,
We then would have a tale to tell,
  If we should live to state,
And how these sneerers ran like H—ll
  To get inside the gate.

At least 300 people arrived in Custer City in the last week, and many are daily arriving.

This will go via Sidney, and will leave Custer City to day, April 29th, 11 a. m., by Mr. James Madding, who is going to Sidney for freight for Mr. John Bueter, from Nebraska City, now doing business here. There is a large train on the way in from Sidney with passengers and provisions. We received a letter from J. W. Dear, Esq., notifying us that his stages will be ready to start May 1st from Sidney through via Red Cloud, and as the mail has been accumulating at Sidney nearly all winter, and being the nearest postoffice to the Hills, Custer will be greatly benefitted by this line. Custer City built a stable for the Cheyenne stage line, but as yet only the fast freight has reached Custer, although Mr. Moulton informs us that the stages will soon arrive, as the line is nearly stocked. They will also run a line through from here to the north, connecting with all the principal mining camps. We will give you another letter early next week.

CAPT. JACK.

[*Omaha Daily Bee*, 13 May 1876]

THE BLACK HILLS.

(Special Correspondence of the BEE.)

CUSTER CITY, May 3.

Nothing of very great interest has occurred since our last letter; yet, as your correspondent is commencing his fourth night of attending to the sick and wounded, and to keep our eyes open, we will write a few lines.

We have received a letter from Dr. Wm. Robinson, of Omaha, now in Rapid City. He informs us that flour is $25 per hundred—and hard to get at that—and all other provisions high in proportion; and yet the papers and parties interested in the Missouri river route, via Fort Pierre, tell us that they are shipping freight to Rapid City and other points north for 3½ cents per pound. If this is the case, why these terrible prices? $16 is the highest we have ever paid for flour in Custer, and yet it costs from $6 to $8 to get it here.

Whiskey by the wholesale is cheap, and the supply is far in excess of the demand. We warned the whisky men in our former letters against bringing in large stocks of this elevating drug, yet they have brought it in by the car-load; and some we know of wish it were back home in their cellars. As I remarked before, flour is needed more than whisky.

May 1st was an unusually busy day with our people. It was representation day on French creek, and merchants, mechanics, lawyers, doctors, and everybody, might be seen in the afternoon, between the hours of 8 and 10 o'clock, with rifle, pick and shovel, hastening to be on their ground. Nearly every claim was represented, and many are working their claims every day. After this, four day's work must be done every week to hold a claim, which will in a short time open up and develop this gulch, and we think we can soon show the people that French creek is paying. We saw one nugget taken out on last Friday by the Hoosier company, on claim No. 67, below Custer City, weighing $9.15. The company are J. A. Robinson, O. P. Thorp, Chas. Pardol and J. M. Shutt, M.D.

While representing our claim discovery above the city, we saw the Franklin boys strike it on the bed rock, six feet seven inches from the surface, and near the centre of the gulch. Yet some of those dissatisfied get-up-and-get-out fellows tell you it is 10 to 30 feet to bed rock on this creek. It is nothing of the kind. No doubt there are places where the bed rock pitches into pockets, but as a general thing the bed is not over 6 to 10 feet.

Mr. George Worlie, of whom we spoke in our last letter, as coming from Sand Creek with $200 in dust for provision, returned this evening to Custer, having got as far as Castle Creek, where he came across the dead bodies of three men; their wagons were ransacked, and the contents scattered all over the road. Mr. Worlie and party at once retraced their steps to Custer, and wait until a larger outfit can be mustered to go over. And so it is, the old, old story, men who will not believe there are any Indians in the country, and bidding defiance to old Sitting Bull and his whole band, start out in parties of three to five, and just so long as the miners act in this careless manner, so long will these cursed red skins take them in. There is no danger from them if men will go in large parties well armed.

The marshal and eight men have just gone out to Castle Creek for the dead bodies of the three men referred to. There were five in the party, and, as the other two have not yet been heard from, they are supposed to have been killed.

A quarrel occurred yesterday between a boy, about 19 years of age, and another young man, in a dug out. The boy stabbed the other in two places, and cut him in both hands. The boy is captured, and the wounded man's life is despaired of.

Messrs. [W. A.] Laughlin & [A. W.] Merrick will have their paper out in a few days. They would have issued it before this, but the man whom they contracted with to bring their material from Cheyenne, with horse teams, is on the road with oxen. This is why Mr. Laughlin went to Rapid City, as he knew his material would not be in in time. Rapid did not please him, and he has cast his anchor in Custer. He is full of life and energy, although troubled with rheumatism, and we wish him success.

News of five companies being ordered to Custer, and that the Hills are thrown open by Congress, has given us new life.

The Governor of Wyoming has sent a messenger inquiring if he could assist us and find out officially regarding Indian depredations. His messenger returns to-day with official documents from Mayor Bemis, and as Col. Wynkoop, of the Rangers, with a party, is about to start for Sidney, I must close. Will post you regularly.

Capt. Jack.

[*Omaha Daily Bee*, 18 May 1876]

CUSTER CITY.

(Correspondence of the BEE.)

CUSTER CITY, May 5.

It has been snowing steadily all day. Since dawn yesterday snow also fell for several hours, and now everybody is hugging a comfortable fire-place, as the atmosphere has been cooled to a very perceptible degree. Immigration and emigration, to and from the Hills, continues unabated. The feeble-minded and timorous take occasion to leave at every opportunity, some even turn back before they reach the Hills, upon mere reports of the dissatisfied. Still there are hundreds of good and true men who remain with the utmost confidence in the future.

The Indians are continually skulking about the outskirts of the city and on the roadway, stealing at every opportunity, and when it requires little risk they go so far as to take scalps. The night before last eight head of horses and two yoke of oxen were taken right out of town by the reds. The oxen were recaptured, but the others are permanently missing. Last night seven more horses were taken, two from Monaghan's saw mill, on the Minnehaha or Laughing Water, within the limits of Custer City.

It certainly does seem strange, especially to people abroad, that such raids can be successfully carried on almost within the heart of our settlements. One of the prime causes of this state of affairs is the reluctance of many of our citizens, chief among whom are a lot of whisky dealers, to take public measures to prosecute and drive off the Indians. They seem to regard such steps as having a tendency to damage the city and its interests, and for this reason they discourage all efforts towards publishing the actual condition of affairs, or a proper pursuit and punishment of these red devils. There are some liquor dealers, however, who are exceptions to this class—the ones referred to are mostly such as deal in whisky exclusively.

I feel in a measure justified in condemning such men, because I have personally taken every opportunity towards making the Hills safe from these red devils, and on numerous occasions acted as guide or captain of scouts in pursuit of the small thieving parties who prowl about for plunder. A week ago a scouting party was organized here to scour the country and ascertain the haunts of these marauding Indians. After a most untiring effort, they succeeded in getting *one horse* for that purpose.

A train of about fifty men arrived here last evening, and on top of one of their wagons was the dead body of Mr. J. Leggette, who was killed near a camp called "The-spring-to-the-right," about twenty miles from Custer, on the Cheyenne road. A jury was summoned this morning by the coroner, and as your correspondent was foreman of said jury, will give you the particulars. About sundown on the evening of the 3d inst the train was moving along looking wistfully for the camp yet two miles distant, when suddenly a volley of ten or fifteen shots was fired into the train from one side of the road, the horses and men, as if by mutual consent, stampeded, only about four men out of thirty or forty having their guns out of the wagons. Mr. Liggite was near the rear of the train, and being an old man sixty-eight years of age, could not keep up with the flying stampeders. When the train was distant about two hundred yards Mr. L. was seen to fall and eight Indians rushed up to him firing pistols and rifles at him while down; this was the last seen of him until his body was recovered and brought in by a party of men the next day. The body on being brought in was duly examined. Underneath his clothing was a belt which contained three rolls of bank notes, one on each side, and one in the back portion. The money was counted; one roll contained $1,660; another, $1,150, and the third, $1,030, making in all $3,840. This was counted and in the presence of witnesses placed in the hands of Mr. Sergeant from Denver, who knew Mr. Legette years ago in Pennsylvania. He once owned a large tobacco and cigar house in Lancaster, Pa.; he was four times in California; his home before coming here was Louisville, Kentucky. We do not know as yet what disposition will be made of the money, but we believe Sargent will stick to it if he is not forcibly relieved of it. One of the rolls of bills was cut through by a slash of a knife which entered near the spine, through the belt; his pockets were rifled and his shirt pulled out, the breast of his shirt opened, etc., to find money, but the Indians did not notice the belt; had they been white men they certainly would have found it. Mr. L. was a batchelor and we do not know where his relatives reside, if he had any, and if any of them should see this article they would do well to see that the settlement of business is quickly attended to. Mr. Sargent told us to-day that he was going to take the body to Cheyenne at once; if so, there will be the place for inquiry.

Flour is selling at from $18 to $20, and parties coming in would do well to bring a good supply of flour, bacon and sugar. Bacon is 45¢ and sugar 40¢. There are so many false rumors going out from here by dissatisfied scarecrows that freighters are afraid to come in with provisions, and that is the only way they can get us out of here—starve us out. Yet we know of some who won't be starved out, but will take the war path and feed on the Indians, and we belong to that 'ere crowd.

CAPT. JACK.

[*Omaha Daily Bee*, 19 May 1876]

BREVITIES.

—A postscript to Capt. Jack's letter, from Custer City, in yesterday's BEE, says: "The judge of the Superior Court has appointed Judge Kuykendall and Mr. Ward, the saw mill man, as administrators of Leggat, deceased, on whose body was found $3,840. Sergeant, the man who got possession of the money, has turned over $3,500, retaining $340, but for what purpose is not known. If he does not give it up he will be arrested for embezzlement."

5

DEADWOOD AND THE NORTH, MAY–JUNE 1876

The stampede to Deadwood Gulch and elsewhere in the northern Black Hills in the spring of 1876 was nothing if not inevitable. A nearly endless tide of prospectors filled the valleys of French, Spring, Iron, Castle, Battle, and Rapid creeks in the central and eastern Hills as the rush ensued and then spilled onward in the zeal to explore and exploit the entire mineralized region. The lure of the northern Hills was intensified by the nature of the gold being recovered there, which was not the fine flake gold of the French Creek diggings but coarse, highly concentrated placer gold, often existing in shallow pay streaks in narrow canyons. The news from the north always seemed to be good: a rocker cleanup of $165 taken after eight and a half days of work on Bear Creek; a nugget weighing one and a half ounces recovered from the same creek; and yet another nugget worth $147 plucked from Claim No. 5 below discovery in Bear Gulch west of Deadwood, all hinted at the riches awaiting the prospector.[1] The northern Hillers loved Bear Gulch, which they called "coarse-gold gulch."[2] But the climate in the northern Hills was different from what prospectors had come to know in the central and southern Hills. In the north, winter snows were deep and long lasting; water courses froze over; and the placers could not be worked for four or five months at a stretch.

The focus of the northern rush was Deadwood Gulch, a picturesque, branched drainage named for the tangle of fallen pines cluttering its slopes. Deadwood Creek itself was actually a three-mile-long tributary of Whitewood Creek, the trunk stream of the area that ran some fourteen miles from southwest of Deadwood and Lead northeast to the open prairie. But the Deadwood and Deadwood Gulch names came to represent a mining region encompassing Whitewood and Deadwood creeks, their slightly expansive confluence being the area where the town of Deadwood blossomed early in the boom. The region also included a host of tributary creeks and gulches, including Whitetail, Fantail, Black Tail, Gold Run, City, Spring, Englewood, Strawberry, Sheeptail, Spruce, and Peedee, among others, all bisecting a mineralized area that had acquired considerable renown in America. This larger Deadwood contained gold that had eroded over eons of time from a complex formation of granite, quartz, and iron and had eased its way down the mountains and into the sinuosities of the water courses. Those liberating forces had deposited the placer gold not just at bedrock but also on an array of benches above the flowing creeks, sometimes hundreds of feet above, a detail confounding Jack Crawford and others when they finally explored and reported these diggings.[3]

While Horatio Nelson Ross is credited with the discovery of gold on French Creek on 30 July 1874 during the Custer Expedition, the story of discovery in Deadwood and Whitewood gulches is not nearly so simple. The individual most commonly credited with discovering gold in Deadwood Gulch is Frank Bryant, a member of a party that included John Pearson, Thomas Moore, Richard Lowe, James Pierman, Samuel Blodgett, and George Hauser, who prospected the area in August 1875. Bryant found gold on Deadwood Creek, near the mouth of City Creek, on 11 August, but neither he nor any member of his party recorded claims or lingered in the area. James Verpont, prospecting with a small party led by A. S. Blanchard, made a second discovery on Deadwood Creek near the mouth of Black Tail Gulch on 6 September. Verpont recorded a Discovery claim; thereafter, claims above and below keyed on Verpont's claim. Yet a third party was prospecting the area at the same time, and on 7 September, one of its members, William Smith, staked the first claim on Whitewood Creek, about one-half mile below the confluence of Deadwood and Whitewood creeks. Within weeks, the gulches were alive with prospectors, all during that hazy time when Captain Edwin Pollock and

The rush to the northern Black Hills commenced in earnest following rich placer discoveries on Deadwood Creek in September 1875. Soon thousands of prospectors, such as these working the Discovery claim in Deadwood Gulch in June 1876, were combing the labyrinth of gulches along Whitewood and Deadwood creeks and beyond. *D. S. Mitchell photograph. Paul L. Hedren*

his infantry companies at Custer City were still charged with searching for and evicting illegal miners. Pollock evidently never dispatched his infantry to the northern Black Hills; in any case, there were many ways of skirting the army's scrutiny.[4]

As Crawford's letters to the *Bee* made clear, the winter of 1875–1876 was harsh in the northern Black Hills, with little prospecting or mining occurring despite the glowing reports of promising recoveries filtering south. Finally in mid-May, Crawford embarked on his long-anticipated exploration of the northern diggings, traveling with a small party of friends. The landscape beyond Custer City was still thawing, drying, and wetting again from incessant springtime rains. Crawford's 16 May account of the perplexing chaos of rutted, muddy, and often impassable roads and broken wagon axles, purloined wagon parts, straying horses and mules, troublesome rains, and convoluted messing and camping arrangements comprises a delightfully candid and vibrant look at a dimension of travel and life that is typically missing from most accounts of the Black Hills gold country during the peak of the rush. Moreover, poet-linguist Crawford relates these details with a wry wit, and readers today can sense his inevitable transition from plainsman-prospector to thespian of the American stage.

Commencing with the 16 May travelogue and continuing through 31 May, Crawford's letters proved to be his crowning accomplishment as a *Bee* reporter and were almost certainly the great delight of his editor and readers. His unabashed favoring of Custer City and his chronicling of day-to-day happenings there in the preceding months pale when measured against the vitality he discovered and reported in the northern Black Hills. Everything on Whitewood was hustle and bustle; an inescapable mirth was evident on the faces of old friends who had struck it at last; placer gold was measured by the bagful; and Crawford saw more dust, the coarsest gold, and the largest nuggets yet known in the Black Hills. Here indeed was the Black Hills gold rush in full flower, engaging thousands of Americans and ebulliently reported by one whose own reputation as a Hiller was earned and solid.

Crawford's fixation with gold played heavily in his reporting from Deadwood. On Deadwood Creek on 24 May, he watched an evening clean-up that netted fourteen ounces of placer. Elsewhere in Deadwood Gulch, Crawford watched a miner haul pay dirt from a hilltop above Gay City and rocker-out $890 in dust. He also talked about the construction of a roaster, a wood-fired furnace useful in breaking down cemented auriferous sands and gravels to free the gold. Today's readers, however, may be equally struck with the movement of sawmills and the miners' insatiable demand for lumber that are also apparent in Crawford's letters. Within the three months of Crawford's residence in Custer City, three sawmills had set up for business, and one or more of those had joined the rush to Deadwood that Crawford discusses in his 31 May letter. While miners used rough timber for the diggings and for fuel, the mills also supplied lumber for businesses and dwellings. Historians estimate that miners and sawmills logged over a billion and a half board feet of Black Hills timber in the first decade or so of the gold rush, destroying large portions of the forest before conservation measures took hold.[5]

Crawford's letters in May and early June 1876 also reported on other booming communities of the north, including Crook City, Centennial, Gay City (later Gayville), and Spearfish, which, at the invitation of Judge William Kuykendall, Crawford helped to lay out. Each community had its own unique attributes, quirks, and residents, and Crawford delighted in telling of them. The prospect of a telegraph connection to Deadwood earned a comment, too, particularly because its principal advocate was John A. Creighton of the prominent Creighton family of Omaha.

On 9 May, Crawford noted the appointment of a deputy United States attorney "for this district." Captain Jack and others made much of the lawlessness in the Black Hills, which had obliged citizens in Custer City and elsewhere to form their own governments and promulgate specific ordinances purposeful to them. In fact, however, a functional federal district court for Dakota Territory existed and was based in Yankton, the territorial capital. Different from the existing territorial court system functioning in areas where the territory was well organized and separate from the justice of the peace courts of the sort Crawford had helped establish in Custer City, the federal courts adjudicated claims and disputes grounded in federal laws and on federal property, including Indian reservations. The prosecution of the case that Crawford matter-of-factly mentioned in his 8 March 1876 *Bee* letter, in which the plaintiff was accused of selling liquor on an Indian reservation in violation of federal Indian trade and intercourse laws, and the Jack McCall murder trial in December 1876 in Yankton for the killing of Wild Bill Hickok were both actions that occurred in the federal jurisdiction.[6]

In late May, Crawford returned to Custer City to renew interests there. He owned Placer Claim No. 1 above discovery on French Creek, among others. When visiting this claim on representation day, he found two jumpers working it, one deep in a hole throwing out gravel and the other standing guard with a rifle. Captain Jack challenged the two, evidently charging aggressively with a raised shovel as if preparing to bash the interlopers. Both leapt up and scurried off.[7] By then, however, the communities of the central Black Hills were showing the effects of the northern boom. On his way back south, Crawford observed on 2 June that Hill City, centrally located on the Spring Creek diggings, was entirely abandoned, with freighters and travelers using its cabins as they passed from Custer to Deadwood. Custer City presented a gloomy appearance, too, its population having been reduced, as Crawford said in the same letter, to about two hundred souls. The French Creek claims were being worked, he noted, but the seasonal shortage of water hampered meaningful production.

Despite the gloom in Custer, other activity was apparent and drew Crawford's attention. Photographer Daniel Sedgley Mitchell, or simply D. S. Mitchell as he was known professionally, had arrived in Custer City from Omaha and was organizing for continued travel north. While photographers had accompanied Custer to the Black Hills in 1874, and Dodge in 1875, Mitchell was the first to work the Black Hills gold country during the height of the placer boom, though many others soon followed. In 1876, the Black Hills gold rush was national news, and the market for stereographs, that popular dual-imaged photographic medium of the day, had reached its most profitable era. One senses in Crawford's 2 June *Bee* letter that he and Mitchell were previously acquainted, for Crawford immediately announced his intent to guide the photographer north to Deadwood, promising to bring some of the photographs with him to Omaha on his anticipated visit there in July. Ultimately, Mitchell took nearly one hundred photographs of Black Hills placer claims, thriving and dying camps and towns, businesses, creeks, geological landmarks, freighters, and trails in a collection that Black Hills historians widely regard as the finest visual documentation of the early gold rush. Not surprisingly, Captain Jack found his way into several of Mitchell's photographs.[8]

Crawford also remarked on the appearance in Custer City in May of Captain James Egan (mistakenly spelled Eagan) and Company K, Second Cavalry, from Fort Laramie, who had escorted a large wagon party over the Cheyenne Road northward to the Black Hills. The deployment of the company was in direct response to the killings of the Metz party and "Stuttering" Brown in the Red Canyon-Cheyenne River countryside in April and the continued Indian raiding occurring where the Cheyenne Road intersected with the so-called Powder River Trail. The Indians used that trail when traveling between the White River agencies in northwestern Nebraska and the hunting and warring camps in northern Wyoming and southeastern Montana.[9] Crawford also noted the travels of writer Edwin Curley, who visited Custer, Deadwood, and points between in June while researching another of his popular travel guides, this one exclusively devoted to the resources, mineral attributes, and social and business qualities of the Black Hills.[10]

Back in Omaha, the editor of the *Bee* also fixated on the golden riches of the Black Hills, offering gleanings from returning Omahans, reprinting stories from other newspapers, and, in all, dishing Black Hills boosterism at a fevered pitch. In mid-May, the newspaper reported that Omaha's First National Bank displayed some fifty ounces of Black Hills dust and nuggets that miner John Burrill had single-handedly collected, mostly from Spring Creek. The same column also noted that Daniel Allen, of Omaha's Kurtz & Allen auction house, showed Editor Rosewater a bottle containing fifteen ounces of shot gold received from Custer City. Two weeks later, Cheyenne stage company owner Matthew Patrick visited Omaha and reported that nearly seventy thousand dollars in gold dust awaited transfer from the Black Hills, but shipments were stalemated because of Indian troubles.[11] In mid-June, the *Bee* reprinted a story from the *Sioux City Journal* noting that miners were sluicing ten dollars to fifty dollars per day from claims on Whitewood Creek above Crook City and were asking from five hundred dollars to five thousand dollars for the outright purchase of those claims. The *Journal's* correspondent, Ben Andrews, assured readers, "The Whitewood and Deadwood gulches are no doubt the richest that have been found for many years, and some old miners assert that they will beat the famous Alder Gulch, of Montana."[12]

The *Daily Bee*'s greatest display of gold-rush boosterism came on 13 May with the production and distribution of another of its lavishly illustrated supplements. From time to time, the newspaper produced these wraps. This particular four-pager, titled "The New 'Short Cut' to the Black Hills," covered the *Bee*'s regular Saturday edition and served largely to promote the Sidney route to the gold fields. Included among thirteen steel-cut illustrations were a map of the Black Hills gold region, bird's-eye views of Sidney and Custer

FOURTH ILLUSTRATED SUPPLEMENT

TO

THE OMAHA DAILY BEE.

"There's colors in that 'ere pan stranger."

SIDNEY BARRACKS. BIRDSEYE VIEW OF SIDNEY

HARNEY'S PEAK

COLD SPRING CANON.—Entrance to Custer City.

CAPTAIN JACK, Special Correspondent of the "BEE."

DISTANT VIEW OF HARNEY'S RANGE.

THE SIDNEY BRIDGE, Across the North Platte River on the Custer City Route. Erected by H. T. Clarke.

RED CLOUD AGENCY.

City, a panoramic view of the Hills, close-ups of the newly completed Sidney or Clarke Bridge across the North Platte River, Red Cloud Agency, Harney Peak, and a placer miner at work. Even Captain Jack, the *Bee's* touted "Special Correspondent," was featured in an illustration, giving readers a glimpse of a gregarious, if garishly outfitted, reporter. The Chicago Engraving Company rendered the illustrations, mostly copying sketches that Second Lieutenant James E. H. Foster of the Third Cavalry had executed when he accompanied the Dodge Expedition in 1875. Excerpts from several of Crawford's letters, interviews with returning Hillers, practical advice on methods of mining and taking claims, particulars on the Sidney road, and Omaha and Sidney business promotions associated with the gold rush filled out the supplement, adding fuel to the ongoing stampede.

(opposite) The *Omaha Daily Bee's* four-page illustrated Black Hills supplement of 13 May 1876 offered advice for potential prospectors. An array of images featured trail landmarks, gold rush towns, Black Hills panoramas, and even correspondent Captain Jack Crawford, bedecked with outlandish flamboyance. *Paul L. Hedren*

[*Omaha Daily Bee*, 24 May 1876]

CUSTER CITY.

(Correspondence of the BEE.)

CUSTER CITY, D. T., May 9, '76.

Your correspondent will leave Custer to-morrow morning for Deadwood and the north, for the purpose of seeing for himself and making a correct statement regarding that country for the benefit of your readers. Hundreds are leaving here for the north daily, and to-morrow there will be about sixty men in our party, well armed and well provisioned. We would have left to-day, but the mail from Red Cloud came in as we were about to start, and as mails are so rare a luxury we concluded to lay over a day and wait for the news. Every soul is eagerly awaiting every scrap of news, and men hastily scan each paper for the purpose of learning if there is any hope of assistance from Uncle Samuel. We were not a little surprised to-day when we went for our mail to find Judge Dougherty, who is trying to run the pony express, charged twenty-five cents each for letters and papers. This is an outrage on our people, who cannot afford to pay such exorbitant prices. Besides this mail was not carried by Judge Dougherty's pony express—which has not been heard from for two weeks—and two mails sent out never reached the agency. This mail was sent in with a party coming through from Sidney, who carried the mail free, until within two miles of Custer, when Dougherty hitched up a team to a light wagon and drove out for it, brought it in, and charged 25 cents per letter or paper. This is, the man who claims to be an old pioneer, a judge, and a gentleman. God save the mark.

We expect to be gone about eight days from Custer, and will gather all the news possible in that time.

Another man was wounded yesterday, one-half mile from Custer, above, while he and partner were prospecting. One man was killed at Rapid last Saturday, and one farther north.

Miners on this creek are working with rifles by their side and revolvers on each hip. These are the men who don't scare worth a cent.

We have been working our claim since May 1st, but scarcity of water is all our trouble. We are on a high bar, and must cut a ditch at least one mile long to get water up so high.

All the boys have returned from Rose Bud. Indians are the cause. Prospects, they say, are good enough to pay, but the danger is too great for the reward.

Forty-two head of stock was stolen from Hill City last Saturday, and on Monday, fourteen more, leaving them all on foot. A letter was received by our mayor at half-past four Saturday evening, asking for twenty-five men to follow, but too late; besides, we are as helpless as if we had not a hoof in town. Our stock is poor and unfit for the trail, and in a short time we expect to have no horses here. As for myself I have got a bridle and saddle, and will take it with me; perhaps may ride back—it depends. We have some good sandy men with us, and if we strike a trail or camp of Reds, we may get some horses.

I hope your thousands of readers will bear with this hurried style of writing we have lately acquired; we do not seek notoriety as a flowery writer, we merely want people to know that we are telling the truth.

I forgot to mention the fact that ten more horses disappeared this forenoon, and seven or eight night before last; but this horse stealing is of so frequent occurrence that we forget it a few minutes after.

To-day, while a crowd of the boys were standing together, it was amusing to hear the reports which came in in different papers—parties going out and reporting Custer burned and all hands murdered, and that the Indians were having a war-dance on our streets. Well, your correspondent still lives, and so does the editor of the BEE. We fear no attack from Indians here, because every cabin is a fortress, with loop-holes sufficient to stand off old "Sit" and his whole tribe.

There have been two weddings in Custer. Mrs. Allen and a gentleman from Denver were married two weeks ago, and last evening Mrs. Maggie Post and Mr. James Hines, both of Salt Lake, were married by Judge P. J. Keefer. Jim and his fair young bride will depart for the north to-morrow, to seek their fortune. They are both industrious and love each other.

We wish them every joy in life;
  May fortune crown them with success;
May Maggie be a loving wife,
  And Johnny's love be none the less.

Building is again in operation, and confidence is being established with the mail routes. The soreheads will be sorry for being so rash, but we cannot blame them, and we must confess it is dangerous to be safe around here.

Two oxen were killed by the Indians three miles from Custer last evening; they took part of one hind quarter. We went out and got the balance last night; it was good meat, too. There has been no other death warrants of late that we know of, although no doubt many have been killed of which we do not know. You can rest assured, however, we will tell you of every raid, murder or theft that comes under our observation.

Thomas E. Harvey, a young and promising attorney from Nebraska, has been appointed Deputy U. S. District Attorney for this district. Mr. Harvey is well worthy of the position; he is highly respected and has the confidence of our people. We are glad to hear of his appointment, and wish him success; or, as Rip says, may he liff long and brosber.

And now I reckon I'll jest let up,
  And prepare for a jolly old time;
I'll pack my grub, and wipe my gun,
  As soon as I close this rhyme;
And to-morrow, when day begins to dawn,
  With hearts as light as the air,
We'll start for the far-off northern land,
  For they tell us the gold is there.

JACK.

[*Omaha Daily Bee*, 20 June 1876]

THE LAND OF GOLD.

(Correspondence of the BEE.)

DEADWOOD CITY, BLACK HILLS,

May 16th, 1876.

A few words explanatory of our trip from Custer and then some facts. We left Custer at 10 o'clock Wednesday, the [10th] inst. Quite a large party were together on the start, but some fell behind, for good, grassy camps, while others went ahead for the same purpose, until there were but six in our party: M. B. Goodell, a merchant from Colorado; Dick Brown, his pard from California; John Powers, Newburg, N. Y.; Charles S. Slone, Boston; James T. Irion, Birmingham,

Ala., and your correspondent. A better set of boys we never met in the mountains.

On our way the first day out we met 22 teams going to Custer and some to Cheyenne for goods. We camped on Dunlap's ranche. Here your correspondent was unanimously elected captain of the outfit. We put on a guard after putting down our supper. He and Goodell were relieved by Stone, when at daylight Dick and Jack were awakened to take the morning watch, when the Indians are most likely to make an attack. The night was a dreary one; thunder, lightening and rain continued all night, and our beds being spread under the wagon tongue with only two rubber blankets lengthways, stretched from the tongue to the ground over our heads. We were considerably wet before morning.

We broke camp at 7 a. m., stopped for dinner at a place called "Robber's Roost," and camped over night six miles from there, in a pretty little ravine, but a spot where the Indians could give us a bad deal if they were so inclined, as we were surrounded by sloping hills, studded with large trees. The roads from here were very heavy, and we got stuck in the mud several times. We had to unload our wagons while crossing Box Elder creek, and shortly after joined another party, who camped with us in the woods five miles from Judson's ranche, where we passed a very pleasant evening. From this point our trials began.

The road from our camp to Elk creek, about five miles, was fair, but after that it was terrible—mud holes, stumps, dead mules and oxen, broken wagons, rocks and side hills, corderoy crossings made of willow branches, and mud to the hub. In the early part of the morning we passed 150 head of beef cattle on the way to Deadwood to supply the market. These cattle were in very fair condition. Many cows were among them and some little calves which had just seen day light. About 4 p. m., after getting over five miles of the worst road ever traveled, we struck a stump, and crack went our front axle. There was no time to be lost, however, so three of the boys started back to look for another axle among the many broken wagons behind, while the balance of us unloaded the wagon, pulled it out and took it apart. Another axle was got larger than ours, and was cut down with a dull hatchet.

On Sunday, the 14th, some of our horses were missing, but were found several miles away after a troublesome search. Mule teams and oxen were passing us all day long, and ye Gods! what swearing, it was terrible to bear on the Sabbath morning, sometimes ten and fifteen men around each wagon, pushing and lifting, while the crack of the teamster's whip, as he flung it around his team with an oath accompanying every cut, was a scene which was certainly characteristic of the people and the country. About 2 p. m. we had our wagon loaded once more and under way, but alas, it was not destined to stand the rough highway to Deadwood and hopes of fortune. We again broke down two miles from where we had our first break. Messrs. Brown and Goodell now unhitched the team and started for Deadwood to borrow a wagon, leaving the balance to take care of the wreck. About a mile from us they found a wagon, borrowed it, and returned, leaving our wagon. We started once more; before leaving, however, Dick wrote on one of our cards the following:

> *Pards*: If you have one drop of the milk of human kindness, or humanity, about you, don't take the balance of this wagon.
> Dick B.

And the following piece of machine biz by we'ns:

Deadwood or bust was our motto,
  When from Custer we started away;
Busted, by Jove—couldn't help it—
  There were too many stumps in the way;
But, pards, we must go back to Custer,
  So don't take a stick of what's left;
Besides 'twouldn't be very pleasant,
  To accuse honest miners of theft.
Jack.

After placing the above in a conspicuous place we started once more for Deadwood, and having a stronger wagon we considered that we had the "dead wood" on the stumps this time. Two miles further on we struck a large camp of about one hundred miners on Two-Bit Gulch, and here we camped. Many old familiar faces were recognized among the boys, and after supper singing and a good

When borrowing wagons or parts on his initial trip to Deadwood, Crawford scribbled notes to owners or passersby on small *Omaha Bee* business cards like this one. Crawford's business card likely looked similar, although this example belonged to John "Ranger" Pierce, another of the *Bee's* gold-rush correspondents. *Barbara Case*

time generally was the order of the night until nearly midnight. We kept no watch here, as we considered ourselves safe in so large a camp.

On Monday, the 15th, we reached Deadwood, having just traversed the worst part of the road, but all down hill, and at times having had to let our wagon down with ropes, while we snubbed them around the trees. Everything was life and bustle on our arrival. Gold dust by the bag full was shown us on the streets by nearly every miner we met, and many were the merry faces of old friends, who shook our hand and told us that they had struck it at last, and so indeed they have. Since our arrival here, and before we were in town more than ten hours, we saw more dust than we have seen before in the Hills.

Jim Sanders, an old and experienced miner, came to town from Iron creek to buy provisions. We were all surprised to see Jim, as he was reported killed, but he pulled out his buckskin and showed us that he still lived. His gold was the coarsest we have yet seen, many pieces averaging from $1 to $3. He tells us he has nine men at work on Iron creek, five on Sand, and three in Bear Gulch. He said his claims are not very rich, but will pay $6 to $8 per day to the hand all through. He bought in our presence the following goods, paying for them in dust: 450 lbs of flour at $23.00 per 100 lbs.; 350 lbs. of pork at 35¢, and $7.25 of tobacco. He promised to bring us a nugget at least one inch long next Saturday, to make a pin.

We had quite a long talk with Judge Hollins. He said this is the best country in the world. He is as busy as a tailor, building, prospecting, &c, and intends to make this his headquarters.

Lots are worth from $50 to $500 in Deadwood to-day.

Last evening Messrs. Goodell, Brown, Stone, Powers, [W. H.] Coder (former discoverer of Whitewood), and several others, started for Gay City, two miles from here. We took a lantern along, as the woods were dense, and the road very rough and full of prospect holes, drain ditches, etc. We had Dick's banjo along, and although the Gay boys were in bed when we arrived we soon made them get up, and a good time ensued. While there we were shown $150 in dust, rocked out by two men the same day, who carried the dirt from the top of a hill to wash it. Mr. Gay informs us that the finest quartz ledge ever discovered has been found in that section, and hundreds are out at present prospecting for more.

I do not intend to write a very long letter from here until I have seen and found out every fact possible to get at. I intend to go to the different claims and pan out some myself also and see the mines clean up at night and report as ever truthfully. There are over 100 houses built here already and one month ago there were not five. Elizabeth joins Deadwood on the east, and is nearly as large, while Gay City is two miles up the gulch, and will no doubt be a large place. Crook City is nine miles from here, at the mouth of Whitewood, and it is thought will be as large a town as is in the foothills, where there is good grass and every facility for shipping goods from Ft. Pierre on the Missouri river, said to be 150 miles distant. There is no grazing here whatever, and all the stock is being sent to Crook for feed. Herders are engaged and scouts are paid $5 per day by the miners to watch the movements of Indians. We visited Crook City on Sunday, and found out what the prospects are there. The miners are paying green hands $4 per day, and old hands $5; $4 is also being paid for men chopping logs and building cabins. Greenbacks, especially small change, is very scarce in camp. Dust is far more plentiful. Hundreds of wagons and tents stand all over the place, and there is scarcely room to move around. The city is very narrow, not being over 200 yards wide across the gulch in any place, and less than 50 in some places. Yet there are many cabins going up on the hill side north of the road, where the roof of the cabins in the rear are under the surface.

Notices are posted calling for a miner's meeting for the purpose of opening a toll road between Deadwood, Spearfish, north of here, Box Elder and Rapid, south. Some think that Spearfish will be the largest and best city in the Hills. A large party are now out there prospecting for the notorious Father De Smet mountain of gold.

A party of forty niners started last week for the Big Horn, and another party of 200 is being organized to go next week. We were invited to join them as scout on good salary, but declined, as we intended going there with General Crook if he comes this way.

There are too many men here for the amount of diggings discovered, and many are still coming in who expect to find claims, all ready to work, at their disposal.

A party of cut-throats arrived here last week and undertook to run things their own way. They organized, elected a recorder, started up and down the gulch, and took by force every claim that was open. Some miners they would come to and ask, "How many claims have you got?" "Only one." "How much ground?" "Three hundred feet." "Well, that's too much; we'll just take half of it." And others just took it all. They even pulled shot guns on inoffensive unarmed miners who protested. In about two hours, however, there were 400 miners (claim holders) gathered in Deadwood. A meeting was held, and the jumpers were waited upon by a committee who wished to know their intentions. No satisfactory answer could be got from them, and after the miners' committee had reported, the same committee were sent back with instructions to the jumpers to leave the gulch and this part of the country by 12 o'clock next day, and they left in a hurry. We are only surprised that the miners did not give them their just dues—a rope's end. A few hours after they left a report came in that they had killed a miner, and 150 of the boys started out after them. The miner whom they shot was fortunately only wounded, and is now lying here, and will recover. We have heard nothing of the jumpers since. They took a tumble, as one of the miners remarked, and, like Hascall, concluded to get.

It won't work. The men who prospected this country last winter, in snow from three to five feet deep, and lived most of the time on meat "straight," will never relinquish their claims except by purchase or lease on shares. They will die in their tracks first; and when any set of tricksters come here to impose on the honest miners they will have no child's play. A man's a man for a' that.

CAPT. JACK.

[*Omaha Daily Bee*, 21 June 1876]

DEADWOOD.

(Correspondence of the BEE.)

DEADWOOD, May 24, '76.

We took another trip up the creek yesterday and feasted with our gay friend William, who treated us with baker's bread, tea and condensed milk, with a nice piece of ham, etc. There are 37 houses in Gay City, and every lot is now taken, and an addition is being made on a ranche adjoining the town site.

A new discovery was made on the 10th of April by Jerry McCarthy on a hill about 100 feet above the level of the creek. Jerry is hauling his dirt from the top of the hill to the base in Gay City in bags, then carting it to the creek, a distance of about 800 yards, and has rocked out over $890 in dust in two weeks with only one man and himself, with the additional assistance of a horse and cart. These are the most peculiar diggings in the country, and many wonder that a man would go there to find gold, while most miners try to find it on the bed rock, or in the bed of the creek.

Jerome Bentanio, an Italian, is working the next claim to Jerry. We asked him for one pan of dirt, about three shovelsfull. He gave it to us, and in the presence of several gentlemen we washed out 50 cents, which we weighed at Mr. Gay's house. There are three working this claim, and now that they have sluices at the foot of the hill they say they can haul the dirt down and wash out $150 per day; $50 to the hand. But we hope this will not excite any one. It is the only hill diggings yet found, and they may not be another such in the Hills. The Gay claims are paying from $25 to $50 to the hand. Mr. Farnham, of Wheeler, Farnham & Co., just below the Gay boys, tells me they are taking out $100 per day to the hand. I only have his word for it. We next visited No. 5, below, owned by a very intelligent old gentleman, Mr. D. G. Cheezum. He has ten men at work and yesterday only run one side of sluices most of the day. We saw him clean up in the evening and 14 ounces of fine gold was the result, which, at $20 per ounce, would be $280. This, he tells me, is not on the pay

Gay City, or Gayville, was named for founders William and Alfred Gay. *D. S. Mitchell photograph. South Dakota State Historical Society*

streak, as they have run more than double that. Mr. Cheezum is an old California miner, and says he was in Alder Gulch [Montana] in ['62], and he believes that Deadwood will show more clean profit when it is worked out than Alder ever did, as this is so much easier to work. He also informs us that there has been three quartz leads found here which beat any he ever looked at for richness. One of these claims is owned by a French company. The ledges vary from 6 to 9 feet in thickness, and the French claim will pay to run a roaster, which they are now constructing. It must be rich if they can take out wages by this means. We saw seven ounces of quartz crushed, and three ounces of gold taken out of it. We have some of the same quartz, and will forward it to the BEE from Custer as soon as we return. Mr. Cheezum says there is just enough placer in this country to give it a good start, and quartz enough to make it permanent, together with a bounteous supply of pure water, and unbounded forests of timber, as well as the other building materials, such as lime, stone, brick clay, slate, etc. Mr. C. thinks that the country is too cold for corn, but that no frosts that may occur will affect barley, oats or wheat in the valleys.

We might add hundreds of interviews we have had with the miners since our arrival, as we are well known to most of them; but it is useless. What we see we know, and that is all that it is necessary to write.

We did see the hide of the large bear killed just at the upper end of town, and Mr. Theo. Loebeck, who killed him, tells us he only weighed 800 pounds; he was very nice eating—we tasted part of him. Mr. Loebeck was packing his pony prior to starting out on a prospect, when bruin came right down to the cabin, within forty feet of him, when his pony gave a jump sidewise, lighting on Theo's corns; which made Theodore mad, and as he pushed the pony back he saw his royal highness, and bruin saw him and made haste up the mountain. Theo. started for his cabin, got his needle-gun, and shot at the bear 240 yards distant, shooting him through the lights [lungs], and he came tumbling back and rolled dead at his feet, and many a healthy miner feasted on his meat. When we were parting from Theo., he said to Dick Brown: "See here, Dick, you don't look a d—n bit like ye did when I saw ye in 'Frisco, with that ar' camp-kettle hat and boiled-faced shirt; camp life, bar meat and dust kinder makes ye look healthy; eh, pard?" Talk about your life in the cities, but if you could see some of those young counter-hoppers with a pick and shovel in their hands, or nailing stakes (substitutes for shingles) on a house, as I am now looking at one from Pennsylvania, with a face like a copper-kettle and an appetite like an elephant, you would say with me, this is the land for ye young men who are dying behind the counters.

A little shooting, just for fun, took place yesterday, the facts being as follows: We were on top of Dick Brown's cabin hewing the last log, when we heard the crack of a shot gun, and heard Dick exclaim, "There, by Jove, that means biz," and looking down street we saw a man take a dead aim and fire. The man fired at walked on without making any haste whatever. This is how it occurred: A man by the name of Giddings, who was running a keno game, went into Matt

Lee's saloon, and, being about half drunk, pulled his pistol twice on Mr. Lee, who is a very inoffensive man, and one who is more in the habit of making friends than enemies. Matt persuaded him twice to put away the revolver. He afterwards asked for a drink. Matt refused, saying, "Go home and take a sleep; you will feel better after it." In the meantime two men came in and called for drinks, and while Matt was making change, Giddings said, (pulling his pistol) "Well, I'll shoot the pudding out of you, anyway, just for fun." Matt, hearing the remark, turned quickly, receiving the bullet in the arm. Giddings then put away his pistol and immediately started for the door. Matt asked for a pistol. "Yes," said Giddings, very coolly, and walking on slowly; "let him have a shootin'-iron." Matt got a shotgun and rushing into the street fired after the crowd had got out of the way. The second time he fired he shot him in the finger, and then, having emptied both barrels, he got a revolver and followed him. The crowd, however, dissuaded him from shooting, as he might hit some innocent person. Giddings was brought down to the saloon by Wm. Lee (Matt's brother) and several others, and we thought at first that Judge Lynch would have a job; but Matt told them to let him go, as he was drunk, and he (Matt) would settle it with him, himself. He escaped to the woods and has not been seen since. They say he is very badly hurt in the shoulder, a buck shot having lodged therein, and his finger will have to be amputated, although it is feared he may live to shoot some one else.

To day is the Sabbath, and yet how unlike it. Workmen are busy building, although no mining is going on. About forty teams arrived to-day from Custer and Cheyenne, and some from Sidney. A dozen or more stores are opened to-day on the streets, and the town is a perfect mass of humanity. From 500 to 600 miners and laborers are in town, some purchasing provisions, others on a spree, squandering that for which they have undergone so much.

Judge Hollins will start to-day with a large party to the head of the Little Missouri on a prospecting tour, and has promised us letters from there regularly. It is a dangerous undertaking for a party of 150 men, but there is a man with them who is willing to forfeit his life if he does not bring them to big pay diggings.

J. H. Creighton, formerly of Omaha, visited our tent to-day, and we had quite a long and sociable chat. Mr. Creighton informs that he came here for the purpose of ascertaining positively whether this country was to be a prominent mining camp or not; and he is perfectly satisfied both with the placer, and quartz, and says he intends to establish a telegraph line to the Hills at an early day; and no doubt you are better acquainted with Mr. Creighton than we are, and can judge whether or not he is a good authority to quote from.

Messrs. Bowten & Berry's saw mill will be in about next Tuesday, and will be in running operation in about five days after. There is a saw mill at Crook City now, and they charge $60 per 1,000 feet for lumber. Messrs. B. & B. will sell theirs for $40.

We started for Crook City to-day, but returned after learning that the books would not be open until Tuesday, and as we leave for Custer to-morrow, and had not much time to spend there. Will visit Crook City on our return, when we hope to see her in a flourishing condition. Gold sells here for $20 per ounce.

CAPT. JACK.

[*Omaha Daily Bee*, 19 June 1876]

THE BLACK HILLS.

(Correspondence of the BEE.)

ELK CREEK.

(Fifteen miles from Deadwood.)

On Custer road, May 31, 1876.

Sitting once more by the camp fire alone (the two boys who are with me having gone to tie the horses for the night). I will give you a sketch of matters and facts coming under my observation since my last letter. I said in my last that I intended to start for Custer from Deadwood, and so indeed I did, but fate willed it otherwise inasmuch as one of our horses was mysteriously got away with the night before our departure through the negligence of Smith & Co. who took the stock to herd and we have not been able since to regain it. A new town has been commenced and in one of the prettiest spots in the Hills. It is named Centennial City, and is on the road from Deadwood to Crook, seven miles distant from the former and two from the latter. It is situated in a beautiful valley bounded on the west by a lovely forrest, and on the east by barren hills, whose sides are of a blood-red color capped by a summit of fine white gypsum, on the south and upper extremity of the city is another hill of the same kind which seems to cut the valley in two, while to the north or northwest as far as the eye can see is a natural sloping valley from one to two miles in width and bounded by trees on the west for twelve miles and on the east by the Red, White and Green Hills before mentioned. This valley is taken up for farming purposes for ten miles from Centennial city, and cabins can be seen at regular intervals of one-half mile all the way to the Spear Fish. We believe that the Centennial will be the City of the foot hills from the fact that it is the only site near the mines in the north that is within a mile of the diggings. Water has been found at a depth of sixteen feet and enough to supply a good sized town.

Spear Fish is ten miles from Centennial, and one of, or we will say the finest, stream in the Hills. We were invited some time ago to join a party to lay out a city there, and had forgotten all about it until yesterday, when about 4 a. m. Judge Kuykendall came to our ranch and wished to know if we were going to help lay out the new town. We immediately prepared, and to the sparkling Spear Fish we went; arriving there we found thirteen of the original locators and found our name among the number, and soon fifteen more men arrived, who, hearing of the intended location of a city, wanted to be in. A meeting was called and it was decided to give the fifteen new arrivals each one share in the city; the original locators having the privilege of choosing a friend to take a share, or hold two shares themselves. A town one mile square was laid out on a piece of ground through one-third of which the Spear Fish goes dashing, making a noise like a cataract, so swift is the stream; the ground is as level as a floor, and is *riant* [laughing; bright] all around; beautiful round hills, red clay, and white with gypsum, and grass at their base already fit for the scythe. After driving the final stakes, a meeting was held and your correspondent appointed secretary. The town was called Spearfish, and Mr. James Fitzsimmons was elected recorder. A committee of five was appointed to draft rules and regulations governing the city, and a team put to work to haul logs for the recorder's office, after which the meeting adjourned to meet this evening at 7 p. m. to attend to other business. After the meeting twenty-eight men, most of them belonging to the company, started down the valley (which is too beautiful for your correspondent to describe) for the purpose of locating ranches. One hundred and fifty Montana boys came in on last Monday a week, and took up ranches for 10 miles up and down this valley. They came in via the Big Horn, and had no trouble with the Indians until within a few miles of the Hills, on the Spear Fish, when one of their pards named Charles Miller was killed while out hunting; six bullets went into his body, and the Indians stripped him, took his rifle, ammunition, spy-glass, &c. The Montana boys informed us that the day before their arrival they met our Big Horn party mentioned in our last letter, and advised them not to go into the Big Horn, as it was suicidal to attempt it with an outfit not well armed, poorly rationed, undisciplined and with horses barely able to keep on their feet, but still they kept on, excepting a few who looked at the matter in a reasonable light. The gold is still panning out, but there are more men here now than can get work. They have stampeded from Spring, French, Rapid and Castle creeks, from Bear Gulch, Bear Buttes, Rosebud, and in fact every other part of the country, even where some of them were making from $4 to $8 per day, but they heard that miners were paying hands $5 on Dead and White Wood, and there might be a chance to get a claim, but the only chances now are to go prospecting and find other streams and other gulches not already taken up by claims.

To give you an idea of the influx of travel to this country I will mention the teams that passed us on the way north to-day. Since 10 a. m. thirteen single horse teams, sixteen double horse teams, seven packed animals, Judge Dudley's saw mill, with fourteen wagons and eighty-four head of cattle. Street & Thompson's saw mill with two hundred and two head of cattle or one hundred and one yoke loaded with saw mill, flour and other provisions, and thus it is. Every day hundreds are arriving; two saw mills are at work, and three more will be in a week. Messrs. Bowter & Berry are sawing lumber, and getting good sale for it at reasonable prices, while the same mill which got in here first charged $60 to $70 for lumber because they had no opposition, they are not doing so rushing a business as heretofore. As the boys are turning in and I feel somewhat fatigued I too will spread my blanket on the green sward and—

With the moon and stars above us,
  And the green upon the sod,
We'll dream of friends who love us,
  And put our trust in God.

Good night to all.

CAPT. JACK.

P. S.—No Indians have been seen lately, hence we are careless and no watch to-night. J.

[*Omaha Daily Bee*, 19 June 1876]

THE LAND OF GOLD.

(Correspondence of the BEE.)

CUSTER CITY, June 2.

One more—not by the camp fire this time, however, for it is snowing, blowing and freezing, and resembles a March evening more than the first of June. After retiring last evening, our wagon sheet under us, on the grass, and a pair of blankets on top of that, then two pair over us, and a rubber to catch the dew, we felt O. K. until about 2 o'clock this morning, when snow took the place of the rain. It became uncomfortably cold even at the fire place, which we hugged very closely while mixing the batter for our pancakes. After a light breakfast of cakes and coffee without sugar, we hitched up and started on to Custer.

We camped on the evening of June 1st on the road at a place termed "Robber's Roost," and continued our journey the next morning, though the weather was still snowy and stormy. Ice was one-eighth of an inch thick in the water pail.

At Dunlap's ranch, a few miles from our morning camp, we found a company of Montana boys building a tressle work across the gulch to carry the Spring creek water to a dry gulch, where they found good prospects. They are expending over $1,000 to bring this water to the diggings, and whether the mine will pay, remains to be seen. The tressle is about 50 feet above the creek, and about 150 yards long. This is about three miles above Allen's claim, which is still being worked.

Yesterday we passed 35 teams loaded with freight and passengers for Deadwood. Flour took a grand drop in Deadwood the day we left, from $30 and $38 down to $15. A large train from Ft. Pierre, and several large trains from here, is the cause, we suppose.

IN LUCK. On arriving at Hill City we found seventeen wagons and about sixty people camped for dinner; we also stopped and entering a fine hewed log cabin made a fire and cooked dinner. Hill City is entirely deserted—not one solitary soul remains—and the cabins are being used now as shelters and comfortable quarters for freighters, miners, prospectors, and the traveling public of the mountains. Every one has stampeded to the north; yet, there is certainly from $3 to $8 diggings on any claim on the creek, and as soon as the excitement north has abated, hundreds will return to their comfortable quarters; but this is not the part referred to, when I say, as above, "in luck." During the time we were eating dinner, we heard a conversation going on outside regarding a white mare which some one had bought and which was balky. This caused us to make inquiry and we learned that the mare we lost was on the way to Deadwood, and the party who had her was trying to trade her for another horse, and that he had paid $10 for her to a man who said he caught the mare at Buffalo Gap. We hurried and ate dinner, started toward Custer with all haste, met the party of four who had the mare. This man who paid the $10 remarked, "Hello, Jack, I heard you was killed." We replied that we thought it was a mistake, and we believed we were still alive and kicking. "Well," said he very familiarly (never remembering seeing the man before), "Jack, old boy, I've been trading hosses all day." "Where is your stock?" we asked. "Well," said he, "there is the one I traded for a white mare that wouldn't pull." "My friend, that mare is mine, and if old Nick is riding her when I come up I will take possession of her. So to save trouble you had better bring her back." He tried to explain matters, etc., but contradicted himself in everything. He finally rode back toward Custer, got the mare, rode back and met us within three miles of town. "Now," said he, "I will hold the mare till I get the $10 I paid for her." But he didn't. A six-shooter kind of persuaded him to dismount, when our lariat took the place of his bridle, and the mare is ours once more.

P. McKay had a pony stolen from him yesterday, and a man rode into town on him to-day. Pete claimed the horse, proved property, and is now happily in possession and will start for Deadwood tomorrow.

Custer City presents a gloomy appearance. The northern fever has reduced its population from over 1,000 to about 200 souls. There are but nine stores, four saloons and one billiard hall still remaining, and many property holders have left their buildings without a representative. Yet from our knowledge of the country we believe Custer will be the winter resort for the majority of the people who will re-

Although Custer's population diminished significantly as the gold rush shifted from French Creek northward, the town proved resilient. Photographer Stanley J. Morrow, who followed General Crook's troops through the Black Hills at the conclusion of their summer-long Indian campaign, took this photograph in September 1876. *South Dakota State Historical Society*

main in the Hills. There are many reasons for business men leaving Custer: In the first place, French creek has almost dried up and for three miles below town the miners could not get a sluice lead of water in the creek. Yet there are many working below the stockade. We met a young man from below to-day, who says he can make from $5 to $8 as soon as he can get his sluices to work, and a company are now putting in a flume to wash out the bed of the creek. Dave Olston, who has been with his partner one mile above town working his claims all winter, told us this morning that after damming the water and running one hour yesterday he took out one ounce of gold. We have referred to Dave heretofore and believe him truthful.

Merchants will go, however, where the most gold is being taken out and build their stores in a bank on the side of a rock, or in the creek, to be near to the wealth.

There are still two doctors in town. The lawyers, however, have all gone north, and that is one reason why we have still greater faith in Custer, for as soon as the people discover the lawyers coming into Deadwood, many who left here to avoid them will return to live in peace.

In compliance with suggestions, I have made arrangements with Mr. D. S. Mitchell, the artist, to photograph all points of interest between Custer and Deadwood. Tomorrow morning Mr. M. and your correspondent will commence on Custer, and start day after to Hill City, and take the [studio] of [his] popular business [there] and [then north]. Will then forward or bring the photographs to Omaha, perhaps the latter, as we wish to make a trip to Omaha about the 4th of July, and if the wind is favorable on that glorious day, will be happy to point out the way for Ranger [John Harwood Pierce], and accompany him on his aerial flight to Harney's Peak. *Don Caesar de Bazan* [the title of a French comedic opera] *dadah*. The above we believe (although we would not swear to it) is hog Latin or Greek, so to speak.

Messrs Cornell & Williams, partners of Mr. W. H. Wood, are just in from Castle creek, and they are taking out good wages on bar diggings there, but have not reached bed-rock as yet. Mr. J. D. Trask & Co. are digging a drain ditch, which they have been steadily working at since February, and soon will be finished, after which they will work off the bed-rock. Mr. Wood started for Deadwood yesterday, to see the country prior to his commencing muscular exercises on his leads and placer diggings here and on Castle.

D. K. Linvely, one of the oldest residents of this place, and a practical miner, is just up from below Stockade, and says there are at least 75 men working there and all doing well, making wages. Water is scarce, however, and they cannot make full time.

We are placed in a rather bad position, it seems to us. According to private letter from a friend at Omaha, he says: "Jack, old boy, the New York *Tribune* says you own considerable property in Custer, and that you give too many glowing accounts of the country." Now, I scarcely know how I am to act; whether it would be better for me to depart from the course heretofore pursued, and lie like a trooper, or still go on telling the truth and receive the censure of the *Tribune*. If Horace Greeley was alive he would not censure a poor youth in the Hills for telling the truth, but he would have a little sense about him and say to some enterprising reporter; "Go west, young man, go west, and find out if that rooster is telling the truth or lying." This, we think, would be the better way, and if the *Tribune* wishes to find out the real condition of the Hills regarding gold, timber, water and other agricultural resources, let them send one of their fine-haired ducks to me and if I do not convince him that there is *gold in paying* quantities on nine creeks, from French in the south for 100 miles to Spearfish in the north, and from there I will escort him (and not charge him a cent either) to the head of the Little Missouri, thence to Tongue river, Powder river and the Big Horn, and if I say, after we have prospected all these creeks and tributaries, I do not convince him that there is gold here in paying quantities, I will present him with my rifle and give him ten shots at twenty paces. But I would have him do as I have done, take no man's word for it, but take off his coat and go to work and take it off the bed rock from ten to fifteen feet from the surface, pan it out, and if she did not pan then let him blow his horn, but till then, ye *Tribuneists*, hold thy peace, and give us a rest.

Another large party has just arrived from Grand Island, consisting of Captain John Cummings, with 33 men and 12 wagons, and Captain Dudgeon, with 23 men and 8 wagons, all in good spirits and looking well. They left Grand Island on the 8th of May, made the trip in 27 days, and Dr. B. B. Kelley, one of the party, informs us that it is a fearful bad road, sandy and marshy. He thinks that Sidney is the only route to the Hills. Most of the party will leave for the north on Monday.

CAPT. JACK.

[*Omaha Daily Bee*, 20 June 1876]

CAPT. JACK.

(Correspondence of the BEE.)

CUSTER CITY, June 3.

A man named Doc Miller, who has been running a herd at the stockade, has been shooting and threatening to kill people down there. He rushed at another man (a miner) with a knife, a few days ago, and the miner let him have it through the body. It was thought he would die, but now he seems in a fair way to recover. Too much tanglefoot was the cause.

John A. Smiley is superintending the making of a new road to Deadwood, via Palmer's gulch, cutting off fifteen miles and avoiding some bad hills. It is to be a toll road.

Two thousand dollars has been subscribed towards bringing the water from Beaver or Spring creek to French creek, and a committee appointed by the miners of this district to survey out the best way to bring it.

How people can be duped, and even old miners, will be seen by the following: A miner by the name of B. H. Barker, who was in the Hills last summer and who is an experienced miner, tells your correspondent the following story about a piece of quartz: "When I first struck French Creek I was kind'r taken with the country. I went at prospecting for gold in the gulch. I found it and made up my mind that there must be rich quartz here as well. I prospected for quartz but found none with free gold, altho' I could get the color by pulverizing it; so thought as how I would jest play a little innocent trick by stuffin' of a piece. So I found a piece as didn't resemble the quartz of Montana, as little as I could help, and with some gold as I brought with me, I jest salted of it. Ye see I didn't feel as if I was doin' wrong, as there was gold in the bloody country. So I bought it down to Custer, and stuffed it right on the hill opposite to the town, an' I showed it to the miners, an' there wasn't a dog gone one of 'em could tell it from the genuine. I carried it a few weeks, and old Zeb Swaringen was a goin' east, so I let him have it, and many is the good square drink he got on it. But Zeb, mind you, didn't know any different but what it was the real stuff, and after he came back from the States he had the same bleedin' piece with him. Now the country is safe; there is plenty of gold here, and, Jack, I don't give a continental whether ye tell the people about it or not; and some of 'em can have a good square laugh over the thing when they remember how Zeb fooled 'em."

Capt. Eagan has visited Custer since our departure to the north. He was entertained by the mayor and citizens, who gave him and his officers a grand ball and supper at the Van Daniker and McGavock house, the finest and best finished hotel in Custer. Captain Eagan is very highly spoken of by our citizens as a gentleman and a soldier. He condemns the Cheyenne route as being impractical and extremely dangerous, so much so that the government has seen fit to stop all travel on that route, and now perhaps people will believe that Jack told them rightly when he advised them to come by way of Sidney and Red Cloud, it being at least 80 miles nearer to Custer overland and 100 miles nearer from Omaha by rail. Captain Eagan escorted a large party, the last that came over the Cheyenne route, and left for Ft. Laramie to report; but expected to return to Custer in twenty days. His genial countenance will be eagerly looked for by our people, and he will always find a hearty welcome for himself and the boys in the miner's camp, and when he returns we hope to enjoy with him many a pleasant ride over hill and dale.

Some time last winter, we believe, we mentioned the fact that Fritz Drougmond, a saloon-keeper, was arrested by a marshal from Yankton, and was taken to that place and for a time imprisoned. During his absence his young wife—about nineteen years of age—was left alone. A hotel was in course of construction, and Mrs. D. hurried on the work and boarded the workmen. Everything seemed to go on smoothly, until D. B. Moody, a saloon-keeper and proprietor of a gambling house, proffered his services as confidential friend and business manager, and finally as partner of Mrs. Drougmond in the hotel business. And still matters and things seemed all serene, until it began to be whispered around that Moody was not only managing the business affairs of old Fritz, but was also attending to family matters.

And was, in fact,
Caught in the act
Of kissing the fair young bride—

of old man Fritz. Only this and *nothing more*; but when Fritz returned, some three weeks ago, he looked at the matter in a different light. He drove Moody from the house, remarking at the same time, "You make von tam—off my wife." Fritz left Custer for Deadwood, his hotel having burned down shortly after his arrival, with several other buildings. On his arrival in Deadwood he opened a small saloon, and one day, just before we left Deadwood, he remarked to us, "Jack, I dinks I do a poody goot bishnes here in a few days. I sent for mine wife und ged her away from does tam fellers off Cushter, den I make me a leedle more money, und I am all ride, don't it?"

Alas! how little old Fritz knew that at that very moment his young wife, as he called her, was

Over the hills and far away;
  Poor Fritz had lost his game;
It seems he stayed too long away,
  So Moody had jumped his claim.

When the woeful tidings reached the ears of Fritz, the atmosphere was black and blue with oaths of vengeance. He dropped everything and started for Custer on foot, not even taking a bite with him to eat. After traveling six miles and not overtaking any teams, Fritz, who is rather corpulent, played out. He returned, sold out his saloon, bought a pony, and yesterday morning arrived in Custer, just one day after us. He immediately traded his tired pony, got another, and left Custer without even a revolver, and the last we saw of Fritz he was galloping over the hills towards Red Cloud.

Another snoozer known as Bilky Adams, from Salt Lake, a speculator in town lots and other people's money, left the country, and just before leaving he went to Deadwood and being deputized by the deputy U. S. collector here, he collected between one and two hundred dollars, returned, borrowed Mr. Hartley's watch, worth $250, and gone he is also. He is one of these fine haired gents; a pretty talker and a "hard russler."

CAPT. JACK.

[*Omaha Daily Bee*, 22 June 1876]

CUSTER CITY.

(Correspondence of the BEE.)

CUSTER CITY, June 5.

I forgot to mention in yesterday's letter that I would enclose the gold taken out of one pan of dirt from the Hill claim on Deadwood. It contained just 50 cents, but I may have lost some of it since.

Smiley is just in from the new road northeast of Custer, and brings fine specimens of quartz. He says that there will be some fine mining ground opened up on this line of road. Twenty-five wagons left here to-day for Deadwood, among whom is the entire party from Grand Island. Captain Cummings informed us, two hours ago, that he and his party came here to see the country, make money if it was in the country, and to be found; and if they had to go to the Big Horn, they would satisfy themselves. We shook his hand and called him a veteran, and we are satisfied he will have success.

Seventeen teams arrived from Deadwood to-day, most of them going to Sidney or Cheyenne via Red Cloud. Mitchell photographed Cummings' party before going to Deadwood. The picture will be a fine one when printed.

From an interview with several freighters from Ft. Pierre, we learn that water and wood is very scant on that route, and nearly 100 miles must be traveled without water fit to drink. They say for about three months, or four at the most, out of the year is the only time the route will be fit for travel.

Mr. Corlette and two other gentlemen just came in this evening with a live cub, a mix between a cinnamon and a grizzly; also the meat and hide of another. Yesterday they killed the mother, weighing about 900 pounds, seven miles up this creek, and hung the meat up. They returned with a wagon for it this morning, and instead of going straight for their meat they went after another large bear which chanced to cross their trail, and this afternoon when they got to their place of destination the buzzards had spoiled their meat.

Two fine mountain sheep were brought in this evening, which were killed near Custer, and now that the north is being so thickly populated with emigration the game is returning south.

Mayor Bemis had a horse stolen this evening. The lariat was cut about two hours ago, and the Doctor is now out on the fly after the thieves. We hope he will make it hot for them. Were we not very busy preparing for our trip north we would take a hand.

Mr. S. R. Gwin, a capitalist from California, has undertaken the work of opening this gulch, as follows: Mr. G. showed us a paper this evening containing the names of fourteen claim holders above Bear Rock, (discovery,) on French creek, turning over to him their claims to be worked, each claim holder to receive one-quarter of the money taken out. I own a discovery myself, and with others have also assigned my claim to Mr. Gwin. He will at once commence a drain ditch and get the water off the bed rock, and if there is not then sufficient water he will bring in Spring or Beaver. He will start for San

Most early Black Hills photographers captured views of Bear Rock and the recorder's cabin on French Creek, west of Custer City. While gold was actually discovered elsewhere on French Creek, the Bear Rock claim served as "discovery" for the Cheyenne Mining District, which followed the creek from Gordon Stockade upstream to its headwaters. Charles Howard of Fort Sanders, Wyoming, took this view of the landmark in 1877. *Larry Ness*

Francisco as soon as he gets his men at work on the ditch, and bring in 100 Chinamen. He says: "I'll show these people whether or not there is gold in this gulch. I can get Chinamen to work this creek if white men can't do it." Mr. Gwin is full of business and energy, and we believe he will succeed. He is also buying town property cheap, and says, although here only a few weeks, he is fully convinced of the richness of the country, and is confident that "there's millions in it."

Capt. Jack.

[*Omaha Daily Bee*, 23 June 1876]

THE GOLDEN ELDORADO.

(Correspondence of the BEE.)

CUSTER CITY, June 6.

A large outfit, consisting of 27 wagons and nearly 100 men, commanded by Henry Homan, arrived in Custer yesterday from Sidney. Henry is lively as a cricket. He expects to start north from here to-morrow with the whole party. There are two ladies with the train. No Indians were seen by them on the trip from Sidney.

We are informed that there are three thousand letters at Red Cloud, and several hundred pounds of papers, and that the postmaster there has received orders not to deliver any more mail to the representatives of Judge Dougherty. So honest men will now be deprived of their mail on account of one mean trickster. We were also informed that a gentleman from this place—one of James Roberts' store-keepers, named McTellar—had written to the post office department that Dougherty's express was a swindle and an outrage on the people; which, if so, is correct, and we would rather be deprived of our mail, as would every honest miner, for six months, than to pay 25 cents for letters to such imposters. Miners consider it a great injustice that, notwithstanding over six thousand souls are here, no post office accommodations should be extended. Yet, we live on hope. Perhaps Crook will settle the matter soon, otherwise Sitting Bull will.

Edwin A. Curley, author of Resources of Nebraska [*Nebraska: Its Advantages, Resources, and Drawbacks*], paid us a visit to-day. He is writing a book on the Black Hills, and is accompanied by Mr. Lewis Braunhold, of Chicago, a fine young artist, who is making sketches to illustrate the book. They returned from Deadwood and the north yesterday, and will leave for Chicago to-morrow. Mr. B. made a sketch of Custer to-day. We had a long interview with Mr. Curley, and we were delighted to find that he felt as we did regarding the Hills, and is confident that French, Spring, Castle, Rapid, and all other gulches that prospect will be worked extensively before long.

This morning, (June 6th), Mr. Homan remarked to me, while alluding to the country's future prospects: "Jack, did you know that there was a fresh scalp in our outfit." We were surprised, as Mr. H. had told us yesterday that no Indians had been seen, nor was he aware at the time of the following facts, which were too good to be kept, although the boys who did the work, were extremely reticent about the matter.

C. C. Clifton, a young man about thirty years of age, who has spent the last 15 years on the Buffalo range, carries a rifle No. 50, (Sharp's)—a regular buffalo gun. Clifton was coming in behind Homan's train, with but two wagons, and in his hurry to catch the big outfit, broke one of his wagons so much that it delayed him some time. Finally, he got started again all O. K., sending one man to scout the bluffs on his right front.

After traveling for a few miles, the scouts dropped back and reported a large train coming from the opposite direction, which afterward proved to be Capt. Haserodt, of Omaha. Clifton, being an old Indian fighter, thought he would try a little ruse, and immediately turned his train from the road into a valley out of sight of the train and in a fine place of ambush. His idea for doing so and his reasons are, that hearing of so many trains being attacked and followed by Indians, he thought some of the reds might be on the trail of the train, for the purpose, if chance should offer, of running off the stock, and he was correct. In fifteen minutes after the passage of the train along came two Indians on horseback; and said Clifton: "Jack, thar's the pair who took it; it hain't no odds; but there was only three of us in the party, and thar's the Ingin's horse; as good a piece of flesh as ever ye straddled," and so he was a fine poney, as white as snow, and as pretty as a picture. We tried to get Clifton to tell us which of the three did the business, but he remarked, "Jack, suppose you had a scalp to-morrow, would you tell whether you took it, or somebody else, or would you let people suppose for themselves?" "That settles it," we remarked, and the conversation ended. Our opinion is, however, that that old buffalo gun had something to do with the matter.

Dr. E. T. Pierce, of Omaha, gave us a few notes this morning, jotted down on a piece of paper, which he had not time to explain, as he was mounted and about to start on a hunt with some of the Homan party. The note, the particulars of which I presume you have already heard, are as follows:

J. D. Hunter, known as "Pony," of Grand Island, killed at Spring-to-the-right; John Coyer, of Grand Island, was wounded, and died afterward; 3 horses killed, and Hunter's party killed two Indians and one pony. There were but six in the party attacked and were corralled by the Indians. One of the party got out in the night, after

In the second of two photographs that D. S. Mitchell took on Spring Creek when he ventured north in June 1876, Crawford stands in the center of the view. *Robert Kolbe*

carrying stone and building a kind of fortification out of stone, and several of the boys, among them Maj. Beamis and Maj. Wynkoop.

Must now close as our wagon is packed and ready to start on our photographic expedition. We will camp to-night at Cold Spring, about five miles from Custer, and make two pictures at that place.

CAPT. JACK.

P. S.—Capt. John Cummings and a party of 33 men and 12 wagons, also Capt. Dudgeon with 23 men and 8 wagons, who left Grand Island on the 8th of May, arrived here on the 3d. They report the road very sandy and bad, and Capt. Cummings would not recommend any party to come over that route. He thinks the Sidney route the best. Dr. B. B. Kelley is with the party and proposes to go north.

JACK.

6

DEADWOOD AND OMAHA, JUNE–JULY 1876

Jack Crawford complained often in his *Bee* letters about the annoying and untimely delays that Black Hillers suffered in dispatching and receiving mail, a service never greatly improved upon during his time there. His May travels from Custer City north to Deadwood only made matters worse, adding additional mileage to the irregular service. Crawford's letter from Deadwood dated 16 May had taken nearly five weeks wending its way to Omaha, and his communiqué eight days later was nearly four weeks in transit. These delays perplexed his editor, Edward Rosewater, who in mid-June had worried visibly for his special Black Hills correspondent: "Unless we receive a letter or otherwise hear of Capt. Jack, . . . we shall be inclined to entertain grave fears of his safety. His last letter, published about two months ago, stated that he had started for the Deadwood from Custer City, and would write again in about eight days. He has since that time not been heard from personally or otherwise."[1]

Hardly had Rosewater expressed his concern for Jack's safety when he received five letters in near succession, which he published over the course of three days. In several of those letters, Crawford forecasted his intent to depart temporarily from the Black Hills later in June. Quietly, Crawford acknowledged that he was in severe financial straights. His travels did not permit meaningful opportunities to work his claims, which were an apparent sideline anyway, and one senses that he had not received payments of any sort from Rosewater. Jack's public explanation focused on requests he says he had received from miners in Deadwood and Gayville to go to Chicago to show off specimens of the gold ore he had been writing about. To that end, in mid-June he shipped sixty pounds of ore by stagecoach to Cheyenne, intending to follow on horseback. Crawford admitted, too, that he had been corresponding with "capitalists" whom he hoped to meet in order to solicit financial support for the construction of quartz mills in the northern diggings. He did not intend to remain away from the Black Hills long, however, and publicly expressed his intent to lead followers from Chicago and Omaha on his return in two or three weeks.[2]

Before departing the Black Hills, however, Crawford returned again to the northern diggings. This second visit north appears to have been at the request of photographer D. S. Mitchell, who welcomed Captain Jack as a guide. Crawford had closed his 6 June letter to the *Bee*, written from Custer City after having just returned from his first visit to Deadwood, with the quip that his wagon was packed and he was ready to start on "our photographic expedition." But no letters to the *Bee* followed. Crawford indeed went north with Mitchell, who photographed industry and landmarks along the way, and for two weeks combed Deadwood and Gayville, met with old friends, and was allowed to explore some of the new hardrock mines opened when prospectors began probing the innumerable quartz outcroppings evident on the hillsides above the gulches. He returned, too, to the budding hamlet of Spearfish and once again came away extolling its agricultural merit. We can trace his journey through a letter sent to the *Black Hills Pioneer* on 21 June, a face-to-face interview in Omaha with Rosewater on 6 July, and a letter written while in Omaha on 12 July.

Before leaving for Omaha, Crawford visited with editors W. A. Laughlin and A. W. Merrick (Albert to his friends) of the *Black Hills Pioneer*, whom he had first met in Custer City several months earlier. In the late winter, these enterprising newspapermen had transported a press from Denver, paused briefly in Custer where they published the first issue of their newspaper, but then continued on during the general migration to the northern Hills. The ever-obliging Crawford promised reports to the *Pioneer* recounting his travels to Omaha and Chicago and the anticipated opportunities there to show off placer gold and mineralized quartz. Crawford's name was already regularly noted in the *Pioneer* and remained commonly seen thereafter.[3]

Crawford shared a few details of his trip in a second letter he wrote to the *Pioneer* on 13 July. He had gone southwestward to Cheyenne and had not traveled on the familiar and tirelessly promoted Sidney route. He had last traversed a part of this road, through Pleasant Valley and down Red Canyon, chasing Indians and outlaws in April with the Black Hills Rangers. But much had changed since he had exited the Black Hills nearly a year earlier with General Crook on the same route. Fully operating stage stations and related roadhouses dotted the trail every eight or ten miles from Custer City to Cheyenne, and the army's infantry encampments bracketed the dangerous Powder River Trail, one located at the mouth of Red Canyon, several miles north of the Cheyenne River crossing, and the other at the head of Sage Creek in the Hat Creek breaks near the western end of the Pine Ridge escarpment. In his letter to the *Pioneer*, Crawford praised the hospitality the officers at each station had offered. Certainly, too, Crawford must have marveled at Fort Laramie's stout iron bridge spanning the North Platte River and at the continuous stream of freighters, Hillers, and stagecoaches he encountered on the Cheyenne-Black Hills Road. Also apparent were laborers stringing a telegraph wire north from Fort Laramie bound for Custer City and Deadwood.[4] By Crawford's own reckoning, this incessant traffic certainly validated his outspoken embrace of the golden prospect of the Black Hills El Dorado. Unseen at the moment, Crawford's familiarity with the Cheyenne Road would take a providential turn two months hence.

In his letters and interviews, Crawford was curiously silent about the prominent individuals he almost surely encountered on his southbound travel. Somewhere between the Hat Creek stage station and Fort Laramie, he passed a thirty-wagon caravan bound for Deadwood that counted among its members James Butler "Wild Bill" Hickok, John "White Eye" Anderson, and Charles "Colorado Charley" Utter, plus a bevy of colorfully monikered harlots destined for the saloons and cribs of the booming northern city. Along this road, too, Crawford most certainly passed the celebrated thespian Jack Langrishe leading a fourteen-member troupe north from Cheyenne to establish a new theater in Deadwood.[5] But easily the most distinguished encounter of all occurred at or near the Hat Creek stage station itself on 28 or 29 June when Crawford's trail intersected that of William F. "Buffalo Bill" Cody and Colonel Wesley

Merritt of the Fifth Cavalry. Cody had closed his show tour earlier than usual that spring to join this regiment as its chief scout when it was called from Kansas to service in eastern Wyoming. Its mission was to impede Indian traffic on the Powder River Trail. During the third week of June, Cody had been momentarily sidelined from the column to escort Lieutenant General Philip Sheridan and other officers from Fort Laramie to Camp Robinson and Red Cloud Agency to investigate matters there. Cody next escorted Merritt, the Fifth's newly appointed commander, north to the regiment's camp, then located along the Cheyenne River in eastern Wyoming, during which course he ran into Crawford.[6]

Crawford's encounter with Cody may have been one of the most providential experiences of his life. Already emulating the popular showman in dress, grooming, and outlook, Crawford now had his chance, brief as it may have been, to become acquainted. With what followed in mere days, a genuine friendship must have flowered almost spontaneously. The two men were eleven months apart in age, Cody then thirty and Crawford twenty-nine. Cody was already a celebrated buffalo hunter, friend of Wild West luminaries like Hickok, Omohundro, Custer, and Sheridan, successful showman, and genuine army scout. And here he was, engaged again with the Fifth Cavalry in what many observers presumed would be a hard-fought but climactic Indian war, with the Black Hills gold fields among its acknowledged causes. For Crawford, the meeting provided an opportunity to regale Cody with stories of his own Black Hills adventures, of the bustle in the gulches and especially at Deadwood, and of the prominent and sometimes nefarious characters he had consorted with. Likely, too, Crawford showed him the specimens of placer gold and quartz he carried and explained his present intent to promote the Black Hills in Omaha and Chicago. Perhaps, too, he declared that he would show the gold to General Sheridan. Almost certainly, Captain Jack expressed a desire to join the Indian war, for what happened in the coming days had to have been prompted, and this face-to-face encounter offered that opportunity.

Crawford's passage through Cheyenne on 3 July was briefly noted in the *Daily Leader*, and from there, he most likely caught the 3:35 P.M. passenger train for Omaha. As he passed Sidney later that evening, he found a moment to converse with Joseph Gossage, editor of the *Telegraph*, and again obligingly extolled the worthiness of the Sidney route to the Black Hills over the just-traveled Cheyenne route. On his arrival in Omaha, Rosewater interviewed him on 6 July. These dates indicate the hurried and compressed nature of Crawford's travels in July, in spite of the momentous encounters occurring along the way. Rosewater also observed that Crawford brought with him a large number of D. S. Mitchell's Black Hills photographs, which were subsequently framed and exhibited at the *Bee* office.[7]

In early July, stories about or from Captain Jack or about the almost always lurid Black Hills gold rush became secondary news in Omaha and elsewhere in America, at least for a while. Splashed above the front page fold of the *Daily Bee* on 6 July were the glaring headlines that George Armstrong Custer had been annihilated on the banks of the Little Big Horn River in Montana on 25 June. "Custer's Command Cleaned Out" proclaimed one *Bee* header; "The Massacre" topped another column. The Great Sioux War had taken a terrible turn in late June, and Custer, easily the most prominent commander in the field that summer, died leading five companies of his celebrated Seventh Cavalry in a grave clash with Lakota and Cheyenne warriors. The linkages between this catastrophic battle and Custer's Black Hills gold discovery in 1874, the Dodge-Jenney exploration in 1875, the futile attempts by the Grant administration to purchase the Hills from the Sioux, and the gold rush now so fully beyond undoing were inescapable even then and are, of course, crystal clear in hindsight.

Jack Crawford's immediate reaction to the news of Custer's annihilation, evidently prompted by a telegram received from Cody on 10 or 11 July wondering whether he had "heard of the death of our brave Custer?"[8] was to compose an eleven-stanza poem that became his most famous:

CUSTER'S DEATH.

To Hon. Wm. F. Cody (Buffalo Bill)
by his friend Capt. Jack.

Did I hear the news from Custer?
Well, I reckon I did, old pard;
It came like a streak o' lightnin',
And, you bet, it hit me hard.

I ain't no hand to blubber,
And the briney ain't run for years;
But, chalk me down for a lubber,
If I didn't shed regular tears.

What for? Now, look ye here, Bill,
You're a bully boy, that's true;
As good as e'er wore buckskin,
Or fought with the boys in blue.
But I'll bet my bottom dollar
Ye had no trouble to muster
A tear, or perhaps a hundred,
When ye heard of the death of Custer.

He always thought well of you, pard,
And had it been heaven's will,
In a few more days you'd met him,
And he'd welcomed his old scout, Bill.
For if you remember at Hat Creek
I met ye with General Carr;
We talked of the brave young Custer
And recounted his deeds of war.

But little we knew, even then, pard,
(And that's just two weeks ago).
How little we dreamed of disaster,
Or that he had met the foe—
That the fearless, reckless hero,
So loved by the whole frontier,
Had died on the field of battle
In this, our centennial year.

I served with him in the army,
In the darkest days of the war;
And I reckon ye know his record,
For he was our guiding star.
And the boys who gathered round him
To charge in the early morn,
War jest like the brave who perished
With him on the Little Horn.

And where is the satisfaction,
And how are we going to get square?
By giving the reds more rifles?
Invite them to take more hair?
We want no scouts, no trappers,
Nor men who know the frontier;
Phil, old boy, you're mistaken,
You must have the volunteer.

Never mind that two hundred thousand,
But give us a hundred instead;
Send five thousand men towards Reno,
And soon we won't leave you a red.
It will save Uncle Sam lots of money,
In fortress' we need not invest;
Jest wallop the devils this summer,
And the miners will do all the rest.

The Black Hills are now filled with miners,
The Big Horn will soon be as full,
And which will present the most danger
To Crazy Horse and old Sitting Bull?
A band of ten thousand frontier men,
Or a couple of forts with a few
Of the boys in the East now enlisting—
Friend Cody, I leave it with you.

They talk about peace with these demons
By feeding and clothing them well;
I'd as soon think an angel from heaven
Would reign with contentment in h—ll.
And some day these Quakers will answer
Before the Great Judge of us all,
For the death of the daring young Custer
And the boys who around him did fall.

Perhaps I am judging them harshly,
But I mean what I'm telling ye, pard;
I'm letting them down mighty easy,
Perhaps they may think it is hard.

But I tell you the day is approaching—
The boys are beginning to muster,
That day of the great retribution,
The day of revenge for our Custer.

And I will be with you, friend Cody,
My weight will go in with the boys;
I shared all their hardships last winter,
I shared all their sorrows and joys;
So tell them I'm coming, friend William,
I trust I will meet you o'er long;
Regards to the boys in the mountains,
Yours truly, in friendship still strong.[9]

This epic poem came to be known by several titles, including "Custer's Death," given here as taken from the *Bee* on 11 July in its first appearance; it was reprinted under the same title in the *Black Hills Pioneer* on 6 August and on the back cover of Cody's Combination Show program of 13 June 1877 in San Francisco. "The Death of Custer" is also common, and Crawford gave it that title when he reprinted the piece in his 1879 anthology, *The Poet Scout*. Stanzas have occasionally been subtracted, but the poem became a featured presentation in Crawford's subsequent stage performances and is recognized even today in Western literary anthologies.[10]

Crawford continued his journey to Chicago, where on 17 July a reporter from the *Chicago Times* interviewed him, inquiring carefully about the Black Hills gold prospects and general lay of the land. Crawford then proceeded on his program of showing quartz specimens and placer gold to bankers and businessmen whom he hoped to entice to return with him to the Black Hills and, of course, to underwrite the costs of bringing in quartz mills. Crawford also seized an opportunity to show his mineral specimens to Lieutenant General Sheridan.[11] "Captain," Sheridan supposedly remarked, "this is the first substantial evidence I have seen of gold-bearing quarts in the Black Hills."[12]

[*Black Hills Pioneer*, 1 July 1876]

COMMUNICATION.

DEADWOOD CITY, June 21st, 1876.

ED. PIONEER: As I am about to start for Omaha to-day, and as many of the boys (*and girls*) will miss me during my absence, I will say a few words in explanation, and as my time is limited to a very few moments, I will make it short. As you are all well aware who have read my letters to the *Bee*, I have stood by the country ever since my arrival last January, and although other correspondents, tender-feet and milk-and-water men, who had neither the sand to stay in the country, or the ambition to take their picks and shovels and find out what was here, as I have done six months ago—these men left the country because a few redskins were stealing our stock and scalping one of our men occasionally, and for an excuse for their cowardice and laziness told the people East that there was no gold in the country; that it was a bilk, a fraud, and a sell. Well, my friends, you are the men to say what there is in this country. You have a first-class paper in the Hills now, at Deadwood—THE PIONEER—managed and owned by gentlemen of pluck and intelligence; men after your own hearts. It is in your power to do much for these men. Send in your items of news and tell the truth, while you will at the same time shame the devil as well as the "tender-feet" liars who called you fools for remaining. Subscribe for the paper and send it regularly to your friends in the East. It will be gratifying to them, and satisfy Eastern capitalists that we have something here worth coming for. I start for Omaha to-day in your interest, and in the interest of every man who is trying to develop the country. I take with me quartz from your leads, nearly all of them, and will have them asseyed as soon as I get there. I will show the capitalists what we have here, and prove to them that our country is at least worthy of investigation, and if they wish to come, will lead the way.

And now let me say a few words regarding the Spearfish. I have just come from there to-day, footed it, and am pretty tired. It is, without doubt, the finest farming and stock-raising country I ever saw, millions of acres of land that is a feast for the eye to look upon. Over one hundred of the Montana boys have taken up ranches there, and I saw them planting their crops. They say if they can raise crops in that country they have all the claims they want. They are now building cabins and preparing for the winter. The Spearfish is the largest stream in the Hills, and must be seen to be appreciated. There is an immense water power there. The town of Spearfish is, we believe, destined to be a large city. Buildings are going up fast, and many are locating daily. Two other men and myself caught 65 pounds of fish in one hour. You have no doubt seen some of the fish which we caught there. And now, as my time is limited, I will say to all the boys

GOOD-BYE.

Good-bye, but for a little while;
  I wish you all success;
Prosperity I trust will smile
  On every claim and mess.
And don't forget that pluck will win;
  I know you've got the sand;
And though at times it looks too thin,
  Keep working heart and hand.

The darkest hour is just before
  The dawning of the day,
So don't stampede to *Bottoms False*,
  Or any other way.
Stick to your craft until she sinks
  Away below the rim,
Until you've worked out all the chinks,
  Then let her rip, and swim.

Those tender-feet who ran away
  And told their little tale,
And swore the dirt would never pay,
  While you stood in the gale—
I'll meet some of them by-and-by,
  'Tween here and Omaha,
And maybe bust them in the eve
  If they should give much jaw.

Again good-bye, stick to her pards;
  She'll loom up now ere long;
And while you think of other bards

And sing your evening song,
Just think of Jack so far away,
And while I'm on the go
I'll always have a word to say
And praise you all I know.

Yours truly,
J. W. C. (CAPT. JACK.)

[*Omaha Daily Bee*, 30 June 1876]

CAPT JACK.

(Special to the BEE.)

[FORT] LARAMIE, June 30.

I arrived here last night from Spear Fish, Deadwood and the Hills; will be in Omaha in a few days with quartz and all the latest news; came through with one companion, and no harm done; the country is safe; more new discoveries, and crops on the Spear Fish and at Custer in bloom. No late depredations by the Indians. CAPT. JACK.

[*Omaha Daily Bee*, 6 July 1876]

CAPT. JACK.

A BEE reporter this morning interviewed Capt. Jack—the BEE's Black Hills correspondent, who has just returned from the gold fields,—and obtained from him many items of interest, especially concerning the many Omaha people who are now in the Hills.

"On the 23d of June," said Jack, "I left Spearfish, and came to Gay City, and there went to seven of the different leads and found thirty-seven quartz leads recorded. I got a number of specimens of quartz from Woolsey's lead, and the Terry, about sixty pounds in all. I have got it all with me, so I can pan it out, and show Omaha folks what it will yield. I intend to try to get some capitalists interested, as I can show them where some money can be made

"At Gay City there are about 300 people, and about 150 houses. It is about three miles from Deadwood.

"The Spearfish country, by the way, is the most beautiful tract of agricultural land that I even saw. About 125 Montana boys have taken up ranches there, and their crops are up. They say that if they can get good crops this year they will not want any more mining in theirs, as they will have a fortune right there. There are about 25 houses in Spearfish, which is a new town, and about fifty people. There is plenty of beautiful timber within a mile and a half of the town. There is a valley, 12 or 15 miles long, from the woods down to the Red Water, where it comes together with the Spearfish, forming the Belle Fourche.

"Charley Heck, of Cheyenne, who came out ahead of me, had twelve pounds of gold dust. There was a great deal of gold dust there, but the miners were afraid to ship it on account of the Indians.

"A new discovery was found, called False Bottom, running into the Spearfish, three days before I left. I had three pans panned out for me, and it yielded 75 cents. Every claim was taken up there within ten hours after discovery.

"Well, now, about Deadwood, Gay City, and Elizabeth—they are all within three miles of each other.

"Capt. [E. G.] Dudley, of Omaha, by the way, is doing splendidly with his saw mill, which is located within 300 yards of the centre of Deadwood. He told me his receipts were $400 a day, and I believe they are. He is sawing out lumber night and day, and the trees are felled within a few rods of his mill. He is making lots of money and no mistake. There are four other mills there, but none so well located as that of Dudley's. He said I was instrumental in bringing him out there, and gave me enough lumber to build a house on my lot in Gay City, and also presented me with a revolver.

"Deadwood has 2,000 people in and around it, living in tents, dug outs, shanties, wagon covers, log houses, cabins, and in the brush. No greenbacks are to be seen. Gold dust is the circulating medium. The reports about the richness of the Deadwood district have not been exaggerated.

"There are a lot of Omaha people there. Henry Homan is doing a fine business, and as soon as he sells out his stock of provisions he will bring another supply from Sidney. Tom Short is doing a rushing trade in crockery, furniture, stationery, hardware, &c., and is the only man who has a 'rocker'—it is a rocking chair, and he uses it himself almost exclusively. Ragan has nearly sold out of his stock of provisions, and expects soon to come out of the Hills. Mrs. McKelvey keeps a boarding house, and sets the best table in Deadwood, and is making money. Jim VanDaniker is running a saloon, boarding house

This photograph of Deadwood on 15 June 1876 is heralded as the first one taken, and most likely it is, although D. S. Mitchell also took at least one stereo view at the same time but with a slightly different camera setting. Mitchell labeled this view as "No. 1, General View of Deadwood City" and noted making prints measuring 6 x 8 inches (which this original is) and mounted on fine cardboard (again as is this original). Critical details confirming this early date are the standing trees in the mid-foreground, including a skinny pine almost obscured behind the prominent trunk at center, and the substantial framed but unroofed building on the right margin. Deadwood was obviously still blooming. *Adams Museum, Deadwood, S.Dak.*

and restaurant, and charges $1.00 per meal. He showed me two bags of gold dust, and said, 'Jack, I am making lots of it.' Bill McHugh has about sold out his stock of goods and will be home soon. Natusch, who used to keep books for Max Meyer & Co., is selling tobacco, cigars, stationery, etc., and is doing well.

"John Smiley is at Custer, where he is in the herding business, taking care of 150 horses. He also has a fine quartz lead there.

"Captain A. P. Sanders is opening a claim on Whitewood on shares.

"Charley Weston has gone to the Bear Lodge country to locate a claim found by his partner.

"Well, I am pretty tired of talking, and I'll write you out some notes for to-morrow."

[*Omaha Daily Bee*, 12 July 1876]

CAPT. JACK.

OMAHA, July 12, 1876.

Quartz is what makes a mining camp permanent, and as we told you about the Omahosses a few days ago, we will now give you a description of the Big Bonanzas, or at least a few of them; and let it be remembered that we are right from there, with proof of our little story. On June the 20th we started from Deadwood to Gayville, three miles above, on Deadwood creek, and at the mouth of Bobtail and Split-tail, and after tying our pony, securing a gunny sack and feeding the cayuse, we started afoot to the head of the gulch. The first mine we visited was the Clara.

This lode is located on the divide between Gold Run and Bobtail, about a mile and a half from Gayville. One shaft was 26 feet deep, about five feet wide and eight feet long, and showing well defined foot walls. The quartz resembles the Wolsey, some sixty pounds of which I have now with me at the BEE office. It is much decomposed and shows considerable free gold, and is easily worked. Mr. McMasters, one of the owners, informed us that he would be in Omaha soon after us with a ton of this ore, and having found 10 cents to the pan several times in the decomposed quartz and clay. Mr. M. and his partners believe that they have a very rich gold bearing quartz mine, and from all indications we feel certain their belief is not without foundation. The Clara was located on April 24th by August McMasters, John Dawson, John Hinch, Frank Coyle and Wm. Traynor.

The General Terry is the Frenchman's lode, of which so much has been said. On arriving at the mouth of the tunnel, Hank Harney, one of the hard-fisted, bronzed, whole-souled partners, hailed us with "Hello, Jack. Heard you was a coming. Come right in." And in we went, about 85 feet, where a single candle was burning, and Hank's

Jack Crawford explored quartz lodes like this one when examining Deadwood Gulch in June 1876. Photographer D. S. Mitchell labeled this picture the "Chief of the Hills" lode in Blacktail Gulch. *Paul L. Hedren*

partner, Mr. Manuel Wild, was unwelding the rock from the front or face of the tunnel as fast as picks would bring it. He took the candle after Hank had introduced us, and showed us the vein from the face to the mouth of the tunnel.

She looks fine and prospects very well. We pounded about one half pound of the quartz while Hank was preparing dinner, and got over a thousand colors. There was no gold visible before we pulverized it. We have that prospect with us. About fifteen feet from the mouth of the tunnel, they have sunk a shaft twelve feet and were offered $200 for one ton of it by parties to break it up and rock it out. We have also specimens of this lode, which is a grayish color, not like the Woolsey or the Clara. This is the first ledge located, and recorded in Deadwood February 21, by Manuel Weld, X. C. Harris, Alex Haing, and Mr. Harney. Harris sold out his interest some time ago.

The Yellow Jacket is an extension of this lode. The ore is similar in appearance to the Terry, and the boys claim that it is just as rich. About one hundred feet from the Yellow Jacket has been discovered an old mine. Hank insisted on our visiting this spot, and sure enough there was the evidence of miners at work twenty years ago. The two trees at the opening of the cut bear evidence of bullets and arrows having pierced them, but when we arrived there the miners had cut most of them out as relics. Who these hardy pioneers were, and what became of them, is a mystery yet. Old Bridger [probably Jim Bridger] tells of twenty miners having gone to the Black Hills twenty years ago, and never being heard from afterwards. They may all have died in this old hole. That they were slaughtered at their work by the noble red-pelts is only too plain. They had just struck the ledge, when their work and lives were brought to a tragic termination. The claim is now being opened in a different place. The owners are Coleman, Anderson & Co., who discovered it by the old hole only a week before.

Our next stopping place was the celebrated Alpha, owned by J. W. Woolsey & Co. We spent a very pleasant hour with the old man, who is an old '49er. He showed us around and told us to take a pan off the dump and "see what we could get." We did so, and got $1.15, besides several pieces of quartz, containing free gold, which can now be seen at the BEE office. We also brought with us about 70 pounds of decomposed quartz and clay from near the top of the ledge, and which we are prepared to pan out as soon as we can make arrangements to show it to our friends in a large hole, or where our moneyed men will come and see for themselves. We will show the capitalist, if he wishes to invest, where he can coin money by the thousands, and will take a party to the spot, and without much danger to their scalps, and will show them every nook and corner of the Hills, and it won't cost them a cent. Wake up, ye Omaha sleeping capitalists, and look to your interests. I am talking square, and have always done so. The filthy lucre is in the Hills, and you know it.

JACK.

[*Black Hills Pioneer*, 12 August 1876]

FROM OMAHA.

OMAHA, July 13, 1876.

EDITORS PIONEER: We promised you a few lines after our arrival in Omaha, and now as we are about through with the handshaking, visiting, eating big dinners and taking anchovies and deserts of chin music, we will endeavor to tell you and our hundreds of friends and acquaintances in the Hills how we got here, and what we are trying to do, never for a moment losing sight of that little world of ours—the home of the brave, and the land of gold.

A hundred years have passed away,
A hundred years and more,
Since first our fathers blessed the day
They struck our Yankee shore.
The stars and stripes are floating still,
The banner of the free;
And now we hear of Little Phil—
"Hold on, enough," cried he.

Old Sitting Bull is in the north,
His braves are with him, too;
He murdered brave young Custer
And many boys in blue.
He swears he'll murder many more
Before another year;
Yet Phil. refuses fighting men,
Who know the whole frontier.

And now for fifteen days no news
From Crook. What does it mean?
Is he too murdered, with his men,
In some vile, dark ravine?
We trust that such is not the case,
That Crook is still all right;
But if the reds have got his hair,
Then, pards, you too will fight.

And fight ye will with heart and hand,
I know your feelings well;

But not in solid mass to stand
Before these fiends of h—ll.
A rock is good enough for you,
Or shelter of a tree,
To fight this brave and noble Sioux,
And that's the style for me.

Offers from Omaha, Salt Lake and other places have been made to the War Department to furnish five thousand frontier men and miners to clean out General Sitting Bull and his gang; but Sheridan says he can whip them with what soldiers he has. Well, let him go; time will tell. If Phil. wishes to whip these Indians, he will have to order a change of tactics, and fight in Indian style. This marching into Indians in solid mass is a good way to reduce the army, but a poor plan for securing peace and safety to us, who have made our homes in the Hills.

W. B. Goodell and myself left Deadwood on the 23d of June, and alone reached Cheyenne on the 2d of July. We had no trouble from Indians, although two parties whom we met had been attacked, one at Red Canon and one five miles from the soldiers' camp on Hat Creek. We were treated finely by the officers at both camps, Major [Captain William S.] Collier and Lieut. [Rufus P.] Brown at the mouth of Red Canyon, and Lieuts. [George M.] Taylor and [Julius H.] Pardee at Hat Creek.

Since my arrival here I have been doing all in my power to induce capital to come to the Hills, and have in a great measure succeeded. Many here are deeply interested and awake to the necessity of introducing quartz mills, and I am also corresponding with capitalists in Chicago, and have received a telegram this morning to meet them there as soon as possible. Will leave here to-morrow for there, and will organize a party and soon be with you once again.

I feel grateful and satisfied since my return to know that my letters during all last winter were read with so much interest, and copied extensively all over the Union by such papers as the N. Y. *Herald*, Chicago *Times*, St. Louis *Globe-Democrat,* San Francisco *Call* and *Bulletin*, and in fact all the leading papers. I tried to tell the people facts, and no one but tenderfeet and weak-kneed pilgrims ever contradicted me; and now I can say, after all these roosters have left the country, there are five thousand as brave men as ever banded together in any country, in the Black Hills to-day, and on our return we know we will meet the tried and true, who will be glad to give us the right hand of friendship, for we remember—

Last winter, when the snow was deep,
And all seemed dark and drear,
When danger haunted us in sleep,
And redskins ever near;
When roads were blocked with crusty snow,
And grub was hard to get,
And, pards, our cakes were only dough—
'Twas rough now, you can bet.

Our horses, too, were poor and weak,
Not one was fit to ride;
And some while hunting near the peak,
Beneath their riders died.
And many more unfit to go
Were stolen by the Sioux,
And then the mules were mighty slow,
Which gave us all the blues.

There will be a terrific emigration to the Hills just as soon as the Indian business is settled. The quartz brought in lately by McMaster, Adams, Bennett, and myself has been examined by hundreds, and the excitement is general throughout the country.

Excuse brevity this time, and I will send you a long letter before I return.

Yours truly,
CAPT. JACK.

7

CAPTAIN JACK AND THE GREAT SIOUX WAR, JULY–SEPTEMBER 1876

Jack Crawford's promotional visit to Chicago proved short but fated. Early in his tour, he met General Sheridan, commander of all regular army troops on the Great Plains. He also received a telegram from Buffalo Bill inviting him to join General Crook in fighting the Sioux. By now, Captain Jack had developed and relished a substantial public following, and this invitation from none other than Cody himself and his own prompt response played prominently in the pages of the *Omaha Daily Bee* and other newspapers. "Capt. Jack Wanted at the Front," the *Bee* headlined on 21 July, announcing that the editor had received the following dispatch, which it forwarded on to Crawford in Chicago:

> FT. LARAMIE, July 21.
> Capt. Jack Crawford, care Omaha Bee:
> We have had a fight; are now on way to join Crook. Will leave Fetterman about July 27th. Can you join us?"
> W. F. CODY
> (Buffalo Bill.)

The "fight" Cody referred to was the daybreak clash on 17 July between Colonel Wesley Merritt and the Fifth Cavalry and Northern Cheyenne warriors at Warbonnet Creek in extreme northwestern Nebraska, about thirty miles east of the Hat Creek stage station. The episode figured immediately in Cody's life (and would soon in Crawford's) because Cody killed and scalped a young warrior, Yellow Hair, and held that scalp aloft as troopers rode by, loudly proclaiming it the "first scalp for Custer." Within days, Merritt's report of the action reached Sheridan's headquarters in Chicago and splashed into regional newspapers. When the Fifth Cavalry reached Fort Laramie on 21 July, additional accounts of the action included the first mention of Cody's scalping of the Indian. Those stories drew national attention, especially in the wake of Custer's death a few weeks earlier.[1]

Crawford's response to Cody's invitation was prompt and surely delighted his readers. From Chicago the next day, Crawford telegraphed his reply "special to *Bee*": "Have received telegram from Buffalo Bill, asking me to join Gen. Crook. Will leave here to-night for the front. Have had an interview with Gen. Sheridan about the Indian campaign. CAPT. JACK."[2]

By midsummer, the nation fully comprehended that a calamitous Indian war had erupted on the northern plains. If asked, most literate citizens probably understood that the war was somehow related to the Black Hills gold rush then so fully and visibly underway in Dakota Territory. In subsequent years, historians would point to many complexities underlying this aptly named Great Sioux War, acknowledging the inextricable links to the Black Hills gold rush but also pointing out such matters as the completion of a northern transcontinental railroad, unfettered citizen access to all of the lands of the northern plains, and, ultimately, the attempted confinement of the Sioux people on the designated Great Sioux Reservation, which, moreover, soon had the Black Hills cut from it. But the matter was simpler in Jack Crawford's day. More likely than not, individuals then viewed this Indian war as just and right in contexts relevant to themselves, whether a cattleman wishing to graze a corner of the northern buffalo range, a railroader at Bismarck peering across the Missouri River wondering when it would be safe to advance the line, or a Black Hiller seeking riches, safely, in the gulches. General Crook probably captured the citizens' view best when he told President Grant at their pivotal White House meeting on 3 November 1875 that Black Hills miners had told him that they viewed it as their sovereign right as citizens to go and do as they pleased. That, of course, is an axiom as old as the United States of America.[3]

During his Black Hills adventures thus far, Captain Jack had remarked on the heightening Indian tension and bloodshed enveloping the northern plains. He had experienced it personally in April and May while in Custer City and during his escapades with the Black Hills Rangers. His letters matter-of-factly reported on the Indian troubles occurring on the margins of the Black Hills, especially along the Cheyenne and Sidney roads. He witnessed the coming and going of cavalry companies escorting freighters and Hillers. He most certainly had heard of the two army camps established on the Cheyenne Road in mid-June to provide additional security for that road and had then visited each on his way to Chicago. By June, regional newspapers such as the *Laramie Daily Sentinel*, *Cheyenne Daily Leader*, and *Omaha Daily Bee* (copies of which were always finding their way to the gulches) were increasingly filled with stories about the Sioux war. Every fourth or fifth day in June and July, for instance, the *Bee* carried a dedicated column headlined "The Indian War" that recounted the current movements of troops under the commands of Brigadier General Alfred H. Terry and General Crook, who were then operating in the Yellowstone and Powder River countryside. Appearing too were stories about Crook's day-long fight on Rosebud Creek on 17 June in Montana, travails with Indians in the proximities of Fort Laramie and Camp Robinson, and continuing reports about the still barely comprehensible Custer disaster in Montana. By mid-June, stories in the region's newspapers about the escalating Sioux war had visibly eclipsed those concerning the Black Hills gold rush.[4]

Crawford's return to the West from Chicago was hurried but included a luminous reception in Omaha on 24 July, a reflection of his emerging celebrity status. He carried a letter of commendation from General Sheridan to Colonel Merritt of the Fifth Cavalry, for whom Cody was scouting, which urged that Crawford be hired as a scout.[5] During his brief visit in Omaha, Captain Jack's friends outfitted him at lavish expense, providing a "new and elegant" fifty-dollar Winchester repeating rifle and a hunting knife purchased at Julius Meyer's Indian Wigwam, a unique emporium filled with all manner of Indian curios; a cartridge belt and knife sheath presented by Gilbert H. Collins of the celebrated Collins saddlery company; and a new buckskin outfit sewn by Kahn & Wedell, a local haberdashery. "So Capt. Jack started for the front well heeled," crowed Rosewater of the *Bee*, who also noted that Crawford would continue to correspond with the paper.[6] A day later, Collins forwarded by way of Cheyenne and Fort Laramie two ornate leather pistol holsters, one intended for Crawford and the other for Cody.[7]

Crawford's immediate destination was Fort Fetterman, Wyoming, the point of rendezvous Cody had suggested. From Omaha, the most direct route there went by way of the Union Pacific Railroad to Medicine Bow, Wyoming, west of Laramie City, and then overland to Fetterman on a well-traveled freight road. Jack departed Omaha on the morning of 25 July, passed Sidney on the twenty-sixth, and made Cheyenne on the twenty-seventh.[8] Local newspapers followed his movements closely; the *Cheyenne Daily Leader* reminded its readers that this "noted scout and correspondent" was bound for Crook's camp to "take a hand in the Sioux unpleasantness."[9]

During Crawford's brief pause in Cheyenne on 27 July, he was approached by G. M. Jones, proprietor of the Railroad Hotel, one of the city's more popular inns and restaurants convenient to the Union Pacific depot, and asked to carry a small parcel to Buffalo Bill. Captain Jack obliged him but asked to know the contents of the package. "Sour Mash," said Jones, identifying a unique form of bourbon whiskey. Crawford successfully delivered Jones's present to Cody several weeks later, much to Bill's surprise and delight. Cody admonished Crawford to keep the matter quiet, "for there were too many dry men around us." He also remarked later that Crawford was the only man he knew who could have brought that bottle of whiskey through without incident, for he was one of the few "teetotal scouts" he had ever met.[10] Crawford did not tell of this lark in his *Bee* letters, but it was a featured anecdote in his 1879 book *The Poet Scout.*[11]

As Crawford's brief correspondence from the road indicated, he did not tarry long in Medicine Bow, only taking a meal and tending his horse, which the Union Pacific had also transported from Omaha. From Medicine Bow, he rode steadily north to Fort Fetterman, intending to rendezvous with Cody and the Fifth Cavalry and then continue on to Crook's camp in the lee of the Big Horn Mountains. He reached the fort at 2 A.M. on 29 July and received accommodations in the barracks of Company C, Fourth Infantry. Cody and the Fifth Cavalry had departed the post several days earlier. Undeterred, Crawford reported that morning to Captain Edwin Coates, Fourth Infantry, commander of the fort, and expressed his desire to follow Merritt's trail as quickly as possible. One senses in his manner of relating these details in his letter of 31 July that he was unsure of what perquisites came to a scout in the regular army and what demands he dared to make. He may even have been uncertain as to when his employment officially began, although quartermaster records later confirmed that he entered into army civilian service on 22 July, probably when in the company of General Sheridan in Chicago. Those records officially carried Crawford on the civilian rolls as a scout for the Big Horn and Yellowstone Expedition, paid at the rate of $150 a month, the same amount that William F. Cody earned, providing yet another indication of Captain Jack's now glowing reputation.[12]

Crawford's ride from Fort Fetterman north to Crook's quartermaster camp on Goose Creek in northern Wyoming was arduous but without interruption. Jack and a companion gained at the fort, John H. Graves, traveled mostly at night and laid over by day. Graves, a Montana miner whom Crawford had known in the Black Hills, had departed Deadwood in May to prospect the Big Horn Mountains. That venture was not paying, however, and Graves had signed up as a courier for General Crook. From the officer in charge of the quartermaster camp, Captain John Furey, Crawford learned that Crook's command had departed two days earlier. After overnighting with Furey, and despite the captain's remonstrance, the two men pressed on. The country to the north swarmed with Indians, Furey warned, and the trail was cross-country and no longer followed the well-defined Bozeman road. Ultimately Crawford and Graves reached Crook's camp on Rosebud Creek, Montana, in the wee hours of 9 August, having traveled some four hundred miles since departing Fort Fetterman on 1 August.[13]

Among the first to greet the newly arrived scout at daybreak was Cody, who fed him a soldier breakfast of coffee, bacon, hard bread, and cold beans, and then led him to Merritt's and Crook's bivouacs.[14] Crawford's reputation had preceded him. First Lieutenant John G. Bourke, one of Crook's aides-de-camp, confided to his diary that Captain Jack's poems were "assaults upon rhyme, reason and good grammar," but he remembered him as a "brave man and a genial, good-natured liar, whose stories were welcomed at every fire-side. He made friends readily and preserved his popularity throughout the trip."[15] Captain Andrew S. Burt of the Ninth Infantry similarly recalled an affable companion. "Our camp fires were lively after Captain Jack joined us," Burt wrote. "He sang his songs, told his stories,

In 1876 and 1877, Buffalo Bill Cody mentored Captain Jack in the ways of scouting and showmanship. Cody wore this unique vaquero outfit at the Warbonnet Creek skirmish in Nebraska in July 1876 and later when joining General Crook's campaign in Montana. The broad-brimmed hat, wide belt, and large silver buckle were Wild West trademarks throughout Cody's long career as a showman. *Buffalo Bill Historical Center, Cody, Wyo.; Original Buffalo Bill Museum Collection, P.69.30*

recited his poems, and kept his tireless jaw constantly wagging for our edification. He at once went on duty as a scout and served in that capacity until the chief of scouts left us, then Jack was appointed to fill his place, which he did in a most commendable manner."[16]

Jack Crawford, in fact, had joined a notable assembly of scouts who variously served with the Fifth Cavalry regiment (which was a mid-summer reinforcement for Crook's flagging Big Horn and Yellowstone Expedition) or with the headquarters component of the expedition itself. With the Fifth, Cody was recognized as Chief Scout, but among his immediate cohorts were long-time plainsmen such as Baptiste "Little Bat" Garnier, William Smiley, Julius M. Green, and Richard Stirk, while Crook's command counted among its stalwart scouts such highly respected plainsmen as Frank Grouard, Louis Richard, and Baptiste "Big Bat" Pourier. These men were often old fur traders and sometimes mixed-bloods who had grown up in Sioux Country on the northern plains; they often married Indian women and certainly knew the native people, their languages, and, most important of all, the land.[17]

The business of scouting for the army obliged these men to follow trails, guide troops, carry messages from one command to another, and undertake reconnaissance forays. But in such credible company as Grouard, Garnier, Richard, and Pourier, who were all steeped in the geography and people of Sioux Country, the worth of showman and outsiders like Cody, Crawford, and Cody's young traveling companion this season, Jonathan "Buffalo Chips" White, was debatable.[18] As Crook's command was about to break camp on Goose Creek and head north toward the Yellowstone River in Montana in search of General Terry, one of the newsmen covering the campaign, John F. Finerty of the *Chicago Times*, questioned Cody about his abilities as a scout and whether he had ever been in this country before. Bill's reply was quick, short, and confident. "Not exactly here," he said, "but a man who is educated to prairie life is at home anywhere. Lieutenant [Joseph] Lawson, there, can tell you how I once guided him correctly through a country I had never set eyes on before." Lawson, nearby, nodded assent.[19] Clearly, confidence and bravado counted for much in the manly world of Indian campaigning, as did, certainly, amiable companionship on the trail and around the evening campfire.

Crawford also had the dual responsibility of corresponding for the *Omaha Daily Bee*. In this secondary role, he was among a sizeable contingent of reporters filing stories on the Sioux war for some of the nation's foremost newspapers. In the wake of the Custer disaster, the Indian war was national news, and Crook welcomed reporters. He knew that men got credit for what appeared in newspapers, a lesson he had learned in the Civil War when others around him received credit for accomplishments more nearly his own. On this campaign, Crook welcomed Robert Strahorn, writing for the *Rocky Mountain News*, *Chicago Tribune*, *Omaha Republican*, *Cheyenne Sun*, and *New York Times*; Thomas C. MacMillan, covering the campaign for the *Chicago Inter-Ocean*; Joseph Wasson, reporting for the *New York Tribune*, San Francisco's *Alta California*, the *Philadelphia Press*, and the *Owyhee Avalanche* of Ruby City, Idaho; John Finerty, corresponding for the *Chicago Times*; Reuben B. Davenport, reporting for the *New York Herald*; Cuthbert Mills, who arrived with Merritt's column and reported for the *New York Times*; and, now, Jack Crawford, writing for the *Omaha Daily Bee*. As when accompanying Dodge's expedition in the Black Hills in 1875, Crawford was again the least heralded of the lot, and the other reporters or officers on the campaign rarely mentioned him, at least in the context of reporting for a newspaper.[20]

Crook's newspapermen were generally remembered as a tireless and genial lot and as excellent campaigners. Finerty rather candidly explained the exposures these men faced. "Let no easy-going journalist suppose that an Indian campaign is a picnic," he cautioned. "If he goes out on such business he must go prepared to ride his forty or fifty miles a day, go sometimes on half rations, sleep on the ground with small covering, roast, sweat, freeze, and make the acquaintance of such vermin or reptiles as may flourish in the vicinity of his couch; and, finally, be ready to fight Sitting Bull or Satan when the trouble begins."[21]

Of the cast of correspondents, Crawford quickly associated with Reuben Davenport of the *New York Herald*. Davenport was the youngest of the reporters at age twenty-four and the most cantankerous and outspoken on virtually everything he witnessed and experienced. He was especially critical of Crook, whom he faulted for ignoring the fundamental principles of military leadership. His campaign, Davenport suggested, bore a close resemblance to the fruitless generalship of McClellan during the Civil War. Davenport's ceaseless unflattering commentary from June onward created tension among the troops and often brought open derision from officers and even other reporters.[22] Topping it, Davenport had a rather peculiar habit of emblazoning the name *New York Herald* on his personal belongings—bridle, blankets, haversack, and canteen. One observer noted sarcastically, "He has not branded his horse '*Herald*,' but he has got him so he looks like a *Herald* horse."[23] Davenport was already a veteran of another northern plains military expedition, having accompanied Dodge in 1875, and he almost certainly met Crawford at the time. That acquaintance, brief as it may have been, seemed to have evolved into a genuine friendship in 1876. As Crawford indicated in his letter of 18 September, the two men now messed together.

Crawford's handful of letters to the *Bee* from the Sioux war included several that add substantially to our understanding of events at places like Fort Fetterman in mid-summer, where wounded soldiers were sent for hospital care after Crook's battle with the Sioux at Rosebud Creek, Montana. The correspondence also recounted the hubbub of the trails as Jack first chased Merritt's column and then Crook's Big Horn and Yellowstone Expedition from Goose Creek to Rosebud Creek. Crawford's longest letter, written from Fort Laramie on 18 September at the close of the campaign, is riveting, relating details of Crook's march from the Yellowstone River into Dakota, the ride for rations during the notorious "Starvation March," and the consequential Indian fight at Slim Buttes, Dakota Territory, on 9 and 10 September.

The Slim Buttes engagement was the army's largest clash with Indians since the Little Big Horn, and Crawford was in the thick of the fighting. Crawford's account is an immediate and gory story of war, with little sympathy spared for the opposing side and the noncombatants caught in the crossfire. Subsequent to the fight, Jack joined Frank Grouard and others in a renewed dash to the Black Hills for rations. Grouard carried Crook's official report of the engagement and many newspaper dispatches. Crook purposefully added Crawford to the detail because Jack knew the internal roads and trails of the Hills, having traveled them less than two months earlier. But unknown to others, Crawford secretly carried a copy of Davenport's dispatch to the *Herald*. Grouard and Crawford ended up in a pell-mell race through the Black Hills to the nearest telegraph terminal, then at Hat Creek. Crawford also sent his own account of his trials on the trail to the *Herald* on 17 September. This ride, discussed more thoroughly in chapter 8, incurred Crook's enmity and marked the end of Crawford's service as an army scout in 1876.

As had become Crawford's custom in his *Bee* letters, he again mentioned familiar characters. He noted the outlaw Persimmon Bill Chambers, for instance, in his letter of 31 July from Fort Fetterman. A genuine Wyoming and Black Hills pariah, Chambers held a lingering fascination for Jack, who had personally witnessed his murderous legacy on the Cheyenne Road southwest of Custer City. His first killing had been of Sergeant Patrick Sullivan, a Fort Fetterman soldier, in March 1876, and the memory of that event was still raw at Fetterman when Jack passed through. Though unknown then, Chambers's days of mayhem were numbered if not then already over.[24]

Crawford signed his 8 September letter as "Chief of Scouts," and that detail is correct. He had succeeded Cody in that largely symbolic role on 22 August when Bill, at his own request, was discharged from his service and returned to Bismarck by steamboat and Rochester, New York, by rail. In Cody's opinion, the campaign was faltering, and there appeared little prospect of any additional fighting. On the latter point, he was wrong, but he was intent on organizing a new "Dramatic Combination," for which he was having a new drama written based on the Sioux war. That new drama would unite Cody and Crawford later that fall.[25]

Regrettably, Crawford wrote at least one additional letter from the Sioux campaign that the *Bee* chose not to publish. Dated 11 August, it most certainly would have recounted Crook's column joining Terry's, the celebrated personalities marching with Terry, such as Major Marcus Reno of the shattered Seventh Cavalry and the egotistical Colonel Nelson Miles of the Fifth Infantry, the combined columns' tedious march to the Yellowstone River, and perhaps something about the alarming disparities between these two commands. Crook's men had abandoned all excess baggage at their Goose Creek quartermaster camp in Wyoming and united with Terry several weeks later in a frazzled condition, having subsisted on short rations. Terry's men, on the other hand, were amply outfitted, bounteously fed, and had supply and transport wagons immediately at hand. But, said Rosewater, Crawford's 11 August letter contained "no fresh news," and being a month old, he would not publish it, despite its having traveled, he noted, a curious roundabout way via Duluth, Minnesota.[26]

[*Omaha Daily Bee*, 31 July 1876]

A BIG DISCOVERY IN RED CANON.

CHEYENNE, July 27.

Editor BEE:

I learn that a party just in from Red Canon, forty-five miles this side of Custer on Cheyenne road, reports the discovery of a fine body of gold bearing quartz at that place and the indications are that good placer mines will be found there. There is no water, however, near the gulch, and unless water can be brought in, the placer will not in all probability pay, but it is as I have said before, the country is not yet thoroughly prospected, and how can it be in such places as the Red Canon, where murders were of almost daily occurrence last winter by marauding bands of redskins. About forty people have left here for the Hills since my arrival.

JACK.

[*Omaha Daily Bee*, 31 July 1876]

MEDICINE BOW.

(Correspondence of the BEE.)

MEDICINE BOW, July 29.

I am just ready to start for Fort Fetterman. Through the kindness of Mr. Clark, superintendent of the Union Pacific, I obtained free transportation for myself and horse from Cheyenne to Medicine Bow, which is only about ninety miles from Ft. Fetterman, where I expect to join four companies of the 5th cavalry, who left Cheyenne on Monday last to join the command. In case I do not meet them, I will follow them on until I come up with the army. Have met with the best kind of treatment at the hands of the citizens of Cheyenne, and numerous little presents benefitting to my outfit. Ed. H. Merrill, with G. H. & J. S. Collins, presented me with a fine bridle. I cannot thank my friends in words as my feelings would prompt me, both in Omaha and Cheyenne. Will try to do my duty and be worthy of their esteem. Will write from the front first opportunity.

CAPTAIN JACK.

[*Omaha Daily Bee*, 7 August 1876]

FORT FETTERMAN.

(Correspondence of the BEE.)

FT. FETTERMAN, July 31.

Arriving at Medicine Bow on the morning of July 27th, and after drawing two rations of oats for my pony from the quartermaster, struck Fisher's German House for breakfast. At 11 a. m., started for Fetterman, distant 90 miles; made 40 without a stop except to water; came up with Charley Hecht's train of government provisions, 37 wagons in all, loaded with 33,000 pounds of supplies for Crook.

Next morning we were up bright and early, and without breakfast the train moved. We traveled about five miles to good grass and camped for grub, and in about an hour we sat down to a good meal, and it is not to be wondered at that the drivers all say Charley is the boss feeder—a large pot of tomatoes, the remains of a deer and chicken, fried bacon, good, strong coffee, and bread as white as snow, made from the snow-flake—grub good enough for a king. We staid in camp, letting our pony feed, and in about two hours, at 11:30, started to make the other 55 miles, and we did it in just ten hours and thirty minutes.

On arriving at this post I reported to the officer of the day, who ordered my horse put up and my body taken charge—I mean care of.

Next morning I reported to Capt. Coates, informing him that I wished to get to Crook's command as soon as possible. The last company had left two days before for the front under forced marching orders, and he informed me that no other troops would leave Fetterman. I expressed my determination to follow at once if Capt. Coates would furnish me a fresh horse, which he very kindly expressed his willingness to do, but reminded me that there was many chances to be taken and danger on every side, and advised me to wait for Mr. Graves, a courier who came in from Crook's command about a week ago. Graves has charge of 17 Montana miners, now north with Crook. They receive no pay, but get all they can capture. In fact they prefer that to pay. They draw rations, however, the same as the soldiers.

Graves is about 45 years of age, stands six feet high in his stockings, and has a sharp, quick gray eye. His hair is turning gray. He neither drinks nor uses tobacco, and is as wiry a cuss as you will meet

When Captain Jack joined General Crook's Indian campaign, his first destination was Fort Fetterman, Wyoming, on the North Platte River, shown here in the summer of 1877. *Charles Howard photograph. Nebraska State Historical Society, RG2955-PH-0-58*

in a week. I met Graves in the Hills last winter, and he was one of the sixty who started for the Big Horn in May last. He received $200 for bringing dispatches here, and will receive the same when he returns, in case there are dispatches here from headquarters for him to take back; otherwise he gets nothing. We will both start to-morrow whether there are any dispatches or not, as we wish to join the command before there is an engagement. We will leave here about 1 p. m., and ride ninety miles the first afternoon and until daylight, when we will lay over a short time to feed, and then proceed on our way.

We are quartered with Co. C., of the 4th Infantry, and a better set of boys we never met. It brings back old recollections of the past, during the dark days of the war, when we listen to the well-remembered reveille and watch the boys roll into ranks to answer to the roll call. Only two companies, C and I, of the 4th, remain here. Both of these companies were with Crook last winter, and suffered severely, many having their feet and hands frozen, and one man was wounded. They have very fine officers, as I judge from the men themselves, and, to-day being monthly inspection, we noticed particularly that every quarters, dining-rooms, cook houses, and in fact every building was carefully inspected, and every spot was as clean as a new pin.

There are nineteen wounded men from the Rosebud at the hospital here, and nearly all are wounded in the arms. They are all doing well, the most of them being able to walk around camp.

We are under obligations to the old war horse, Wm. McLaughlin, ordnance sergeant and quartermaster, for the use of his writing desk and the freedom of his office. Mac is a veteran of many years' standing, and has been severely wounded. He is *the* business man of Fetterman.

Persimmon Bill, that renegade and horse thief who shot Sergeant Sullivan, of Company F, on the 3d of last March, three miles above here, is now reported as being with Sitting Bull. He is a bad man and a coward, too, for he shot Sullivan in the back without giving him a chance to defend himself. Jack Watkins is said to be with him. With such schemers as these two men, we would not be surprised to hear of some sharp movements on the part of the red-skins.

A man by the name of Hedges came here from Montana with no arms, save a butcher-knife. He has worked here for the government for the last month and is now armed with a good rifle and six-shooter. He starts to-night for the Hills alone.

Sergeant Attix, of Co. B, 2d Cavalry, who was discharged a few weeks ago, is now carrying dispatches between here and Crook's camp at $300 for the round trip. He is a small man, very active and brave, and the quickest courier on the road.

Mr. W. H. Murphy, late of the Western Union at Omaha, arrived here on the 23d of last month and is now operator at this place. He gave us the right hand of fellowship and made us welcome.

Charley Hecht has just arrived; his train will be in this evening.

All mail for your correspondent and the front should be directed via Ft. Fetterman, as there is no mail direct from Ft. Laramie.

Grasshoppers are on the war path here and have destroyed most of the grass, which together with the dry season, makes hay very scarce this year, in fact a patch of bottom land above here which has always yielded 150 tons will not cut more than 50 this year.

I had a long talk with Mr. Graves to-day regarding the Big Horn country, and contrary to my expectations he tells us that neither his men nor himself found any prospects whatever, and that most of his party were still prospecting when he left them. Mr. Graves is a reliable man, and I feel sure he would not tell an untruth. There are sixty miners with Mr. Graves, and they are prospecting yet, except seventeen who are with Crook. I shall find out what the Big Horn is before long if I keep my scalp.

Balcombe, formerly of the *Republican*, now Deputy U. S. M., arrived here this evening from Medicine Bow. What his business is we do not know.

We will carry about two thousand letters and papers to Crook's army, leaving here to-night. Capt. Coates will furnish an extra pack animal to pack mail.

CAPTAIN JACK.

[*Omaha Daily Bee*, 9 September 1876]

HOMEWARD MARCH.

(Special to the BEE.)

CAMP ON HEART RIVER,

D. T., 5th, via Bismarck, Sept 8.

We are twenty-six miles from the Little Missouri. The Indians have dispersed; there are small trails leading in different directions. We have only three day's rations after to-day, and about 150 or 200 miles from Deadwood, where we are said to be going.

We are six days at least from Deadwood and 100 miles from Fort Lincoln. I expect to go to the Hills two or three days in advance of the command. Davenport, of the New York Herald, who scouts and messes with us, will accompany me; from there will telegraph or write further. Starvation stares us in the face; scurvy and dysentery is upon us to some extent.

To-morrow half rations only will be issued, which when done, we may hunt for a living.

Davenport, of the Herald, joined in the chase to-day after thirty Sioux, discovered by our scouts in advance, but owing to the weak condition of our horses, the reds got away.

I think the campaign is virtually over.

CAPT. JACK,

Chief of Scouts.

[*Omaha Daily Bee*, 18 September 1876]

FORT LARAMIE.

(Special to the BEE.)

FT. LARAMIE, Sept 17.

I arrived here last evening at 7 p. m., direct from the field—325 miles in six days, with five changes of horses, beating eight horses and five fresh couriers who were employed to get ahead of me. I was employed as a special courier for the New York Herald, and Frank Grouard, Gen. Crook's guide, followed me with authority from Gen. Crook to purchase fresh horses wherever he found them. He bought two between Deadwood and Custer, and according to his own account killed one. He reached Custer half an hour before me.

We had a fight, 150 men, under Col. [Captain Anson] Mills, being engaged. 25 men charged the village of 34 lodges, under the command of Lt. [Frederick] Schwatka. Lt. [Emmett] Crawford made several splendid charges during the day, driving the reds from every position. Got three days' rations—mostly dried meats—for the whole command, which considering that we lived on horses for three or four days previous, was good. We killed about fifty Indians; three of our men were killed, and about ten wounded. Had no time to note particulars. Took two bucks and several squaws prisoners. The Indians received no reinforcements, and no attack was made except on our rear guard—the 5th cavalry, commanded by General [Lt. Colonel Eugene A.] Carr, who gave them a warm reception, killing eight or ten Indians. Got some scalps.

CAPT. JACK.

[*New York Herald*, 18 September 1876]

THE STORY OF A SCOUT BEARING THE HERALD DESPATCHES—TRIALS AND DIFFICULTIES IN GETTING IN AHEAD.

FORT LARAMIE, Wy. T., Sept. 17, 1876.

After the fight your correspondent engaged me as a special courier to carry despatches to this place. I received permission from General Merritt, after which General Crook requested me to accompany a detachment of fifty men to the Black Hills, as I knew the country. With fifty Indian ponies selected from the captured we started, passing the column about ten a. m. on the 11th, and riding till near midnight. On the 12th at six a. m. we again moved forward, and when within twenty miles of White Wood Creek, after showing Colonel Mills the place to enter, I tried to get away from the command with my despatches, but was prevented twice by Colonel Mills and Commissary [John W.] Bubb.

On arriving at Crook City, and after eating supper and receiving another despatch from your correspondent, I started at eleven o'clock at night for Deadwood. It was pitch dark and my mule fell with me twice, so that I had to walk through a dense forest nearly all the way to Deadwood, where I arrived on the morning of the 13th, at six o'clock. After some difficulty in securing a horse I started for Custer City, being warned by friends to keep a good lookout.

I rode to Box Elder, where I got a change of pony from another friend, and when within ten miles of Custer City was passed by Frank Gruard, who, with General Crook's authority to buy fresh horses, was determined to beat me at Custer. He engaged Frank Smith, one of my Black Hills scouts of last winter, paying him $100 to carry despatches to Red Canyon, forty miles. He told me he sent a courier before nine o'clock, but it was twelve before Smith started, and while I, exhausted, slept.

He also retained duplicates of your correspondent's despatches, which he handed me out of a package of mail matter going to Red Cloud. Next morning Mr. Young, of Custer City, provided me with a horse, remarking:

"Jack, kill him if you want; but beat them if possible."

At nine o'clock next morning I left Custer, and at three p. m. was at Major Collyer's camp at Red Canyon. The Major, being a particular friend of mine, would let me go no further that night as he remarked: "You are nearly dead now, and Gruard sent me Crook's order to forward the despatches, so you might as well give it up. They are twenty-four hours ahead of you."

The Major made me a bed, and I slept; but in the morning I was again on the road, and, on a poor horse, I made Sage Creek at eight p. m. Here I met Lieutenant Taylor, who told me he had forwarded the despatches, and that they were far ahead.

There was a break in the line from here to Fort Laramie, and the operator informed me that he had sent a man to fix the line, and he thought he could use it by ten o'clock a. m. So I left the duplicate with him which Gruard very foolishly handed me at Custer, and I ordered it over the line as soon as he could get a current, and, sure enough, when I reached Government Farm I found the man sent out to fix the wire, and he informed me that my despatch was on the wire and ahead of all others. I rode from Sage Creek to Government Farm—forty-eight miles—in five hours, got a change of horses there and arrived here at seven o'clock last evening only nine hours behind Crook's courier. Five men and seven horses were against me, yet I beat them all.

Gruard informed me that the first horse he bought he killed trying to catch me. Frank is a good friend of mine, but I suppose he was obeying orders.

I will start back tomorrow for the command with despatches from General Sheridan, who interviewed me last evening. I met Captain Egan and supplies going into Indian Creek. I rode 325 miles in six days and am pretty well exhausted.

Crazy Horse's band have been doing all the killing north of and around Deadwood lately. A mail courier was killed near Crook City a few days ago, and a miner was killed on Falsebottom, near Spearfish. Flour was only $3 at Crook City, and Crook can get plenty of supplies.

I believe the General intends to make Custer City his base of supplies for the winter and fight it out on that line. The wagon train from Fetterman would arrive the same day I left Custer. There were many sick with dysentery in the command and a few felt hungry.

Horse meat tasted good on the 4th of this month, and hardtack was more precious than Black Hills nuggets. Lieutenants Crawford and Schwatka deserve great credit for dashing charges and cool bravery; also Pattoozee, or Big Bat, as we call him. Had the whole command been up we would have accomplished much. Four hundred head of stock got away at least.

Your correspondent and myself had first pick out of the Indian herd after the officers who charged got good ones. Lieutenant Von Lentwitz was brave and cool. The Doctor amputated his right leg above the knee. Charley White, one of my scouts, was shot through the heart. He was connected with Buffalo Bill, and was much thought of. I expect to meet your correspondent at Custer City on my return, and will give him all the news as soon as I get rested and collected.

[Captain Jack.]

[*Omaha Daily Bee*, 22 September 1876]

CROOK'S CAMPAIGN.

(Special Correspondence of the BEE).

FT. LARAMIE, Sept 18.

As I am ahead of all other couriers this will perhaps be the first letter published, excepting dispatches giving an account of the fight. On the evening of September 7th, on arriving in camp, Gen. Crook informed me that there was a detachment of troops going into the Hills for provisions with some pack animals, and requested me to accompany them. I consented, and after receiving six hard tack, the allowance of each man, we started with 150 men, under Col. Mills, Lieuts. [Adolphus von Leuttwitz] Von Luettwittz and Schwattka. The night was pitch dark and only by the occasional lighting of a match could we see the compass by which we were guided. About one o'clock a. m. we camped and slept till daylight, when we again moved on. The command was entirely composed of men from the 3d Cavalry, fifteen being detailed out of each company. Frank Gruard and myself were the only scouts with the party. On the 8th, about 3 p. m. Frank discovered some ponies about three miles ahead, and soon after, we found it was a Sioux village. The command was at once given to prepare for action, and accordingly the two battalions formed a line of battle under the brow of the ridge, which hid the foe from our immediate view.

A council was held, and after due consideration it was determined to move back to a deep ravine and wait till daylight. Then said Col. Mills to his men: "Then we will pounce upon them while they sleep, and leave not one to tell the tale." As soon as this decision was arrived at and understood, I volunteered to ride back and inform Gen. Crook of the Indian village, but for some reason the offer was declined, although Gen. Crook was not over 35 miles from us then, and still moving on.

After moving back under cover of the dense fog, which hung like white curtains on the bluffs and peaks around the village, we encamped for the night in mud knee-deep in some places, while the rain fell continually. Not a man in that whole outfit could boast of one dry stitch. All we could do was to take off our socks, wring them, put them on again and walk around, dropping our rifles occasionally to slap our hands around our bodies to warm them, for it was very cold. Small fires were kindled, and those who had coffee made some, while many poor fellows who had none, looked wistfully on; but very few who had any offered to share with the less fortunate.

Davenport, of the New York *Herald*, and myself had about two thimblefuls of green tea, which when made, would scarcely run out of the tin cup, it was so weak. This, with one hard tack each and some bacon rind, was all we had to eat. Nor did we expect any more, when to our great joy, Mr. [Thomas Moore] More, in charge of the pack train, remarked, "Jack, how are you and Davenport faring?" "Very poorly, indeed, sir," said I, trying to be very polite; "only one tack each and very weak tea." "Well," said he, "sit up and try some of our coffee. The packers, you know, have always got a little left." I shall never forget the change which came over the countenance of Davenport. His eyes brightened, and his fingers, numb with the cold, twitched nervously at the tin cup; and in less time than it takes to tell it we were drinking coffee, eating soup and flour paste, two of the happiest of mortals, even in our dilapidated condition. Mr. More afterward gave us a piece of canvas to spread on the mud, and we tried to sleep; but it was impossible, with two wet blankets on top, a piece of rubber canvas below, and every stitch wet; besides, the mules were stampeding all night.

At 3 a. m. every one was ready and we moved forward, Frank and myself in the advance, to find the village; the pack train moved slowly behind, and nothing could be heard save the tinkling of the muffled bell on the bell horse, which, in order to keep the mules from braying, had to be kept in motion. Occasionally, however, a mule would open his mouth and bray loudly. All this time it was pitch dark; nothing could be seen save the white sides of the distant bluffs to our right and front. Once Col. Mills sent me to the right, fearing Frank was not on the right course; but Frank was O. K., and I returned from the ravine.

The guard soon came back from the front and said, "Jack, come this way." I followed him to the front and found five fine ponies, which we brought into our lines, driving them to our rear. Looking back again to our rear I discovered a horseman on a ridge, and reported to Col. Mills, who remarked, "Jack, that is the soldier I sent back for the pack train; he is lost; you go back and bring up the train." In ten minutes more I was back with the train, and ordered Lieut. Bubb forward, which he did. While moving ahead, and when within a few hundred yards of the village, the charge was ordered, and Lieut. Schwatka, with 25 men, swept through the village like an avalanche sweeping with him all the stock in the immediate vicinity—about 125 fine ponies and horses. Col. Mills came after with the main detachment on foot, firing into the tepees, while the reds were cutting cloth and jumping out on all sides. Most of the Indians ran towards a point which we failed to secure, and escaped, carrying with them their dead and wounded. Just as the Indians were escaping and seeking refuge in flight, some one shouted, "Rally on the pack train," but the clear ringing voice of young Lieut. Crawford, whose face seemed to illuminate the scene and inspire the men with all confidence, soon put a stop to such a disastrous move, and soon Col. Mills had a fine position on a knoll commanding the village. In half an hour after the pack train arrived and was safely corralled with the captured herd in a little ravine, where the reds could not reach them. Crawford made some fine charges as soon as it was light, and Frank Gruard and another party charged the reds in different places, for the purpose of getting more stock, but what Schwatka's chargers failed to get, the Indians soon drove to a safe retreat. Owing to the attack being made so premature, Lieut. Von Luettwitz had not time to reach the other side of the village, which would have gained for us a cross-fire and prevented the escape of any. However, the Lieutenant made a desperate effort to make it, but was the second man wounded, the bullet striking him in the right knee-cap, shattering it badly. His leg was amputated next day, and he was doing well when I left. Ed. McKernan, corporal of E company, Third Cavalry, was also wounded in the thigh at the same time. Four of the Indians who escaped hid themselves in a small ravine with bottom of thick underbrush, and acted as sharpshooters during the day. Once we charged them with nine men, expecting to drive them out, but they would not drive, and after killing one and wounding another of our men, we withdrew. In the meantime Col. Mills was placing his men in position, and in two hours we commanded every knoll within a mile of the village. Lieut. Schwatka and myself, with three soldiers, made some rifle pits, which covered the wounded and the pack train, after which we roamed around on our own hook until Col. Mills requested me to go into the village and find out what there was. So with seven soldiers and about the same number of boys with the pack train, we rushed down into the village under a heavy fire from the peaks east of us, and also from the Indians in the ravine. One mule was shot dead and one horse. We went around, however, from one tepee to the other, accompanied by Mr. Strahorn, and found the tepees full of dried meats, skins, bead work, and all that an Indian's head could wish for, and it did seem to us about that time what a pity that Wendell Phillips, or some other philanthropist, was not here to make a plea for the noble reds. Besides these trophies, we found others of far more significance. Col. Mills took from a lodge Custer's guidon, an officer's overcoat, and several saddles of Custer's cavalry. Three horses were also found in the herd bearing the brand of the 7th Cavalry.

The following letters were also found, another proof of the rottenness of the late Indian policy:

"Spotted Tail Agency,
January 14, 1876.
"The bearer of this, Stabber, belongs to this agency, will travel north to visit his people. He will return to this agency within ninety days without disturbing any white man. In case he need any thing you'll not lose by giving it to him. This is true.
T. C. Boucher."

In case he need any little thing—a lock of your hair, I suppose, he means, or your horse, pistol, gun or any "little thing."

Here is another:

"Whitestone Agency, D. T.,
February 18, 1874.
"*To any U. S. Indian Agent:*

"This is to certify that Charging Crow, an Indian belonging to the Sarasac band, is a true man to term of treaty, and uses all his influence with his people to do right. I cheerfully recommend him to favorable consideration of all.

"Yours respectfully,

"E. A. Howard,

"U. S. Indian Agent."

Immediately after the fight commenced, two couriers were dispatched back to the command for reinforcements, and an hour afterwards a third, on good strong horses taken from the herd. Horse flesh had been issued to the men. At a little after noon our lookouts reported the column advancing, which gladdened the hearts of us all, as we did not know at what time the Indians would be reinforced by neighboring villages. By this time firing had almost ceased, except an occasional shot from the ravine close to the village. Two soldiers had already been killed by parties in that hole, and Gen. Crook determined, if possible, to capture one alive, and ordered Frank to get as close as he could, under cover, and talk to him, offering him quarter if he would come out. Frank did so. But the only response was a bullet close to the head of our guide; and for a time this was abandoned.

All day had the soldiers posted opposite the ravine poured a continuous fire into it; yet the Indian rifles would not be silenced. A soldier, not knowing of there being Indians, then rode directly up to the ravine, intending to pass it and ascend the hill, when his horse was shot dead from under him. The second shot took part of the stock off his carbine, and the third, as he scampered off, whistled through his hat. Soon after Gen. Merritt's arrival he ordered our scouts to move cautiously towards the ravine and try to get a shot at the enemy. While so doing, Charley White, one of my messmates, was shot through the head and killed instantly. Then the soldiers and several officers began to muster, and seemed determined to dislodge them if possible. At least two hundred men rushed on to the brink of the ravine, pouring a hot fire into it. But the Indians had with their hands and knives dug into each side of the ravine, and there they lay, under the ground, with their squaws and children. Finally Baptiste, or "Big Bat," as we call him, jumped right into their midst, killed one Indian, took his scalp, and while the gory lock was waved above his head with one hand, he was leading out the squaws and children with the other, at the same time speaking kind words in the Sioux language, telling them they would not be hurt. Bat succeeded in getting all the squaws and children out, but our own men, who could scarcely be restrained, kept pouring their fire in so hotly and close to him that he had to get out, leaving three bucks still in the ravine alive, one dead, and one mortally wounded, a chief, called American Horse, who died next morning (Sunday), the 10th. After the squaws had got out, Gen. Crook got one of them to go in and try to persuade the two remaining Indians to come out, promising them quarter, which she did, and the two are now with us, and look with the utmost contempt upon the whole army, as if their hands had not been dyed in the blood of Custer and his men. After the Indians had evacuated their stronghold, a strange spectacle met the gaze of the hundreds that gathered there. The ravine was deep, and the bottom was covered with low bushes, small trees and brambles. The Indians had small breastworks with mud, roots, &c., across the breach in a number of different places, and the prints of their fingers were plainly visible where they had pressed it down tightly. The mud was drenched with the blood of the wounded and dead squaws and children. One warrior, three squaws and two children lay dead in this awful stronghold. Black Wolf, a chief, is one of the prisoners. There were twenty-one captives in all. One squaw being informed by Bat that this was Gen. Crook, the big chief, rushed up to him and taking him by the arm could not be persuaded to let go her hold, but walked around the village for nearly half an hour looking with horror and fear upon the soldiers and fearing instant death. Another squaw found her dead pappoose in a lodge, and was the very picture of despair and intense woe. The captives informed us that Crazy Horse's village was on the other side of Slim Buttes, and that some of their people had gone for reinforcements. Our skirmish line was strengthened, and about three o'clock mounted Indians began to circle around the entire command, seemingly trying to find a weak point to dash through and re-capture their stock. But though a brisk fire was kept up from that till dark, no charge was made, and a good night's rest, on ground high and dry, with plenty of buffalo robes, blankets, and a big fire, was the result of our day's labor; besides plenty of dried beef and horsemeat, for although the men had plenty of the Indian's provisions, yet they had got so used to horse and mule meat that they seemed to like it.

A battalion of infantry under Major Burt, as gallant a young officer as there is in our command, made some fine charges over the hill, near Buttes, in the evening. About twenty Indians were killed on this side of the camp. The cavalry did some excellent skirmishing also, the line being about 6 miles long around the entire command. As evening fell the discharge of musketry became silenced, Major Burt having charged the Indians from the last and highest raise mid [terrific] cheers from the "dough boys" (infantry); only four men wounded.

And thus when shades of evening fell
The scene was calm and still.
And Crook, he whispered, "all is well
Since Burt has gained the hill.
Our men will have their fill to-night;
'Tis just as heaven wills,
All honor Crawford, boy, to you,
To Schwatka, Bubb, and Mills."

All honor to the boys in blue,
The boys who fought and fell,
Destruction follow every son
Who shot from yonder dell,
And may another sixty days
Bring forth a mighty change;
I think it will, for little Phil
Is now upon the range.

I had not time previous to leaving the command to get a list of the killed and wounded complete, and this letter is written entirely from memory.

The bead work and spoils of the village were distributed among the men, and hundreds of fine robes, skins, etc., with all the lodges, were burned, leaving not one atom of anything useful to the Indians. Several wounded squaws and some children were left in the village, where they would be cared for by their people.

Next morning, when moving out of camp. Lieut. Bubb requested me to go back and drive in six head of horses which were in the rear. After turning five to-ward camp, and about to go for the other, a dozen bullets whistled by my head. I did not insist on driving in the sixth one, but I brought in the five. One was an American horse, and, I think, of the 7th cavalry. General Carr, with the 5th cavalry, was left to bring up the rear, and Carr, as everybody knows, is an Indian fighter out and out.

The following little piece of strategy is worthy of comment: I was about starting for the front, when I noticed the maneuvering of Carr's command, and, sitting on my mule at a short distance off, I watched Gen. Carr. He mounted his cavalry on the brow, or near the top of the ridge. On the other side were the Indians. After the main column had got nearly a mile from him, he started, as if to join them, on the gallop. Then, as soon as out of sight in the valley with the rear battalion, he dismounted every other man and sent them back on their hands and knees to the brow and awaited the Indians, who, seeing the head of the first battalion moving up opposite the hill, charged to gain the ridge to get a shot at the departing Fifth. As soon as they came within a hundred yards, "up, boys, and at them," was the command, and in less time than it takes to tell it, eight *good* Indians were laying on the ground and several wounded, while Carr lost but one man wounded, named [William] Madden, a private.

Your correspondent came near losing his hair on the afternoon of the fight in trying to get that of an Indian. He did get one top-knot, however, which will be sent down to you for inspection. Tell my friends in Omaha who presented me with rifle and equipments that I have kept my word. The captured horses were distributed among the men who charged, commencing with Col. Mills. Your correspondent had the fifth pick, and got a fine mare and colt; will bring her to Omaha when I come down. Davenport, of the New York *Herald*, got one of the Custer horses; he was in the fight all day. I have telegraphed my experience in this scout to the New York *Herald*, for whose correspondent I carried special dispatches, receiving $500 to beat all others. I beat seven horses and five different changes of couriers between Deadwood and here.

CAPT. JACK.

[*Omaha Daily Bee*, 16 October 1876]

RED CANYON.

(Special to the BEE).

RED CANYON, Oct. 14.

General Merritt, with over one thousand mounted men and ten days' rations on pack mules, started yesterday at 10 a. m. for a ten days' scout between the Hills and the agency.

Two horse thieves were shot and killed yesterday morning by a party in government employ. One was a Mexican and the other a white man.

The Mexican is called Lingo, and came to the command on Goose creek with the Snake Indians. They both fought hard and fired the first shot at their pursuers.

The Indians are reported leaving the agency, and many have been seen to day between Custer and Ft. Laramie. We saw the trail of five near Pleasant valley this morning. Fears are entertained that there will be a general outbreak along this route.

CAPT. JACK.

8

CAPTAIN JACK'S RIDE, 11–16 SEPTEMBER 1876

A RECONSIDERATION

Brigadier General George Crook's scattering of the small Indian encampment at Slim Buttes, Dakota Territory, on 9 September 1876 had profound consequences in an Indian war that, until then, had gone decidedly against both Crook and the entire United States Army. The war's objectives were clear enough, especially as the Black Hills gold rush was proving ever more vital to the national economy as prospecting exposed the increasingly valuable hard-rock mineralization undergirding the placer riches. Until this point, however, the war had been marked with devastating setbacks for the army at Powder River in March and Rosebud Creek and Little Big Horn River in June. Colonel Wesley Merritt's small clash with Cheyenne warriors at Warbonnet Creek in July, where Buffalo Bill took the celebrated "first scalp for Custer," provided a glint of good news, but the Lakotas and their Northern Cheyenne friends still dominated the vast northern plains war zone.

The Slim Buttes fight proved to be a turning point. Crook and the army considered it a meaningful victory over the northern Indians, a reality from the war zone that was soon enough widely trumpeted in the nation's newspapers. The troops scattered the nearly three hundred inhabitants; destroyed tipis, possessions, and critical food stuffs; and inflicted casualties, while also sustaining some of their own. For the Sioux, the fight hammered home the point that their remarkable success-filled summer was over. The destruction of the camp was a harrowing implementation of "total war," a brutal strategy characterized by the dawn attack, the wholesale destruction of everything in the village, and the killing, scattering, or capturing of the inhabitants. Many similar attacks followed as the army stepped up its prosecution of the Great Sioux War. Slim Buttes had set a new tone.[1]

Crook's troops discovered an array of Seventh Cavalry relics in the Slim Buttes camp, including a stars-and-stripes guidon, a gauntlet marked with the name of Captain Myles Keogh of Company I, McClellan army saddles, three Seventh Cavalry horses, orderly books, and letters written to and from Seventh Cavalry troopers. There was little doubt that warriors in the village had participated in the Little Big Horn Battle, and many in Crook's column saw the Slim Buttes action as retribution. Certainly Crook needed to forward news of this success to his superior, Lieutenant General Sheridan in Chicago, as swiftly and directly as possible.[2]

After withdrawing from the now destroyed village on the morning of 10 September and moving some fifteen miles toward the Black Hills, Crook again directed many of the same hand-picked men he had selected two days earlier to advance ahead of the column bound for the Hills, some seventy miles away, to procure desperately needed foodstuffs. As Crawford's letters indicated, in their earlier movement, these men had chanced upon the Slim Buttes village and opened the engagement. As before, Captain Anson Mills, Third Cavalry, commanded the advance detachment. Included among its riders were the expedition's chief of commissary, First Lieutenant John W. Bubb, chief packer Thomas Moore, and Lieutenants Frederick Schwatka and George S. Chase, both also of the Third Cavalry. Crook directed his chief scout, Frank Grouard, to accompany Mills and carry his official dispatches. Grouard was under Crook's strict orders to get the official reports transmitted from the nearest telegraph office, at Fort Laramie or anywhere short of there, before any other account was put on the wire. Crook likely had learned from Crawford, who had encountered construction crews on the Cheyenne Road in late June, that the telegraph line was advancing north from Fort Laramie, bound for Custer City and eventually Deadwood. In fact, the line was now operating at Hat Creek, although this fact was unknown to Crook's men. Crook solicited Crawford's assistance both as a guide and in buying supplies because of his familiarity with Black Hills trails and communities.[3]

Crook's admonishment to Grouard to insure that his dispatches were put on the telegraph wire ahead of all others was almost certainly prompted by his understanding that the column's newspaper correspondents had also given dispatches to Grouard. Further, several reporters, including Reuben Davenport and Crawford, intended to travel with Mills. Crook wanted Sheridan reading his account of the action before any reporter's version, especially because some of the newsmen, most particularly Davenport, were annoyingly critical of what they had seen and experienced at Slim Buttes and all along. Indeed, the expedition had been fraught with problems, and its lone battlefield success at Slim Buttes was modest by most measures.[4]

Mills's party, numbering seventy-five men, including scouts Grouard and Crawford and reporters Davenport and Robert Strahorn (writing principally for the *Rocky Mountain News*), departed Crook's camp on the morning of 11 September and rode until midnight. Some in the detachment were mounted on Indian ponies; Davenport rode a Seventh Cavalry horse; Crawford rode a mule. The trail was an ordeal, the riders buffeted by steady rains, shrouded in chilly gray skies, and wearied by interminable mud. By his own account, Grouard lost his way on the first day, and several of the officers quizzed Crawford about the most direct way to the mining camps. Landmarks like Bear Butte and the undulating Black Hills themselves were not yet discernible on the distant horizon, and the officers relied on compass bearings. Crawford later said that he would have directed the party to Deadwood on a more south-southwesterly course by way of Spearfish, but instead they remained on Grouard's southerly bearing. To the glee of Mills's party, the mist broke on the twelfth, and the riders at last glimpsed the Black Hills in the distance. At Crawford's direction, they oriented west of Bear Butte to Whitewood Creek and Whitewood City, reaching the latter at about sundown.[5]

Hospitably received in Whitewood City, most riders remained there. Strahorn, for one, dropped out to partake of a beefsteak and potato dinner. But Mills, Grouard, Crawford, Davenport, and a guard of five soldiers continued west along Whitewood Creek for Crook City, which they reached at about 11:00 P.M. Grouard later wrote that he instructed Crawford to be on hand at daybreak to as-

Located along Whitewood Creek northeast of Deadwood, Crook City was a bustling if short-lived mining camp in 1876 and a critical destination during Crawford's greatest scouting adventure. *Stanley J. Morrow photograph. South Dakota State Historical Society*

sist Bubb in buying supplies and to remain with the command while he, Grouard, continued on with the various dispatches. Crawford supposedly told Grouard that he intended to sleep over with a friend in Crook City and would be on hand at first light. Quietly, however, Jack planned another course in collusion with Davenport, who was insistent on delivering a *New York Herald* exclusive. Soon after the Slim Buttes fight, Davenport, concerned with Crook's increasing animosity toward him and suspecting that no courier appointed by Crook would deliver his report, had asked Crawford whether he knew of a scout in Merritt's command who would carry his communiqué to Fort Laramie. Despite Davenport's offer of five hundred dollars plus expenses for safe delivery, no courier volunteered. Crawford then offered to provide the service so long as he could secure an absence from Merritt. Merritt supposedly assented, and Crawford was given a duplicate copy of Davenport's Slim Buttes dispatch (one had also been given to Grouard). Crawford carefully secreted Davenport's write-up beneath his buckskin shirt. He attempted to steal away from the command twice on the twelfth when within twenty miles of Whitewood Creek but was thwarted on both occasions by Mills and Bubb. Apparently, Grouard did not yet know of Crawford's true intent.[6]

Before Davenport and Crawford parted company in Crook City, Davenport penned a second dispatch and gave it to Crawford, who then quietly struck off in the night for Deadwood. As Crawford later told it, Bubb was already buying provisions there, and Crawford thought he could not be of any more help. It was pitch dark on the trail, and Captain Jack's mule stumbled twice, and rider and mount mostly walked to Deadwood. When Grouard started from Crook City the next morning, he paid no heed to Crawford's whereabouts; he was intent only on reaching Deadwood and forwarding his dispatches from there by courier. But upon reaching Deadwood and going to a livery, he saw Captain Jack's mule in one of the stalls. He asked the stable attendant where that mule had come from and learned that Crawford had been there at about 5 A.M., changed mounts, and embarked for Custer City. Realizing his predicament, Grouard elected to carry the dispatches forward himself rather than hiring someone else for the job. After acquiring the best horse then available in the stable, he sought out an acquaintance who accompanied him to one of the city's banks, where he withdrew five hundred dollars. With that money and a written order he carried from Crook, he figured he had a fair chance of beating Crawford to Fort Laramie, some two hundred miles distant. The other correspondents had also given him money to pay any expenses that might be incurred in handling their dispatches.[7]

Both men followed the same well-defined road south through the Hills from Deadwood to Custer City, Crawford with a five-hour lead. Grouard had the advantage of cash in hand, however, and as his horses played out, he was able to buy or hire fresh mounts along the way, riding some until they gave out and others until they literally dropped dead beneath him. He remembered that he changed horses six times between Deadwood and Custer City, killing three and using up the other three. About five miles beyond his last change of mounts and perhaps ten miles short of Custer City, Grouard caught up with Crawford, whose own horse was completely winded. Grouard asked him whether he remembered the order that he should stay with Bubb and buy supplies, but Crawford replied only that he was taking dispatches through for the *New York Herald.* After informing Captain Jack that he was discharged from his duties as an army scout from the time he left the command, Grouard passed Crawford and continued on to Custer, making the 101-mile ride from Deadwood in four hours and ten minutes.[8]

Crawford may indeed have started from Deadwood on a good horse, but he rode it hard. He was able to change mounts only once, at Box Elder, a landmark about a third of the way south to Custer City, and rode the replacement the rest of the distance. Captain Jack arrived in Custer several hours after Grouard but easily found him and learned that he had engaged Frank Smith to carry Crook's dispatches to the army camp at Red Canyon, paying one hundred dollars for the service. Grouard presumed, rightly as it turned out, that a soldier courier would advance the communiqués from Red Canyon to the next camp and so on to Fort Laramie. Smith, one of Crawford's fellow Black Hills Rangers, left Custer City that evening. Crawford also learned that Grouard had withheld the newspaper correspondents' dispatches and packaged them as mail bound for Red Cloud Agency, all except Davenport's dispatch, which he rather cavalierly handed to Crawford. Davenport had been right to be concerned about a Crook man forthrightly handling a *New York Herald* dispatch.[9]

Both utterly exhausted, Grouard and Crawford overnighted in Custer City on the thirteenth. In Grouard's view, the great race, such as it was, ended there. He later recalled that he wrote a note to General Crook reporting on what he had done and then went to bed for three days: "I could not move around very lively, and it took me that time to recover from my trip." He chortled to his biographer several decades later that the *New York Herald* did not receive Davenport's dispatch until three days afterwards, and by then, details of the Slim Buttes fight were known throughout the land. He likewise presumed that Sheridan had indeed read Crook's reports of the campaign and Slim Buttes fight first, before seeing anything in the press. On that detail, he was right, but his understandings about the newspapers were hazy.[10]

Regardless of the fact that Crook's report had been forwarded from Custer City the night before, Crawford realized that he could still insure that Davenport's stories scooped the other newspapermen's accounts because they had been bundled, so he believed, as mail destined overland for Sidney, by way of Red Cloud Agency. His own horse having died that night, Crawford secured another from a friend, who remarked, "Jack, kill him if you want; but beat them if possible." He departed from Custer City at 9 A.M., 14 September, bound for Red Canyon, Hat Creek, and Fort Laramie. The trail south was familiar to him, for he had traveled it in late June when outbound to Chicago to induce financiers to bring quartz mills to Deadwood. By 3 P.M., he reached the army camp at the mouth of Red Canyon, where Captain William S. Collier, Fourth Infantry, commanded and held him over. Crawford claimed that Collier only wished to protect an exhausted friend. Besides, Collier told Crawford, Grouard "sent me Crook's order to forward the despatches [*sic*], so you might as well give it up. They are twenty-four hours ahead of you."[11]

Crawford spent the night in Collier's infantry camp and resumed the trail the next morning on a poor horse, so he lamented. His travel that day passed the Cheyenne River and Indian Creek stage stations, scenes of so much trouble with Indians and road agents throughout the summer. By 8 P.M., he reached the Sage Creek army camp adjacent to the Hat Creek stage station (the locations were side by side). There, Crawford met with First Lieutenant George M. Taylor, Twenty-third Infantry, commanding the one-company soldier garrison, and again learned that Crook's dispatches had been forwarded as ordered and were far ahead. Crawford also learned that the telegraph line was down somewhere between Hat Creek and Fort Laramie but that a man had been sent to restore the wire. The operator thought the line would be operating by ten o'clock the next morning.[12]

After staying over in Taylor's camp at Sage Creek, Crawford continued his journey to Fort Laramie. Before departing, however, he gave the local operator Grouard's copy of Davenport's dispatch and asked that it be put on the line as soon as it was again serviceable. When passing Government Farm five hours later, and a mere eleven miles north of the fort, he met the man who had been sent to repair the wire and learned that Davenport's dispatch was then being transmitted from Hat Creek ahead of all others. Crawford obtained

The United States Army's camp on Sage Creek southwest of the Black Hills figured prominently in Jack Crawford's Black Hills and Sioux war adventures. He met Cody there in July and in September entrusted the station's telegraph operator with important dispatches. *D. S. Mitchell photograph. Robert Kolbe*

a fresh horse at Government Farm and reached Fort Laramie at seven o'clock that evening, 16 September.[13]

Crawford later wrote General Crook that he had promptly sought out the Fort Laramie telegraph operator and allowed him to interrupt the *Herald* transmission so that Crook's official report could be sent to Omaha. That detail seemed to be an overt placation and nearly irrelevant because Sheridan had arrived at Fort Laramie that same day and was not in Chicago or Omaha. The notion of a "race" between Grouard bearing Crook's report and Crawford carrying *New York Herald* dispatches was instantly unimportant. Sheridan, who had come west to plot the next phase of the Sioux war with Crook

The Government Farm and its immediate environs, eleven miles north of Fort Laramie, served as the locale of a vegetable garden for the fort's garrison and as a way station on the Cheyenne-Black Hills stage and freight road. Crawford exchanged horses there when hurrying messages to the telegraph at Fort Laramie. *D. S. Mitchell photograph. Robert Kolbe*

and others, had received the Slim Buttes report first-hand from Taylor's courier. Even then, Crook was making his own way through the Black Hills to meet Sheridan at Fort Laramie. A scoop was irrelevant in another sense, too. Crawford may well have allowed the Fort Laramie telegraph operator to interrupt the transmission of Davenport's lengthy dispatch, but Sheridan had already had the opportunity to forward a version of Crook's report to department headquarters in Omaha and by that means had scattered news of the Slim Buttes fight to all interested newspapers throughout the land.[14]

Thanks to Captain Jack, however, on Sunday, 17 September, the *New York Herald* did indeed feature Reuben Davenport's long account of the Slim Buttes fight, written on Owl Creek on 10 September, along with his supplemental report written at Crook City on 12 September. They formed the most complete version of the incident of any of the accounts appearing that day. But on the seventeenth also, the *New York Times* featured its own description of the fight, apparently written by its correspondent, Cuthbert Mills. A brief account of the action also appeared that day in San Francisco's *Alta California*, quoting from Crook's official report, evidently courtesy of Sheridan; and Robert Strahorn's version of the engagement appeared in the *Chicago Tribune* that day, as well. Doubtless, there were others. Grouard told Crawford that he had mailed the correspondents' reports from Custer City, but that must not have been so. Still, the *Herald's* account was the most fulsome, and success rested on that fact.[15]

While at Fort Laramie, Crawford penned the three stories that were reprinted in the previous chapter. In a brief "Special to the *Bee*" sent by telegraph on 17 September, he provided Rosewater and his Omaha readers with a clipped account of his adventure-filled ride and the fight at Slim Buttes. When published in the *Bee* on the eighteenth, it served as a sidebar to a longer story of the fight apparently drawn from Davenport's account. Also on the seventeenth, Crawford wrote an illuminating story for the *New York Herald* telling of his long ride to and through the Black Hills to Fort Laramie carrying Davenport's communiqués. Transmitted by telegraph, Crawford's story appeared in the *Herald* on the eighteenth. Of the many versions of the ride that he and others told later, this one is the most complete and accurate, for it was written almost immediately upon completing the exploit. And on 18 September before departing Fort Laramie, Crawford wrote his own careful account of the Slim Buttes fight that adds many important details to our understanding of the engagement. He had been in the thick of the fighting from the start. This story appeared in the *Bee* on 22 September.

Crawford soon realized that there were consequences for having aided Reuben Davenport in securing his *New York Herald* scoop. While he claimed to have made his intention known to Merritt before departing Crook's column on 11 September, Crawford's clarity can be questioned; Merritt surely would not have condoned or permitted putting a newspaperman's interests ahead of the army's. Moreover, Grouard related to his biographer that at Crook City he had told Crawford to remain there and assist Bubb and that Crawford had acknowledged the order. In the hierarchy of Crook's scouts, Grouard was clearly the superior. When Grouard passed Crawford on the trail into Custer City on the thirteenth, he recalled that he questioned Crawford's business, heard only that he was carrying dispatches for the *New York Herald*, and dismissed him as a scout "from the time he quit the command," which the quartermaster interpreted as 15 September.[16] And while Davenport's initial reports of the Slim Buttes engagement appearing in the *Herald* on the seventeenth were forthright and largely praise-filled, his final campaign dispatch, written from Deadwood on 16 September, was not. Instead, it suggested that Crook's march "will hereafter be compared with the retreat of Napoleon from Moscow, and might have been equally disastrous, but for a freak of the fortune which rules the destinies of war, enabling the army to capture a small Sioux village, containing stores of food sufficient to defer the menacing presence of starvation. This action was inglorious."[17] Crook and his officer corps never forgave Davenport for his editorializing on the conduct of the campaign.[18]

For his part, Crawford attempted to redeem himself with General Crook, penning a careful if rationalizing letter from Custer City on 24 September. Jack had returned to the Black Hills and easily located the Big Horn and Yellowstone Expedition then recuperating along French Creek at Custer City. Merritt now commanded since Crook had gone on to Fort Laramie to confer with Sheridan. Crawford wrote Crook that he had just learned that he had been discharged as a scout and felt sure that that action was based upon misunderstandings. Crawford explained that he had received Merritt's permission to carry the *Herald* dispatch, that he believed that Bubb needed no help in Crook City, and that it was he who told the Fort Laramie telegraph operator to break the *Herald* transmission to accommodate Crook's official report. Crook never responded. Crawford's services as a scout with Crook's expedition had indeed come to an end.[19]

The *New York Herald* paid Crawford handsomely for his services, eventually cutting checks for the original $500 that Davenport offered for carrying the dispatches and $222 for expenses.[20] As the *Omaha Daily Bee* noted in their report of the matter, those expenses plus the cost of the reporter in the field "shows what it costs a great

The *New York Herald* presented Captain Jack with this ornate lap desk for delivering newspaper accounts of the Slim Buttes Indian fight. The desk features an inset silver medallion heralding Crawford's services as an army scout in 1876. *Autry National Center, 90.197.2*

and enterprising newspaper to get the news."[21] The *Herald* also later presented Crawford with an ornate lap desk. Its engraved silver medallion noted, "Presented to John W. Crawford for Strength + Courage by N. Y. Herald Co. July 1876."[22]

Despite the consequences, Captain Jack's ride through the Black Hills to Fort Laramie carrying newspaper dispatches reporting the Slim Buttes fight was his crowning accomplishment during the Great Sioux War. Crawford had been in the thick of desperate fighting at Slim Buttes, but so were many others. He ate horse and mule flesh, but again, so did others. He suffered the same long marches, rain, bone-numbing cold, and mud just as every other member of Crook's expedition had. But Crawford's ride was a distinguishing, individual accomplishment that tested his stamina, horsemanship, and perseverance as he rode some 325 miles in six days and, with an added touch of luck, delivered the detailed *New York Herald* stories to the telegraph wire ahead of all others. For that, Captain Jack is deservingly remembered.

9

LOOSE ENDS

Knowledge of Jack Crawford's closing days in the Black Hills is sketchy. His travels were loosely forecast in his letter to the *New York Herald* dated 17 September 1876, where he noted that he was starting for Colonel Wesley Merritt's command the next day with dispatches from General Sheridan, whom he had encountered at Fort Laramie the day before. We know that Crawford conferred with Merritt on the twenty-fourth in the army camp near Custer City where, depending on accounts, his termination as an army scout occurred or was confirmed. He protested this release in a letter that day to General Crook but seems never to have pressed the matter. And his final letter to the *Bee* at the close of this episode as a Black Hills and Sioux war correspondent was written from Red Canyon on 14 October, relating nothing of particular consequence but noting that he was again traveling south toward Cheyenne and Omaha.

At the close of Crawford's participation in the Sioux war, he had one bit of untidy business to wrap up. Three of Crawford's and Davenport's letters in September mentioned that Captain Jack had taken an Indian scalp at Slim Buttes. Crawford's letter to the *Omaha Daily Bee* on the eighteenth noted that he had acquired an Indian's "top-knot," as he called it, and that he had almost lost his own scalp in the encounter. "Tell my friends in Omaha who presented me with a rifle and equipments that I have kept my word," he remarked. In Davenport's letter to the *New York Herald* written on 10 September, the letter

Crawford protested his dismissal as an army scout to Colonel Wesley Merritt, Crook's successor as commander of the Big Horn and Yellowstone Expedition, but to no avail. This photograph shows Merritt's headquarters camp east of Custer City in late-September 1876, about when Crawford visited. *Stanley J. Morrow photograph. National Archives*

Crawford sacrificed his scouting job to carry, he too reported that Crawford had killed and scalped an Indian.[1]

Crawford's patrons in Omaha may indeed have literally challenged him to get a scalp, admonishing or daring him to make good use of the fine equipments they had provided. Just as likely, if such a goading actually occurred, it could have been mere bold or rough talk. That July, Crawford was embarking for Wyoming to scout for the army, joining Buffalo Bill precisely when the big news throughout the country was Cody's having taken an Indian scalp in the Warbonnet Creek skirmish, the loudly proclaimed "first scalp for Custer."[2] Certainly Cody's Nebraska exploit was common chatter as the campaign progressed, particularly when gregarious individuals like Buffalo Bill were called upon to tell of their daring-do around evening campfires. At that time in America, taking scalps and collecting other battlefield trophies, untidy as it seems today, served to authenticate the business of scouting and warfare. Both Indians and whites did so, and one can easily imagine Crawford following suit in an attempt to demonstrate his gratitude for the gifts he had received and to elevate himself to the stature of his prominent patron. But, however motivated, Captain Jack distanced himself from his deed almost immediately.[3]

Edward Rosewater, editor of the *Bee*, noted that Crawford's Indian scalp was received in Omaha on 21 September and was in Rosewater's possession. Crawford apparently mailed it from Fort Laramie during his several-day stay there. Cody had also mailed his Indian scalp from Fort Laramie when passing through on 21 July bound for Crook's camp, and its receipt by a friend in Rochester, New York, was widely reported in the nation's newspapers.[4] Captain Jack returned to Omaha in early November carrying, among other things, a satchel of Indian "plunder," including women's dresses and other mementos that he placed on exhibit at Julius Meyer's Indian Wigwam, a curiosity store in the heart of the city.[5] Among countless items on display and for sale at the Wigwam, Meyer particularly showcased "tomahawks, bows and arrows, pipes, scalps, moccasins, bead work," along with buffalo robes and "all other kinds of Indian dressed furs and skins" collected from the western tribesmen.[6] The extent to which Crawford ultimately sold or gave some or nearly all of his Indian collection to Meyer is unknown, but the *Bee* also noted that he presented a calumet and several Indian curios from the Slim

Julius Meyer's Indian Wigwam was a popular Omaha emporium throughout the 1870s and 1880s and particularly featured Indian arts and curiosities of all sorts. Here Meyer poses with Indian guests in the mid-1870s. *KM3TV/ Bostwick-Frohardt Photograph Collection, permanently housed at the Durham Museum, Omaha, Nebr.*

Buttes village to "Omaha Tribe, No. 2, Improved Order of Red Men," a local fraternal lodge.[7] Thereafter, he seems never to have inquired about his Indian scalp or plunder again.

The *Bee* noted Captain Jack's next adventure on 25 November, informing readers that Buffalo Bill had invited him to join his troupe for the coming theater season. Crawford eagerly accepted the employment but apparently viewed it only as winter work, expressing his intent to lead another party to the Black Hills in the spring. Cody had left Crook's column in mid-August of 1876 to organize another traveling show that featured a stage production drawn from incidents in the Sioux war. The play, *The Red Right Hand; or, Buffalo Bill's First Scalp for Custer*, debuted in December and featured Cody

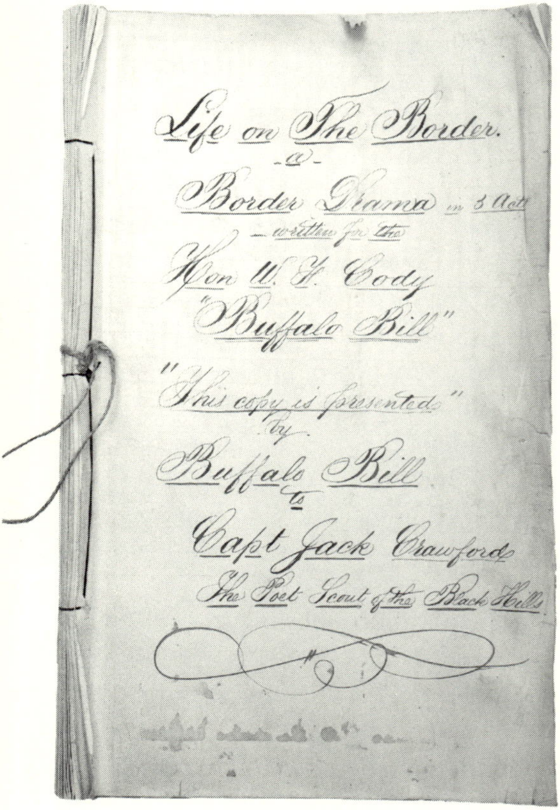

Cody presented Crawford with this handwritten script of the play *Life on the Border* when Crawford joined his acting troupe for the 1876–1877 Combination Show season. Both scouts took leading roles in *Life on the Border* and *The Red Right Hand,* which alternated during the season. *Autry National Center, 90.17.2*

and Crawford as leading characters. Both men also participated in the olio performances presented down front while sets were being shifted. This hodgepodge of dancing, juggling, singing, or lecturing provided Crawford opportunities to read his own poetry and give recitations. The play itself was grounded in the context of troubles between Black Hills miners and Indians.[8] Cody described the new production in his autobiography as a "five-act play, without head or tail," which afforded his troupe "ample opportunity to give a noisy, rattling, gunpowder entertainment, and to present a succession of scenes in the late Indian war, all of which seemed to give general satisfaction."[9]

When Cody's company played two consecutive nights in the same city, they alternated *The Red Right Hand* with another play, *Life on the Border,* to entice repeat patronage. Regarded as one of Buffalo Bill's better melodramas, *Life on the Border* followed the story of counterfeiters, a missing scout, and Indian trouble, featuring Cody and Crawford as themselves. But the lead production for the season was always *The Red Right Hand*, and however staged from performance to performance, the play's concluding act invariably featured a reenactment of Cody's supposed face-to-face encounter with Yellow Hair (or Yellow Hand, a mistranslation), the young Northern Cheyenne warrior killed at Warbonnet Creek. Usually Captain Jack portrayed the Indian, he and Cody wrestling hand-to-hand before shots rang out and Crawford, falling dead, was scalped. The actual episode, which took place on 17 July 1876, involved only long-range shooting before Yellow Hair's scalp was taken, but such unadulterated truth lacked the drama of a manly duel staged nightly. Each night as well, somewhere at the side of the stage or in a theater window, Cody displayed the actual trophies he had collected at Warbonnet Creek, including Yellow Hair's scalp. That scalp had become a trademark that Cody used to authenticate himself as a legitimate scout and plainsman.[10]

For Crawford, Buffalo Bill's invitation to join his so-called combination show provided more than a simple chance to consort again with a highly admired friend. It also offered the unique opportunity to learn the arts of performance and stagecraft. Until now, Captain Jack had been the living embodiment of a plainsman, both in the gulches of the Black Hills and on the Sioux war trail, where he had affirmed his ability to entertain, informally anyway, whether with Banjo Dick Brown in the saloons of Custer City and Deadwood or around an evening campfire in the midst of Crook's army. With Cody, Crawford was learning the power of stagecraft and that audiences would pay to see the talent he possessed. While Crawford could hardly know it then, he was embarking on a career that would consume him for the rest of his life.

The *Omaha Daily Bee* kept readers apprised of Crawford's travels with the show during the winter of 1876–1877. In January, the newspaper featured a review of the *Red Right Hand* production lifted straight from the *Boston Herald*. The Boston newspaper found "grand charm" in the unconventional bearing of real heroes like Cody and Crawford and saw in them "all that was bold, heroic, and noble." And the *Herald's* reviewer was amazed by "the clever manner in which Buffalo Bill and Captain Jack handled their beautiful repeating rifles, from which, at times, a continuous stream of fire seemed to pour, much to the detriment of a considerable band of red-skinned warriors, who seemed to be killed off rather faster than they could run back of the scene and come on again for fresh killing." But the illusion was sustained and the show labeled the "best of its kind."[11]

Crawford himself still wrote to the *Bee* occasionally, as well. From the show's stop in Sharon, Pennsylvania, on 23 February, he reported his elation in traveling with Cody and how he was accosted at every stop by "reporters, intended Black Hillers, and chronic inquisitors" wanting news from the gold fields. Of course, Crawford obliged them by telling "straight and truthful stories," he reported.[12] But some of this inquiry was self-instigated, as the *Bee* revealed when it reprinted Crawford's letter to the *Parker City Daily*, in which the performer announced his pending arrival in that fair Pennsylvania city in early March. "Should any of the boys propose going to the Hills, I can give them more information regarding that country than any other man in the State," Crawford bragged. He also announced that Cody's troupe would end its show season in Omaha in late April and that he and Bill then intended to lead a large party into the Hills. The notion of returning to the Black Hills held powerful sway with Captain Jack, although it never happened as he imagined it.[13]

In due course, the Buffalo Bill Combination played in Omaha on 20 and 21 April, staging three performances at the Academy of Music on Douglas Street. The *Bee's* review on the twenty-first revealed the nature of such melodramatic productions: "Every person in the play is a walking arsenal—armed to the teeth with repeating rifles, revolvers, and knives; the frequent discharge of fire-arms led us at one time to fear that the ammunition would run short." Captain Jack received specific notice. The former correspondent "appeared to advantage last night, and gave evidence of being a good actor," the reporter commented. "The camping scene was very good, and his original song 'Marching on the Rosebud,' was well received. His 'shooting the hat business' created considerable amusement." As always, the fifth and concluding act of the play was the dramatic duel between Cody and Yellow Hair, capped by the scalping episode, after which an allegorical tableau in the background showed the face of Custer. "There is considerable humor in the drama, and upon the whole it was a much better entertainment than we had expected to see," concluded the *Bee* reviewer. The show's unique static accompa-

The Caldwell Block on the south side of Omaha's Douglas Street included the Academy of Music (beneath the arch) among its array of businesses. The Academy was Omaha's sole venue for stage productions in the 1860s and 1870s, and the Buffalo Bill Combination concluded its season there in April 1877. *Nebraska State Historical Society, RG054-PH-0-15*

niment, Yellow Hair's gun, shield, pistol, quirt, and scalp, was exhibited in Omaha, too, in the front window of the Martin and Kennard drugstore across the street from the theater.[14]

The Omaha performances were to have been the last for the 1876–1877 season, and as soon as the curtain dropped for the final time, Cody departed for North Platte to investigate the prospect of acquiring ranch properties there. He had enjoyed a long association with that town and nearby Fort McPherson, where many scouting and hunting adventures had originated.[15] Crawford, meanwhile, prepared to visit Chicago to "get up an excursion party for the Black Hills." But before Crawford departed, he received a telegram from Cody inviting him to rejoin the show and travel to San Francisco. *The Red Right Hand* was being resurrected for a four-week "star engagement," and Cody wanted Crawford along.[16]

Although Cody's Combination played five weeks rather than four in California and Nevada, and almost always to packed houses, matters of Crawford's compensation and a shooting incident in Virginia City, Nevada, strained and then shattered this unique relationship. As an inducement to rejoin the show, Cody offered to make Crawford's salary "all right" in light of Crawford's expressed disappointment with the twenty-dollar weekly salary he had received on the eastern tour. It was the same amount, Crawford carped, that the show's property manager earned. The California tour opened to good receipts and glowing reviews, and Crawford asked Cody for a salary of one hundred dollars per week. Cody offered forty dollars but settled on fifty when Captain Jack threatened to walk out. Crawford fumed over this perceived slight throughout the tour and allowed it to fester for the rest of his life.[17]

The final straw in the mounting Crawford-Cody schism came in Virginia City, Nevada, in the second-to-last performance of the tour. There, during the reenactment of the Yellow Hair fight, with both Cody and Crawford mounted on horses, Crawford shot himself in the groin with a blank round while attempting to draw his pistol. He finished the performance, but when the curtain fell, friends rushed to the stage. Blood soaked his trousers, and a doctor was summoned to examine a four-inch-long ragged wound below his left groin. While painful, the wound was not life-threatening. Crawford blamed the incident on Cody for insisting on using horses that evening, which otherwise rarely or never occurred. After a matinee performance the next day with a stand-in for Crawford, Cody settled accounts, disbanded the company, and departed for North Platte. Crawford was hospitalized in Virginia City for two weeks. Cody did not pay Crawford's hospital charges, and after settling the account himself, Crawford netted a mere fifty-eight dollars from the western tour.[18]

Aware of Crawford's precarious financial situation, leading citizens in Virginia City invited him to stage a benefit on 6 September, and Captain Jack set about assembling a combination show featuring his own play, *Fonda; or, The Trapper's Daughter*, written while he was bedridden, along with customary olio acts. Crawford's hurriedly organized production featured his friend, Gertie Granville, a twenty-six-year-old curly-haired soubrette who had traveled with Cody and Crawford throughout the 1876–1877 season. She later married Tony Hart of the renowned Harrigan and Hart song-and-dance team of New York City. Crawford's production played to a packed house in Virginia City and drew receipts of eight hundred

Jack Crawford and actress Gertie Granville traveled with the Buffalo Bill Combination in 1876–1877 and then partnered in Jack's own combination in 1877–1878. Crawford's show traveled California but ultimately disbanded in financial ruin. *Houseworth & Co. Photographers. Bancroft Library, University of California, Berkeley*

dollars. He repeated this success at another benefit in San Francisco. He then retained his company and toured California throughout the fall and into January 1878. Although reviews of his show were occasionally laudatory, revenues were small, and the Captain Jack Combination proved a financial failure. Crawford disbanded his makeshift company in January and never again organized a similar show. But he also never strayed far from the stage.[19]

When Crawford disbanded his show in San Francisco in early 1878, he closed several significant chapters in his life. Buffalo Bill Cody had showered opportunity and visibility on Crawford in the late-1870s—wondering publicly whether Jack had heard the news of Custer, inviting him to join Crook "at the front," quietly tutoring him on the Sioux war trail, welcoming him to his combination show, and continually mentoring the eager but novice actor. But their relationship had soured, especially as Crawford came to resent Cody's unwavering popularity and the financial disparities existing between the two men. Increasingly believing that he had been financially slighted during their time together, and then abandoned outright in Virginia City, Crawford lashed out publicly at Cody in the summer of 1877 and drew a sharp rebuke. "People have flattered you until you think . . . that you are a great man," wrote Cody. "Jack, go ahead. You will find out that all that glitters is not gold. I wish you success and will never do a thing to hurt you. I am very sorry the accident occurred, but I think you had made up your mind to start out for your self. So good luck."[20] Such exchanges occurred repeatedly in the coming years, Crawford ever resentful of Cody's unflagging draw and Cody defensive but invariably magnanimous. Crawford owed more to Cody than he could ever admit, beginning in 1873 when he attended one of Buffalo Bill's combinations in Pennsylvania. But Captain Jack never rose to Cody's stature, or even got close.[21]

Crawford did return to the Black Hills briefly in early 1878, alone, and not at the head of an organized party. He was noted as a hunter providing meat for a local market and for his prospecting. Some historians credited Crawford with discovering gold in Rockerville Gulch southwest of Rapid City, where the local mining camp was first known as "Captain Jack's Dry Diggings." The discovery gulch immediately south bore the name "Captain Jack's Gulch." The town itself quickly became Rockerville, but the discovery gulch still bears Crawford's name, at least on some maps. These were dry diggings, and a flume and ditch were necessary for successful gold recovery, but that was business for others. Crawford did not linger in the Hills and, later that spring, bounded off for the gold fields of the Cariboo Region of British Columbia. He had come to relish the vibrancy of new gold camps and would repeat that thrill and adventure once more when gold was discovered in the Klondike in 1897.[22]

Although Crawford initially relished the self-proclaimed moniker "Poet Scout of the Black Hills," and many of his poems were grounded there, he soon dropped the Black Hills from his title. It had been a marketable association early in his stage career, but he outgrew it and soon became simply "Captain Jack Crawford, the Poet Scout." Crawford never again resided in the Black Hills, but he did return from time to time. In early 1893, for instance, his one-man lyceum played, as one Black Hills newspaper put it, "all the principal towns of the Hills and . . . met with a rousing reception and crowds at each place," including Hot Springs and Deadwood.[23] In Deadwood, he made two presentations to raise monies to protect Wild Bill Hickok's grave in Mount Moriah Cemetery.[24] Likely he had not seen that particular gravesite before, but he recalled passing Hickok's first grave in Deadwood's Ingleside Cemetery up Whitewood Creek in 1876. Soon thereafter he had written two short poems of remembrance, "Wild Bill's Grave" and "An Epitaph on Wild Bill." In the headnote to the latter, he said that he had penned the little ditty "while sitting on his grave, near Deadwood, on the 10th of September, 1876." While Crawford muddled the date slightly (it was actually 13 September), he did not forget his Black Hills "pard."[25]

In 1895, Crawford chanced onto William Gay in Helena, Montana. A pioneer Black Hiller, founder of Gayville in Deadwood Gulch, and a personality regularly encountered on the pages of the *Omaha Daily Bee* during the gold-rush years, Gay was then in the Helena jail under sentence of death for the murder of a deputy sheriff. Gay, who sought a new trial, appealed to Captain Jack for money to pay lawyers; whether he provided any money is unknown. Gay wrote Crawford in April 1896, again asking for money to mount a campaign to convince the governor to commute his sentence, but two months later, he was executed. Crawford always spoke kindly of Gay and in 1876 had counted him as a friend and mining counselor. But Gay was not recalled so favorably in Deadwood Gulch, where the odor of a hard life and the conviction for a murder in Gayville in 1878 cloud his story.[26]

Several of Crawford's other close Black Hills friends and acquaintances fared considerably better than poor Gay. Charley Whitehead, the *Kansas City Times* correspondent who had shared a number of interesting adventures with Captain Jack in early 1876, including riding alongside him in the Black Hills Rangers, reported from the Black Hills gold fields for nearly a year before returning to Kansas City. He gave Crawford a glowing review as an actor when Cody's combination show played there in April 1877. In 1878 and 1879, Whitehead evidently reported for or edited newspapers in Leadville, Colorado, and Cheyenne, Wyoming, but he had returned again to the *Kansas City Times* by late 1879. The 1880 federal census noted a Charles Whitehead residing in Kansas City, occupation "editor," but his trail drops from the scene thereafter.[27]

Another of Crawford's close Black Hills pals was Richard "Banjo Dick" Brown, a musician who roved the West and was heralded the "Champion Banjo Player of the world" when he first played in Cheyenne in November 1874.[28] Remembered as a "proficient banjo performer, an excellent baritone singer, and a versatile actor,"[29] Brown served-up an enthusiastic entertainment of string music, original ballads, and old standards, especially the always-popular gold rush ditty "Days of Forty-nine." Brown played Cheyenne again late in 1875 before making his way to Custer City in February 1876, arriving soon after Jack Crawford. The two men traveled to Deadwood together in May, Crawford exploring the northern gulches for the first time and Brown apparently relocating there from Custer City. Brown became a fixture in Deadwood's saloons and theaters and, in December, joined Billy Nuttall to operate the Temple of Music. His lasting Black Hills epitaph might well have been his writing and singing of the somber ballad "The Black Hills" ("The Dreary Black Hills" today) had he not killed Edward Shaughnessy one night in November 1876 in an act of apparent self-defense.[30]

The Shaughnessy killing at the Bella Union caused a momentary stir in the Black Hills. Crazed, Shaughnessy had trailed his former mistress, the show-girl Fanny Garrettson, from Laramie City to Deadwood. While the two were never married, they reportedly had lived together for three years until she abandoned him and took

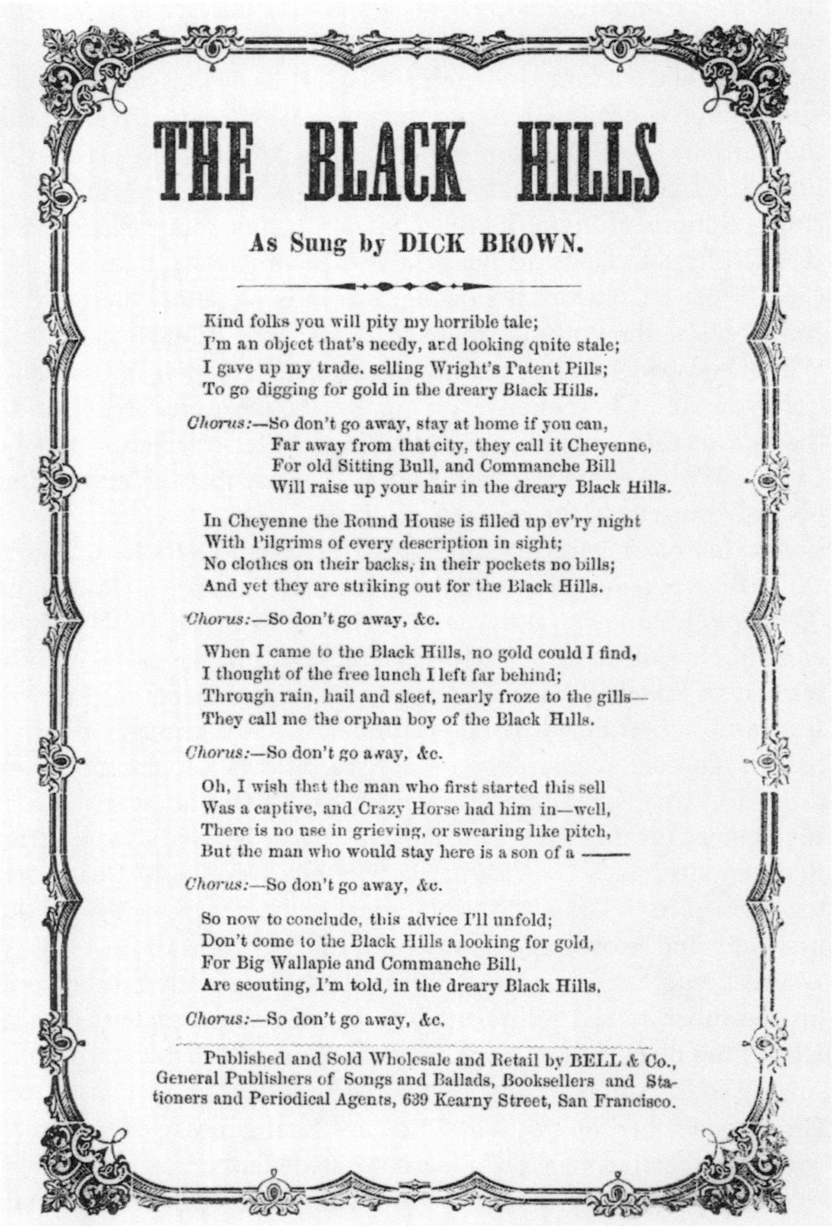

THE BLACK HILLS

As Sung by DICK BROWN.

Kind folks you will pity my horrible tale;
I'm an object that's needy, and looking quite stale;
I gave up my trade, selling Wright's Patent Pills;
To go digging for gold in the dreary Black Hills.

Chorus:—So don't go away, stay at home if you can,
Far away from that city, they call it Cheyenne,
For old Sitting Bull, and Commanche Bill
Will raise up your hair in the dreary Black Hills.

In Cheyenne the Round House is filled up ev'ry night
With Pilgrims of every description in sight;
No clothes on their backs, in their pockets no bills;
And yet they are striking out for the Black Hills.

Chorus:—So don't go away, &c.

When I came to the Black Hills, no gold could I find,
I thought of the free lunch I left far behind;
Through rain, hail and sleet, nearly froze to the gills—
They call me the orphan boy of the Black Hills.

Chorus:—So don't go away, &c.

Oh, I wish that the man who first started this sell
Was a captive, and Crazy Horse had him in—well,
There is no use in grieving, or swearing like pitch,
But the man who would stay here is a son of a ——

Chorus:—So don't go away, &c.

So now to conclude, this advice I'll unfold;
Don't come to the Black Hills a looking for gold,
For Big Wallapie and Commanche Bill,
Are scouting, I'm told, in the dreary Black Hills,

Chorus:—So don't go away, &c,

Published and Sold Wholesale and Retail by BELL & Co., General Publishers of Songs and Ballads, Booksellers and Stationers and Periodical Agents, 639 Kearny Street, San Francisco.

"The Black Hills" was a ballad written and performed by "Banjo Dick" Brown, one of Jack Crawford's closest companions during his Black Hills adventure. Brown was a long-time gold-camp entertainer in California, Colorado, and Dakota Territory before embarking for Australia in 1879. *Paul L. Hedren* up with and then married Brown. On 16 November, Shaughnessy threatened Brown with an axe, and the banjo player drew his revolver and shot him five or six times; he died later that evening. The killing was investigated and ruled an act of self-defense. The Brown-Garrettson marriage survived the event, but in due course the pair drifted on. The *Ford County Globe* of Dodge City, Kansas, noted them playing the theaters of that city in July 1878, with a troupe that included Fannie Keenan, a Saint Louis actress also known as Dora Hand.[31] Several months later, the *Laramie Daily Sentinel* reported that Fanny Brown, formerly Fanny Garrettson, was shot and killed in Dodge City "by one of her numerous husbands," but the Wyoming paper had it wrong.[32] In October, Garrettson and Keenan were rooming together when an unnamed assailant fired into their shanty, narrowly missing Garrettson but killing Keenan. Dick Brown is not mentioned in the story, nor is Garrettson again, but Cheyenne and San Francisco newspapers noted Brown sailing for Australia in 1879, apparently alone. Gold rush towns were booming in Australia, too.[33]

Edward Rosewater, owner and editor of the *Omaha Daily Bee* and Captain Jack's faithful patron during the nascent days of the Black Hills gold rush, ran a thriving newspaper until his own death in 1906. While Crawford's departure from the Black Hills closed out the poet scout's service to the *Bee*, Rosewater had not yet lost his ardor for reporting the gold rush, which engendered an enduring fascination regionally and nationally that had not yet peaked. Even as Crawford moved to join Crook's campaign, Rosewater dispatched his other gold-rush correspondent, John Harwood Pierce, known as "Ranger" to *Bee* readers, to Custer City to ensure the flow of news. Ranger, in turn, was succeeded by another correspondent known today only as "Winchester," whose stream of letters to the *Bee* beginning in early November 1876 had the same quirky charm as Crawford's, including the use of occasional lines of verse. Winchester's coverage of the gold rush began just as Crawford's had, with letters recounting travel from Sidney north to Red Cloud Agency and on to Custer City. He visited and reported on the Black Hills gold towns during wintertime and filled his letters with spirited chatter from the diggings, which proved considerably more robust. Much work was now occurring underground, and quartz mills abounded and were raising their own unique cacophony throughout the gulches. And as in Crawford's time, Rosewater also published an array of Black Hills gold-rush correspondence from returning Omahans, resident Hillers with local connections, and stories drawn from other newspapers.[34]

Rosewater seemed to delight in providing news about gold. Even as Crawford's stories about his Sioux war exploits were appearing in the *Bee*, the paper carried articles about the four-member Wheeler party, owners of the renowned Claim No. 2 below Discovery on Deadwood Creek, near Gayville. The party was then transporting over a quarter million dollars in placer gold dust (1,040 pounds troy), sacked in buckskin bags, through Fort Laramie, Cheyenne, and Omaha, bound for Philadelphia. On their journey from Deadwood to Cheyenne, they employed an escort of twenty armed men. As the Wheeler party trained from Cheyenne to Omaha, they inquired about the express charges for transporting their gold from Omaha to Philadelphia. When they learned that it would cost about one thousand dollars, they chose to carry the gold through themselves. Before departing the Black Hills, the partnership sold its claim on Deadwood Creek for the reported sum of three thousand dollars, thinking that it was played out, but the new owners worked bedrock again and quickly recovered their purchase price and then some.[35]

The Wheeler party's take came from seven months of work, and the *Bee* noted that other prospects in the Black Hills were paying equally well. John B. Pearson and J. A. Pierce, both noted among the earliest prospectors working in Deadwood Gulch and the owners of Claim No. 3 below Discovery on Deadwood Creek, were recovering five hundred dollars to six hundred dollars per day by means of drifting—the always dangerous work of pulling bedrock gravels to the surface through small vertical shafts. William Gay, so often mentioned in Crawford's letters and part owner of Claim No. 9 above Discovery, told Rosewater of an eleven-thousand-dollar take in four days. Large nuggets caught Rosewater's fancy, too, including one valued at $72.47 taken from Potato Creek and another valued at $38.40 from Whitewood Creek.[36] Even though Rosewater endeavored to keep his newspaper in the forefront of Black Hills gold-rush coverage, he also offered an occasional tempering tone. One of his roving correspondents, J. C. Wilcox, reminded readers that while the report of $264,000 taken from one claim on Deadwood was true, "there are many claims which do not pay so well, and many men who have worked hard and made nothing."[37]

As news of Black Hills riches captured imaginations far and wide, the Grant administration finally achieved the opening of the Dakota gold fields. In September 1877, the so-called Manypenny Commission headed by George W. Manypenny, long-time Indian rights activist and commissioner of Indian affairs, concluded an agreement with the Lakotas that relinquished reservation lands west of the 103rd meridian and inside of the forks of the Cheyenne and Belle Fourche rivers west to that line. The issue turned on the promises of continued government support at a time when the Great Sioux War was turning decidedly against the tribesmen and access to the buffalo hunting grounds was diminishing altogether. The Black Hills were opened and riches poured forth freely. Meaningful gold production estimates from the early years are difficult to derive, but the South Dakota School of Mines offered the following recovery figures: 1876, $1.2 million; 1877, $2 million; 1878, $2.25 million; 1879, $2.5 million; and 1880, $3.3 million. The Homestake Mine at Lead itself produced nearly 1.5 million ounces of gold in the nineteenth century valued at contemporary prices in excess of $31 million.[38]

After their collegial adventure on Crook's campaign in 1876, Crawford and Reuben Briggs Davenport of the *New York Herald* maintained an occasional correspondence for some years. Recovering from acute diarrhea contracted during the closing days of what became known as the Starvation March, where Crook's men subsisted on small amounts of unseasoned and sometimes barely cooked horse and mule flesh, Davenport left the expedition. He moved about frequently, sometimes working for the *New York Herald* or as an Associated Press reporter, for whom he covered the Spanish-American War. Davenport spent the last twelve years of his life as chief editorial writer for the Paris edition of the *New York Herald-Tribune* and died in Montpellier, France, in 1932. He last surfaced in a Great Sioux War context in 1890 at the center of a dispute between himself and Captain Charles King, who had scorned him in his book *Campaigning with Crook*, King's best-selling narrative chronicling the Fifth Cavalry's participation in the war. Crawford sided with Davenport and sparred with King, too, as did other participants. King obligingly rewrote several pages in his book.[39]

From time to time, Jack Crawford again worked with large the-

Captain Jack Crawford enjoyed a long career as a playwright, performer, poet, and yarn spinner, entertaining lyceum audiences throughout America until the time of his death in 1917. *Robinson and Roe photograph. Paul L. Hedren*

ater production companies, usually staging his own plays, and for the rest of his life enjoyed reasonable but not overwhelming acclaim as a performer, poet, playwright, and popular hero. He especially enjoyed appearing before such veterans groups as the venerable Grand Army of the Republic, comprised of Union Civil War veterans. He authored six books of poetry, beginning with *The Poet Scout: Being a Selection of Incidental and Illustrative Verses and Song*, published in San Francisco in 1879. It showcased over seventy poems, many set in the Black Hills and many more that recalled friends or events from Crook's campaign in 1876. Several of Crawford's books were reprinted, and many are found today both signed and with a freehand verse added. Selling books at his performances was a quiet but lucrative dimension of his livelihood. Crawford also wrote a handful of plays, all of which were performed during his lifetime but none more spectacularly than when John B. "Texas Jack" Omohundro staged and starred in *Fonda* in Denver in 1880. Crawford had written the play in 1877 while bedridden in Virginia City after the shooting incident with Cody.[40]

A reporter for the *Spokane Spokesman-Review* captured the essence of Crawford's popularity as a stage performer: "Laughter, tears and applause demonstrated the pleasure of an audience of 400 last night at the First Methodist church, while John W. Crawford, better known as Captain Jack, the Poet Scout, spun yarns, recited poetry and depicted the evils resulting from the use of strong drink and the circulation of pernicious literature." Crawford was "one of the best single handed entertainers now before the public," the reviewer concluded.[41] In his lyceum performances, Crawford played to themes, conjuring visions of the authentic West he had experienced personally, and he lectured in support of veterans and railed against drink and dime novels. The latter only led boys, he opined, to tragedies of the sort he himself had witnessed in the Black Hills.[42]

Jack Crawford's life ended in Woodhaven, Queens, New York, on 28 February 1917 at the age of sixty-nine. As he lay on his deathbed suffering from pneumonia, he learned of the death of his old rival, Buffalo Bill Cody. Age and his own infirmities had mellowed him. "So Bill Cody is gone?" he supposedly remarked. "I guess they will be sounding taps over me pretty soon. Well, when we meet Tall Bull and that tough old codger Sitting Bull on the other side and stick up our hands palm forward and say, 'How Kola!' there will be a lot to

John W. Crawford, "Captain Jack, the Poet-Scout," was buried in Cypress Hills National Cemetery, Brooklyn, New York, on 3 March 1917. *Mark Abrams*

talk about." Crawford was buried on 3 March in the Cypress Hills National Cemetery in Brooklyn.[43]

Captain Jack was an unpretentious, openhearted spirit, who once said of himself, "I am simply Jack Crawford, boy soldier, rustic poet, scout, bad actor."[44] Of all his great adventures, one wonders which of them he would have regarded as his most thrilling and important? We can imagine Jack reflecting first and perhaps foremost on his time in the Black Hills in 1875 and 1876, reporting the gold rush, climbing Harney Peak, riding with the Black Hills Rangers, prospecting and panning, and consorting with characters like Judge Kuykendall, Major Wynkoop, William Gay, Charley Whitehead, and Banjo Dick Brown, in what he always called the "real West." Crawford, indeed, had experienced the real West and a time like no other. He knew it, and so do we.

NOTES

Introduction

1. Watson Parker, *Gold in the Black Hills* (1966; reprint ed., Pierre: South Dakota State Historical Society Press, 2003), pp. 8–14; Annie Heloise Abel, ed., *Tabeau's Narrative of Loisel's Expedition to the Upper Missouri* (Norman: University of Oklahoma Press, 1939), pp. 237–38; Harold E. Briggs, "The Black Hills Gold Rush," *North Dakota Historical Quarterly* 5 (Jan. 1931): 72–73; Jeffrey Ostler, *The Lakotas and the Black Hills: The Struggle for Sacred Ground* (New York: Viking Penguin, 2010), pp. 47–50.

2. J. H. Triggs, *History of Cheyenne and Northern Wyoming, Embracing the Gold Fields of the Black Hills, Powder River and Big Horn Countries* (Omaha, Neb.: Herald Steam Book & Job Printing House, 1876), pp. 60–61.

3. Wilcox, "For the Black Hills," *Omaha Daily Bee*, 19 Feb. 1876.

4. Triggs, *History of Cheyenne and Northern Wyoming*, pp. 61–63; Briggs, "Black Hills Gold Rush," p. 73; Parker, *Gold in the Black Hills*, pp. 13–17.

5. Parker, *Gold in the Black Hills*, pp. 19–23; Jane Conard, "Charles Collins: The Sioux City Promotion of the Black Hills," *South Dakota History* 2 (Spring 1972): 131–71; Ostler, *Lakotas and the Black Hills*, pp. 69–70. The reservation was defined in Article Two of the Fort Laramie Treaty of 1868. *See* Charles J. Kappler, comp. and ed., *Indian Affairs: Laws and Treaties*. Vol. II: *Treaties* (Washington: Government Printing Office, 1904), pp. 998–99.

6. Donald Jackson, *Custer's Gold: The United States Cavalry Expedition of 1874* (New Haven: Yale University Press, 1966), pp. 3, 14. Article Eleven of the treaty contained the stipulation that the Indians "will not in future object to the construction of railroads, wagon-roads, mail-stations, or other works of utility or necessity, which may be ordered or permitted by the laws of the United States" (Kappler, *Indian Affairs*, p. 1002).

7. Jackson, *Custer's Gold*, pp. 81–85; Ernest Grafe and Paul Horsted, *Exploring with Custer: The 1874 Black Hills Expedition* (Custer, S.Dak.: Golden Valley Press, 2002), pp. 78–79, 87; Parker, *Gold in the Black Hills*, p. 25; William Ludlow, *Report of a Reconnaissance of the Black Hills of Dakota, Made in the Summer of 1874* (Washington: Government Printing Office, 1875), p. 14.

8. The memorable aphorism of gold "from the grass roots down" appeared first in the *Chicago Inter-Ocean*, 27 Aug. 1874, and Custer reported something similar in his official report of the expedition. *See* Herbert Krause and Gary D. Olson, *Prelude to Glory: A Newspaper Accounting of Custer's 1874 Expedition to*

the Black Hills (Sioux Falls, S.Dak.: Brevet Press, 1974), p. 126, and Ostler, *Lakotas and the Black Hills*, pp. 84–85, 208.

9. John S. Gray, "News from Paradise: Charley Reynolds Rides from the Black Hills to Fort Laramie," *By Valor & Arms: The Journal of American Military History* 3, no. 3 (1978): 37–45; Jackson, *Custer's Gold*, pp. 85–88.

10. Krause and Olson, *Prelude to Glory*, p. 128, reprinting the *Chicago Inter-Ocean*, 27 Aug. 1874. *See also* C. C. O'Harra, "The Earliest Mining Laws and Mining Organizations in the Black Hills," *Black Hills Engineer* 12 (Nov. 1924): 239–40.

11. Grant K. Anderson, "Samuel D. Hinman and the Opening of the Black Hills," *Nebraska History* 60 (Winter 1979): 524–27; Parker, *Gold in the Black Hills*, pp. 26–28.

12. Parker, *Gold in the Black Hills*, pp. 30–33; "Black Hills: Gordon's Statement," *Omaha Daily Bee*, 3 Mar. 1875.

13. Parker, *Gold in the Black Hills*, pp. 33–36, 54; Watson Parker, ed., "The Report of Captain John Mix of a Scout to the Black Hills, March–April 1875," *South Dakota History* 7 (Fall 1977): 385–401; Erik M. Eriksson, "Sioux City and the Black Hills Gold Rush, 1874–1877," *Iowa Journal of History and Politics* 20 (July 1922): 334; Jeffrey L. Patrick, ed., "To the Black Hills Gold Fields: The Letters of Samuel M. Zent, Hoosier Prospector, 1875–1876," *Indiana Magazine of History* 91 (Sept. 1995): 275–76; "Black Hills," *Omaha Daily Bee*, 15 Jan., 22, 24 Apr. 1875; John D. McDermott, ed., *Gold Rush: The Black Hills Story* (Pierre: South Dakota State Historical Society Press, 2001), pp. 12–14.

14. Parker, *Gold in the Black Hills*, p. 63; Lesta V. Turchen and James D. McLaird, *The Black Hills Expedition of 1875* (Mitchell, S.Dak.: Dakota Wesleyan University Press, 1975), p. 1.

15. Parker, *Gold in the Black Hills*, pp. 63–65; Turchen and McLaird, *Black Hills Expedition*, pp. 9–26.

16. Richard I. Dodge, *The Black Hills: A Minute Description of the Routes, Scenery, Soil, Climate, Timber, Gold, Geology, Zoology, etc.* (New York: James Miller, 1876) pp. 104–9.

17. Quoted in Parker, *Gold in the Black Hills*, p. 65.

18. Walter P. Jenney, *The Mineral Wealth, Climate and Rain-Fall, and Mineral Resources of the Black Hills of Dakota* (Washington: Government Printing Office, 1876), p. 56.

19. Jenney, *Mineral Wealth*, p. 14.

20. "Black Hills," *Omaha Daily Bee*, 19 July 1875. *See also* "Gold in the Black Hills," ibid., 26 July 1875.

21. For examples of such letters, *see Cheyenne Daily Leader*, 15 Mar. 1875, and *Omaha Daily Bee*, 26 July 1875.

22. “News from the Black Hills,” *Omaha Daily Bee*, 28 June 1875.

23. “The Black Hills,” ibid., 4 Aug. 1875.

24. Watson Parker, “The Majors and the Miners: The Role of the U. S. Army in the Black Hills Gold Rush,” *Journal of the West* 11 (Jan. 1972): 104–7; M. R. Cordero, “A High Handed Outrage,” *Omaha Daily Bee*, 2 Aug. 1875; Douglas C. McChristian, *Fort Laramie: Military Bastion of the High Plains* (Norman: Arthur H. Clark Co., 2008), p. 358; Wayne R. Kime, ed., *The Black Hills Journals of Colonel Richard Irving Dodge* (Norman: University of Oklahoma Press, 1996), p. 165; Martin F. Schmitt, ed., *General George Crook: His Autobiography* (Norman: University of Oklahoma Press, 1946), p. 188.

25. Schmitt, *General George Crook*, p. 189; Kime, *Black Hills Journals of Colonel Richard Irving Dodge*, p. 167; Parker, *Gold in the Black Hills*, pp. 67, 70. Kime reports that Crook permitted six men to remain behind; Parker names seven men as given in the Claim Recorder’s Book of the Cheyenne Mining District, which is preserved in the archival collections of the South Dakota State Historical Society, Pierre. Doubtless, Camp G. H. Collins was named for Gilbert H. Collins, a trader at Fort Laramie.

26. Fort Laramie Post Returns, Aug.–Nov. 1876, Returns from United States Military Posts, 1800–1916, Records of the Adjutant General’s Office Record Group 94, National Archives Microfilm Publication M617, roll 596; Paul L. Hedren, *Fort Laramie in 1876: Chronicle of a Frontier Post at War* (Lincoln: University of Nebraska Press, 1988), pp. 14–15.

27. Hedren, *Fort Laramie in 1876*, pp. 15–18; Thomas R. Buecker, *Fort Robinson and the American West, 1874–1899* (Lincoln: Nebraska State Historical Society, 1999), pp. 77–78; Eriksson, “Sioux City and the Black Hills Gold Rush,” p. 338; Schmitt, *General George Crook*, p. 189.

28. Betti VanEpps-Taylor, *Forgotten Lives: African Americans in South Dakota* (Pierre: South Dakota State Historical Society Press, 2008), pp. 129–32; Krause and Olson, *Prelude to Glory*, p. 128; “Buckskin Jack,” *Omaha Daily Bee*, 1 June 1875; and James D. McLaird, *Wild Bill Hickok & Calamity Jane: Deadwood Legends*, South Dakota Biography Series, no. 2 (Pierre: South Dakota State Historical Society Press, 2008).

29. Darlis A. Miller, *Captain Jack Crawford: Buckskin Poet, Scout, and Showman* (Albuquerque: University of New Mexico Press, 1993), pp. 1–4.

30. Ibid., pp. 4–5.

31. Ibid., pp. 6–9; Paul T. Nolan, *John Wallace Crawford* (Boston: Twayne Publishers, 1981), p. 28.

32. Nolan, *John Wallace Crawford*, p. 28.

33. Miller, *Captain Jack Crawford*, pp. 9–16; Nolan, *John Wallace Crawford*, p. 28.

34. Miller, *Captain Jack Crawford*, pp. 17–19.

35. Ibid., pp. 20–21; Nolan, *John Wallace Crawford*, pp. 29–30.

36. Jack Crawford, *The Poet Scout: Being a Selection of Incidental and Illustrative Verses and Songs* (San Francisco: H. Keller & Co., 1879), p. xiv.

37. Nolan, *John Wallace Crawford*, pp. 29–30; Paul T. Nolan, "When the Curtains Rise, Scouts Fall Out," *Southern Speech Journal* 29 (Spring 1964): 175; Miller, *Captain Jack Crawford*, pp. 22–27; Sandra K. Sagala, *Buffalo Bill on Stage* (Albuquerque: University of New Mexico Press, 2008), pp. 205, 208, 227–28.

38. Pierce, "The Poet Scout of the West," *Omaha Daily Bee*, 5 Jan. 1896. For Crawford's tour, *see* Miller, *Captain Jack Crawford*, pp. 192–95. A copy of the Hartranft letter can be found in Crawford, *Poet Scout*, p. v. *See also* Miller, *Captain Jack Crawford*, pp. 26–27.

Chapter 1. With the Dodge Expedition

1. Wayne R. Kime, ed., *The Black Hills Journals of Colonel Richard Irving Dodge* (Norman: University of Oklahoma Press, 1996), pp. 96–97.

2. Ibid., p. 8n13.

3. Reuben Davenport's and Andrew Burt's writings are presented in full in Marc H. Abrams, comp. and ed., *Newspaper Chronicle of the Indian Wars*, 16 vols. (Brooklyn, N.Y.: Abrams Publications, 2010), vol. 4.

4. John W. Crawford, "Reminiscences of the Black Hills," n.d., p. 17, Jack Crawford Materials, Box 1, Darlis A. Miller Papers, MS 218, Rio Grande Historical Collections, Hobson-Hunter University Archives, New Mexico State University, Las Cruces.

5. John H. Wells, *Placer Examination: Principles and Practice* (Portland, Oreg.: North American Geology Publications, 1975), pp. 159–61; Watson Parker, *Gold in the Black Hills* (1966; reprint ed., Pierre: South Dakota State Historical Society Press, 2003), pp. 149–50.

Chapter 2. On the Trail to Custer City

1. John W. Crawford, "Reminiscences of the Black Hills," n.d., p. 17, Jack Crawford Materials, Box 1, Darlis A. Miller Papers, MS 218, Rio Grande Historical Collections, Hobson-Hunter University Archives, New Mexico State University, Las Cruces.

2. Ranger [John Harwood Pierce], "The Poet Scout of the West," *Omaha Daily Bee*, 5 Jan. 1896; Don Russell, *The Lives and Legends of Buffalo Bill* (Norman: University of Oklahoma Press, 1960), p. 241; James O. Aplan, "In Search of the Poet Scout," in *11th Annual Dakota History Conference, April 6–7, 1979, Papers*, ed. H. W. Blakely, Karl E. Mundt Historical & Educational Foundation Series, no. 5 (Madison, S.Dak.: Dakota State College, 1980), p. 381.

3. Paul T. Nolan, *John Wallace Crawford* (Boston: Twayne Publishers, 1981), p. 26.

4. Leigh Irvine, "Biographical Sketch," in *The Poet Scout: A Book of Song and Story*, by Jack Crawford (New York: Funk & Wagnalls, 1886), p. xii.

5. Evidence of Crawford's complete transformation begun the previous winter can be seen in the engraving of him that appeared on the front page of the *Omaha Daily Bee*'s Black Hills Supplement of 13 May 1876. The same issue also provided images of Custer City, Harney Peak, landscapes, and trail landmarks. Crawford's plainsman attire is also plainly seen as he poses in two Black Hills photographs, taken by D. S. Mitchell, circa June 1876, which are reproduced in this book.

6. "Brevities," *Omaha Daily Bee*, 1 Feb. 1876.

7. Arthur J. Larsen, ed., "The Black Hills Gold Rush: Letters from Men Who Participated," *North Dakota Historical Quarterly* 6 (July 1932): 308.

8. For details on the Sidney-Black Hills Road, *see* Norbert R. Mahnken, "The Sidney-Black Hills Trail," *Nebraska History* 30 (Sept. 1949): 203–25, and "Description of the Route from Sidney to Custer City via Red Cloud," *Sidney Telegraph*, 29 Apr. 1876.

9. Editorial, 2 Feb.1876, "Sidney," 8 Apr. 1876, and "The Bloody Red-Skins," 24 Apr. 1876, all *Omaha Daily Bee*; William E. Lass, *From the Missouri to the Great Salt Lake: An Account of Overland Freighting* (Lincoln: Nebraska State Historical Society, 1972), pp. 194–96; Paul L. Hedren, *Great Sioux War Orders of Battle: How the United States Army Waged War on the Northern Plains, 1876–1877* (Norman: Arthur H. Clark Co., 2011), pp. 84–87. According to Edwin A. Curley, the mileage difference between the Sidney and Cheyenne routes to Custer City was almost negligible: Sidney route, 235 miles; Cheyenne route, 243 miles. *Edwin A. Curley's Guide to the Black Hills* (1877; facsimile ed., Mitchell, S.Dak.: Dakota Wesleyan University Press, 1973), pp. 81–82.

10. Thomas R. Buecker, ed., "Letters of Carolyn Frey Winne from Sidney Barracks and Fort McPherson, Nebraska, 1874–1878," *Nebraska History* 62 (Spring 1981): 23, 44.

11. "A Bold Black Hiller," *Omaha Daily Bee*, 9 Apr. 1877; Larsen, "Black Hills Gold Rush," p. 308.

12. Tom Buecker, "Red Cloud Agency Traders, 1873–1877," *Museum of the Fur Trade Quarterly* 30 (Fall 1994): 5–6.

13. James D. McLaird, *Calamity Jane: The Woman and the Legend* (Norman: University of Oklahoma Press, 2005), pp. 38–40, 46 (citing Crawford, "The Truth about Calamity Jane," *Journalist* [5 Mar. 1904]: 333).

14. "The Gold Fever," 9 Jan. 1876, and "The New Eldorado," 14 Jan. 1876, *Omaha Daily Bee*. At the 1876 Black Hills twenty dollar bullion rate, the reported nuggets weighed slightly more than 1 and 1.45 troy ounces, respectively.

15. Editorial, ibid., 14 Jan. 1876.

16. "The Black Hills—Letter from an Old Montanian," ibid., 11 Feb. 1876.

17. John H. Wells, *Placer Examination: Principles and Practice* (Portland, Oreg.: North American Geology Publications, 1975), pp. 6–9.

Chapter 3. Custer City

1. Agnes Wright Spring, *The Cheyenne and Black Hills Stage and Express Routes*, American Trail Series, no. 6 (Glendale, Calif.: Arthur H. Clark Co., 1949), pp. 165–66; Annie D. Tallent, *The Black Hills; or, The Last Hunting Ground of the Dakotahs* (Saint Louis: Nixon-Jones Printing Co., 1899), pp. 264–65; Fred W. Whitley, "A History of Custer City, South Dakota, 1874–1900," *South Dakota Historical Collections* 37 (1974): 245–46.

2. Tallent, *Black Hills*, pp. 265–68; Watson Parker, *Gold in the Black Hills* (1966; reprint ed., Pierre: South Dakota State Historical Society Press, 2003), pp. 74–75; Darlis A. Miller, *Captain Jack Crawford: Buckskin Poet, Scout, and Showman* (Albuquerque: University of New Mexico Press, 1993), p. 39; Whitley, "History of Custer City," pp. 293–94; Crawford, "Land of Gold!," *Sidney Telegraph*, 22 Apr. 1876. The Flick-Pollock-Crawford-Flick cabin survives in modern-day Custer in the city park opposite the town's imposing 1881 Courthouse Museum.

3. A discussion of the regulation of society during the California gold rush can be found in Rodman Paul, *California Gold* (Cambridge: Harvard University Press, 1947), ch.12. The Custer City instance almost directly mirrors the California model.

4. Hascall returned to Omaha and is next found interfering with that city's Republican senatorial primary election held on 11 May. The *Bee* followed Crawford's lead, scornfully labeling the lawyer "Hascall, the rascall" ("The Primaries," *Omaha Daily Bee*, 12 May 1876). Hascall's politics and motives confounded the *Bee*, a paper with a decidedly Republican slant, and it later sarcastically labeled Hascall a "*dem-rep*," noting that he courted both the Democratic and Republican parties but belonged to neither. "Conventionalities," *Omaha Daily Bee*, 19 May 1876.

5. [Jerry Bryant], "The Wives and Times of Al Swearengen—Part I," *Adams Banner* 5 (Fall 2004): 1; Harry ("Sam") Young, *Hard Knocks: A Life Story of the Vanishing West* (1915; reprint ed., Pierre: South Dakota State Historical Society Press, 2005), p. 194.

6. Parker, *Gold in the Black Hills*, p. 184.

7. For information on Mix and the Second Cavalry, *see* Watson Parker, ed., "The Report of Captain John Mix of a Scout to the Black Hills, March–April 1875," *South Dakota History* 7 (Fall 1977): 385–401.

8. Captain Jack Crawford, *The Poet Scout: Being a Selection of Incidental and Illustrative Verses and Songs* (San Francisco: H. Keller & Co., 1879), p. xi.

9. Brian W. Dippie, comp., *Bards of the Little Big Horn* (Bryan, Tex.: Guidon Press, 1978), pp. xii–xiii.

10. "On to the Hills," 28 Feb., 1876, "The New Hotel at Fort Laramie," 2 Mar. 1876, and "The New Stage Line to the Black Hills," 8 Mar. 1876, *Omaha Daily Bee.*

11. Spring, *Cheyenne and Black Hills Stage*, pp. 134–35.

12. "Brevities," 25 Feb. 1876, "Black Hills Notes," 10 Mar. 1876, and Ranger, "Cheyenne," 31 Mar. 1876, *Omaha Daily Bee.*

Chapter 4. Indians, Outlaws, and the Black Hills Rangers

1. "Black Hills News," *Omaha Daily Bee*, 6 Apr. 1876, citing the *Kansas City Times.*

2. "Hills City," *Omaha Daily Bee*, 11 Apr. 1876.

3. Watson Parker, *Gold in the Black Hills* (1966; reprint ed., Pierre: South Dakota State Historical Society Press, 2003), pp. 54–55, 64–65; Fred W. Whitley, "A History of Custer City, South Dakota, 1874–1900," *South Dakota Historical Collections* 37 (1974): 247–48.

4. Communication with David Wolff, Spearfish, S.Dak., 18 Apr. 2011.

5. Paul L. Hedren, *Fort Laramie in 1876: Chronicle of a Frontier Post at War* (Lincoln: University of Nebraska Press, 1988), pp. 74–78, and "Garrisoning the Black Hills Road: The United States Army's Camps on Sage Creek and Mouth of Red Canyon, 1876–1877," *South Dakota History* 37 (Spring 2007): 3–7; Arthur J. Larsen, ed., "The Black Hills Gold Rush: Letters from Men Who Participated," *North Dakota Historical Quarterly* 6 (July 1932): 311, 315.

6. Annie D. Tallent, *The Black Hills; or, The Last Hunting Ground of the Dakotahs* (Saint Louis: Nixon-Jones Printing Co., 1899), pp. 290–91; Jesse Brown and A. M. Willard, *The Black Hills Trails: A History of the Struggles of the Pioneers in the Winning of the Black Hills*, ed. John T. Milek (Rapid City, S.Dak.: Rapid City Journal Co., 1924), pp. 84–85; Darlis A. Miller, *Captain Jack Crawford: Buckskin Poet, Scout, and Showman* (Albuquerque: University of New Mexico Press, 1993), pp. 42–46; Hedren, "Garrisoning the Black Hills Road," pp. 8–14.

7. Thomas D. Isern, "The Controversial Career of Edward W. Wynkoop," *Colorado Magazine* 56 (Winter/Spring 1979): 1–18; Louis Kraft, *Ned Wynkoop and the Lonely Road from Sand Creek* (Norman: University of Oklahoma Press, 2011), p. 256. *See also* Flint Whitlock, *Distant Bugles, Distant Drums: The Union Response to the Confederate Invasion of New Mexico* (Boulder: University Press of Colorado, 2006).

8. Paul L. Hedren, "Persimmon Bill Chambers: The 'Scourge of the Black Hills Trail,'" *Annals of Wyoming* 81 (Autumn 2009): 6–8; Hedren, "Garrisoning the Black Hills Road," pp. 3–5; "The Bloody Red-Skins," 24 Apr. 1876, and "Particulars of the Killing of H. E. Brown," 1 May 1876, *Omaha Daily Bee*.

9. John Stands in Timber and Margot Liberty, *Cheyenne Memories* (New Haven: Yale University Press, 1967), p. 162n5. A less embracing view of Semineau, or Seminole, is offered by Harry ("Sam") Young, *Hard Knocks: A Life Story of the Vanishing West* (1915; reprint ed., Pierre: South Dakota State Historical Society Press, 2005), pp. 193–94. Young mistakenly identifies him as a Sioux mixed-blood. The Semineau name is confirmed in "American Horse's Interview" in the *Indian Interviews of Eli S. Ricker, 1903–1919*, ed. Richard C. Jensen, Voices of the American West, vol. 1 (Lincoln: University of Nebraska Press, 2005), pp. 279, 439.

10. Andrew S. Sweetser, "A Correction," *Omaha Daily Bee*, 24 Apr. 1876.

11. *See* Joseph G. Rosa, *Jack McCall, Assassin: An Updated Account of His Yankton Trial, Plea for Clemency, and Execution* (n.p.: English Westerner's Society, 1999).

12. Quoted in Larsen, "The Black Hills Gold Rush," p. 313. The $9.15 French Creek nugget weighed nearly one-half troy ounce.

13. "Black Hills," *Cheyenne Daily Sun*, 18 Apr. 1876.

14. Otis E. Young, Jr., *Western Mining* (Norman: University of Oklahoma Press, 1970), p. 111. Crawford's $14 nugget weighed nearly three-quarters of an ounce.

Chapter 5. Deadwood and the North

1. Walter P. Jenney, *The Mineral Wealth, Climate and Rain-fall, and Natural Resources of the Black Hills of Dakota* (Washington, D.C.: Government Printing Office, 1876), p. 43; "Black Hills News," *Sidney Telegraph*, 1 July 1876. In 1879, Claim No. 37 on Bear Gulch yielded the largest gold nugget ever found in the Black Hills. Valued at $465, it would have weighed nearly 23¼ troy ounces. "Gold Nuggets," *Black Hills Engineer* 19 (Nov. 1931): 362.

2. "Bear Gulch," *Black Hills Pioneer*, 22 July 1876.

3. Watson Parker, *Gold in the Black Hills* (1966; reprint ed., Pierre: South Dakota State Historical Society Press, 2003), pp. 89–90, and *Deadwood: The Golden Years* (Lincoln: University of Nebraska Press, 1981), pp. 12–13; Otis E. Young, Jr., *Western Mining: An Informal Account of Precious-Metals Prospecting, Placering, Lode Mining, and Milling on the American Frontier from Spanish Times to 1893* (Norman: University of Oklahoma Press, 1970), p. 271; Steven T. Mitchell, *Nuggets to Neutrinos: The Homestake Story* (n.p.: By the Author, 2009), pp. 48–49.

4. Mitchell, *Nuggets to Neutrinos*, pp. 105–7; Parker, *Gold in the Black Hills*, pp. 25, 90.

5. Richmond L. Clow, "Timber Users, Timber Savers: Homestake Mining Company and the First Regulated Timber Harvest," *South Dakota History* 22 (Fall 1992): 214–15. For a history of sawmills in the region, *see* Martha Linde, *Sawmills of the Black Hills* (Rapid City, S.Dak.: Jessie Y. Sundstrom, 1984).

6. Boyd Leedom, "Justice—Western Style," in *Dakota Panorama*, ed. J. Leonard Jennewein and Jane Boorman (Mitchell, S.Dak.: Dakota Territory Centennial Commission, 1961), pp. 326–27, 329, 331; Francis Paul Prucha, *American Indian Treaties: The History of a Political Anomaly* (Berkeley: University of California Press, 1994), pp. 100–102.

7. John W. Crawford, "Reminiscences of the Black Hills," pp. 32–34, Jack Crawford Materials, Box 1, Darlis A. Miller Papers, MS 218, Rio Grande Historical Collections, Hobson-Hunter University Archives, New Mexico State University, Las Cruces.

8. On photographer D. S. Mitchell, *see* Ephriam D. Dickson III, "Capturing the Lakota Spirit: Photographers at the Red Cloud & Spotted Tail Agencies," *Nebraska History* 88 (Spring–Summer 2007): 18–20; Robert Kolbe, with Brian Bade, *They Captured the Moment: Dakotas Photographers, 1853-1920* (Sioux Falls, S.Dak.: By the Authors, 2006), pp. 119–21; and Paul L. Hedren, "Garrisoning the Black Hills Road: The United States Army's Camps on Sage Creek and Mouth of Red Canyon, 1876–1877," *South Dakota History* 37 (Spring 2007): 43–45.

9. Paul L. Hedren, *Fort Laramie in 1876: Chronicle of a Frontier Post at War* (Lincoln: University of Nebraska Press, 1988), p. 94.

10. The first version of Curley's Black Hills book was titled *Glittering Gold: The True Story of the Black Hills*, published in Chicago in September 1876. A revised edition, *Edwin A. Curley's Guide to the Black Hills*, was published in Chicago in June 1877; the Dakota Wesleyan University Press, Mitchell, South Dakota, published a facsimile edition in 1973.

11. "Black Hills Gold," 11 May 1876, and "Brevities," 23 May 1876, *Omaha Daily Bee*.

12. "Gold! Gold!," ibid., 13 June 1876.

Chapter 6. Deadwood and Omaha

1. Editorial, *Omaha Daily Bee*, 15 June 1876.

2. John W. Crawford, "Reminiscences of the Black Hills," n.d., pp. 48, 56, Jack Crawford Materials, Box 1, Darlis A. Miller Papers, MS 218, Rio Grande Historical Collections, Hobson-Hunter University Archives, New Mexico State

University, Las Cruces; "Capt. Jack.," *Black Hills Pioneer*, 24 June 1876; "Brevities," *Omaha Daily Bee*, 15 July 1876; Darlis A. Miller, *Captain Jack Crawford: Buckskin Poet, Scout, and Showman* (Albuquerque: University of New Mexico Press, 1993), p. 50.

3. Annie D. Tallent, *The Black Hills; or, The Last Hunting Ground of the Dakotahs* (Saint Louis: Nixon-Jones, 1899), pp. 269–70; Nancy Niethammer Kovats, "*Black Hills Pioneer*: First Newspaper of Deadwood, Dakota Territory, 1876–1877," *South Dakota History* 8 (Summer 1978): 194.

4. Paul Hedren, *Fort Laramie in 1876: Chronicle of a Frontier Post at War* (Lincoln: University of Nebraska Press, 1988), pp. 37–38, 89–90, 103–4.

5. Joseph G. Rosa, *They Called Him Wild Bill: The Life and Adventures of James Butler Hickok*, 2d ed. (Norman: University of Oklahoma Press, 1974), pp. 286–87; William B. Secrest, ed., *I Buried Hickok: The Memoirs of White Eye Anderson* (College Station, Tex.: Creative Publishing Co., 1980), pp. 93–95; "Good Bye, Langrishe," 22 June 1876, "As for Amusements," 25 June 1876, and "Mr. W. A. McLaughlin," 9 July 1876, all *Cheyenne Daily Leader;* Alice Cochran, "The Gold Dust Trail: Jack Langrishe's Mining Town Theaters," *Montana The Magazine of Western History* 20 (Spring 1970): 69. The Langrishe troupe departed Cheyenne on 21 June, camped at the Six Mile ranch southwest of Fort Laramie on the twenty-fourth, and took dinner at Hat Creek on 2 July.

6. William F. Cody, *The Life of Hon. William F. Cody, Known as Buffalo Bill, the Famous Hunter, Scout, and Guide: An Autobiography* (1879; reprint ed., New York: Indian Head Books, 1991), pp. 340–41; Don Russell, *The Lives and Legends of Buffalo Bill* (Norman: University of Oklahoma Press, 1960), pp. 220–21. In his *The Poet Scout: Being a Selection of Incidental and Illustrative Verses and Songs* (San Francisco: H. Keller & Co., 1879), p. xx, Crawford asserts that his encounter with Cody occurred on Indian Creek, north of the Hat Creek stage station. On page 80 of that book, within the poem "The Death of Custer" (which had first appeared in the *Omaha Daily Bee* on 11 July 1876), he reminds Cody of their encounter at Hat Creek. The meeting most likely occurred on 28 or 29 June since he sent a telegram to Rosewater from Fort Laramie, forty miles south of Hat Creek, on 30 June.

7. "Mr. J. Crawford," *Cheyenne Daily Leader*, 4 July 1876; "Here and There," *Sidney Telegraph*, 8 July 1876; "Brevities," *Omaha Daily Bee*, 7 July 1876.

8. Crawford, *Poet Scout*, p. 79.

9. *Omaha Daily Bee*, 11 July 1876.

10. James R. Grossman, ed., *The Frontier in American Culture: An Exhibition at the Newberry Library, August 26, 1994–January 7, 1995* (Berkeley: University of California Press, 1994), pp. 36–37; Crawford, *Poet Scout*, pp. 79–82; James T. King, "The Sword and the Pen: The Poetry of the Military Frontier,"

Nebraska History 47 (Sept. 1966): 240; Brian W. Dippie, comp., *Bards of the Little Big Horn* (Bryan, Tex.: Guidon Press, 1978), pp. 59–61.

11. Crawford, Letter to the Editor, 20 Mar. 1877, *Cincinnati Times*, "Clippings, 1871–1879," Jack Crawford Materials, Box 2, Miller Papers; news item, *Cheyenne Daily Leader*, 28 July 1876.

12. Quoted in Crawford, *Poet Scout*, p. 25.

Chapter 7. Captain Jack and the Great Sioux War

1. "Intercepted," 19 June 1876, "Telegraphic," 20, 24 July 1876, and "Buffalo Bill's Trophies," 7 Aug. 1876, all *Omaha Daily Bee*; "Merritt's March," *Cheyenne Daily Leader*, 20 July 1876; "Col. Merritt's Report," *Laramie Daily Sentinel*, 21 July 1876; "The Indian War," *New York Herald*, 23 July 1876. The story of the Warbonnet Creek skirmish is told in Paul L. Hedren, *First Scalp for Custer: The Skirmish at Warbonnet Creek, Nebraska, July 17, 1876*, rev. ed. (Lincoln: Nebraska State Historical Society, 2005).

2. "Capt. Jack to the Front," *Omaha Daily Bee*, 22 July 1876.

3. Martin F. Schmitt, ed., *General George Crook: His Autobiography* (Norman: University of Oklahoma Press, 1946), pp. 188–89. The roots of the Great Sioux War have been roundly debated, and the prevailing arguments synthesized in three accessible essays: Mark H. Brown, "A New Focus on the Sioux War," *Montana The Magazine of Western History* 11 (Oct. 1961): 76–85, and Harry H. Anderson, "A Challenge to Brown's Indian Wars Thesis," ibid. 12 (Jan. 1962): 40–49, both reprinted in *The Great Sioux War 1876–77: The Best from* Montana The Magazine of Western History, ed. Paul L. Hedren, (Helena: Montana Historical Society Press, 1991), pp. 25–52; and Robert M. Utley, "Origins of the Great Sioux War: The Brown-Anderson Controversy Revisited," *Montana The Magazine of Western History* 42 (Autumn 1992): 48–52.

4. For an overview of the Sioux war to this stage, *see* Paul L. Hedren, *Great Sioux War Orders of Battle: How the United States Army Waged War on the Northern Plains, 1876–1877*, Frontier Military Series, no. 31 (Norman, Okla.: Arthur H. Clark Co., 2011), pp. 41–58.

5. "Personal," 24 July 1876, and "Capt. Jack Crawford," 25 July 1876, *Omaha Daily Bee*.

6. "Capt. Jack Crawford," ibid., 25 July 1876.

7. "Brevities," ibid., 26 July 1876.

8. "Capt. Jack Crawford," ibid., 25 July 1876; "Here and There," *Sidney Telegraph*, 29 July 1876; "Personal Paragraphs," *Cheyenne Daily Leader*, 27, 28 July 1876.

9. "Personal Paragraphs," *Cheyenne Daily Leader*, 27 July 1876.

10. William F. Cody, *The Life of Hon. William F. Cody, Known as Buffalo*

Bill, the Famous Hunter, Scout and Guide: An Autobiography (1879; facsimile reprint, New York: Indian Head Books, 1991), p. 349. G. M. Jones is identified in "Far West Sketches," *Omaha Daily Bee*, 11 Aug. 1875.

11. Jack Crawford, *The Poet Scout: Being a Selection of Incidental and Illustrative Verses and Songs* (San Francisco: H. Keller & Co., 1879), pp. 26, 34–35.

12. Ibid., p. 27; William P. Hall, Acting Regimental Quartermaster, Fifth Cavalry, Report of Persons and Articles Employed and Hired, Big Horn and Yellowstone Expedition, Aug. 1876, Records of the Office of the Quartermaster General, Record Group 92, National Archives, Washington, D. C. This quartermaster report actually accounted for twelve scouts, all earning $150 monthly, but Cody alone was acknowledged as "Chief Scout."

13. Crawford, *Poet Scout*, pp. 27–33. John G. Bourke records that Crawford joined the column on 8 August, but both individuals were likely referring to the same evening. Bourke, *On the Border with Crook* (New York: Charles Scribner's Sons, 1891), p. 350.

14. Crawford, *Poet Scout*, pp. 29–30, 33–34.

15. Charles M. Robinson III, ed., *The Diaries of John Gregory Bourke: Vol. 2, July 29, 1876–April 7, 1878* (Denton: University of North Texas Press, 2005), p. 54.

16. Andrew Burt, untitled reminiscence, n.d., Andrew S. Burt Papers, United States Army Military History Institute, Carlisle, Pa.

17. Hall, Report of Persons and Articles Employed; L. G. ("Pat") Flannery, ed., *John Hunton's Diary: Vol. 2, 1876-'77* (Lingle, Wyo.: By the Editor, 1958), p. 96; Don Russell, *The Lives and Legends of Buffalo Bill* (Norman: University of Oklahoma Press, 1960), pp. 233–34; "Richard C. Stirk Interview," in *The Settler and Soldier Interviews of Eli S. Ricker, 1903–1919*, ed. Richard C. Jensen, Voices of the American West, vol. 2 (Lincoln: University of Nebraska Press, 2005), pp. 203, 282–85.

18. Russell, *Lives and Legends of Buffalo Bill*, pp. 80, 209–10; "Crook's Scouts," *Omaha Daily Bee*, 21 Aug. 1876.

19. Quoted by John F. Finerty, *War-Path and Bivouac; or, The Conquest of the Sioux* (Chicago: By the Author, 1890), p. 212.

20. Thomas Powers, *The Killing of Crazy Horse* (New York: Alfred A. Knopf, 2010), pp. 162–63; Oliver Knight, *Following the Indian Wars: The Story of the Newspaper Correspondents among the Indian Campaigners* (Norman: University of Oklahoma Press, 1960), pp. 159–74; Marc H. Abrams, comp. and ed., *Newspaper Chronicle of the Indian Wars*, 16 vols. (Brooklyn, N. Y.: Abrams Publications, 2010), vols. 5–7 [1876].

21. Finerty, *War-Path and Bivouac*, p. 120.

22. Knight, *Following the Indian Wars*, pp. 172–73. For a lively example of

Davenport's criticism of Crook, *see New York Herald*, 3 Aug. 1876, reprinted in Abrams, *Newspaper Chronicle of the Indian Wars*, vol. 6. For a defense of Crook in light of that particular criticism, *see Cheyenne Daily Leader*, 9 Aug. 1876, also in Abrams, vol. 6, which sarcastically urges that Davenport be sent home or promoted to the rank of field marshal and commander of the Department of the Platte in lieu of Crook. For a sense of Davenport's shaky embrace by Crook's officer corps, *see* Charles King, *Campaigning with Crook and Stories of Army Life*, 1st [unexpurgated] ed. (New York: Harper & Bros. 1890), pp. 153–54. King called the reporter "one of the most unhappy wretches on the face of the globe," "a nuisance," "woefully green," and "a desperate coward, but so zealous in the cause of journalism that anything he fancied might interest the readers of the paper . . . was sent on irrespective of facts in the case." King's retraction, appearing on pp. 153–55 of subsequent printings, also illuminated aspects of Davenport's uneven reputation.

23. Knight, *Following the Indian Wars*, p. 172, citing the *Rocky Mountain News*, 8 Aug. 1876.

24. "Persimmon Bill," *Cheyenne Daily Sun*, 3 May 1879; Paul L. Hedren, "Persimmon Bill Chambers: The 'Scourge of the Black Hills Trail'," *Annals of Wyoming* 81 (Autumn 2009): 2–10. Chambers most likely died in a fight among his Indian partners sometime in the late summer or fall of 1876.

25. Cody, *Life of Hon. William F. Cody*, pp. 355–56, 359; Russell, *Lives and Legends of Buffalo Bill*, pp. 246–47.

26. Editorial, *Omaha Daily Bee*, 8 Sept. 1876.

Chapter 8. Captain Jack's Ride

1. The story of the Slim Buttes encounter is told by Jerome A. Greene, *Slim Buttes, 1876: An Episode of the Great Sioux War* (Norman: University of Oklahoma Press, 1982); and Paul L. Hedren, *Great Sioux War Orders of Battle: How the United States Army Waged War on the Northern Plains*, Frontier Military Series, no. 31 (Norman, Okla.: Arthur H. Clark Co., 2011), pp. 63, 112–13. Hedren discusses the precepts of total war on pages 36–39.

2. Greene, *Slim Buttes*, pp. 72–73.

3. Joe DeBarthe, *Life and Adventures of Frank Grouard*, ed. Edgar I. Stewart (Norman: University of Oklahoma Press, 1958), p. 159; [Jack Crawford], "The Story of a Scout Bearing the Herald Dispatches—Trials and Difficulties Encountered in Getting in Ahead," *New York Herald*, 18 Sept. 1876, in *Newspaper Chronicle of the Indian Wars*, comp. and ed. Marc H. Abrams, 16 vols. (Brooklyn, N.Y.: Abrams Publications, 2010), 7:114–15.

4. DeBarthe, *Life and Adventures of Frank Grouard*, p. 159; Oliver Knight, *Following the Indian Wars: The Story of the Newspaper Correspondents among*

the Indian Campaigners (Norman: University of Oklahoma Press, 1960), pp. 247–49, 276.

5. DeBarthe, *Life and Adventures of Frank Grouard*, pp. 159–60; Knight, *Following the Indian Wars*, pp. 276–77; Crawford to Crook, [24] Sept. 1876, "Clippings, 1872–1879," Jack Crawford Materials, Box 2, Darlis A. Miller Papers, MS 218, Rio Grande Historical Collections, New Mexico State University Library, Las Cruces; [Reuben Davenport], "A Forlorn Hope," *New York Herald*, 17 Sept. 1876, in *Newspaper Chronicle of the Indian Wars*, comp. and ed. Abrams, 7:108.

6. DeBarthe, *Life and Adventures of Frank Grouard*, pp. 160–61; Crawford to Crook, [24] Sept. 1876; Jack Crawford to Editor, *Cincinnati Times*, 20 Mar. 1877, and "Brave as the Bravest," *Milwaukee Evening Wisconsin*, 2 Feb. [1891], both in "Clippings, 1872–1879"; Andrew Burt, untitled reminiscence, n.d., Andrew S. Burt Papers, United States Army Military History Institute, Carlisle, Pa.; Crawford, "Story of a Scout."

7. Davenport, "A Forlorn Hope"; Crawford to Crook, [24] Sept. 1876; DeBarthe, *Life and Adventures of Frank Grouard*, pp. 160–61; Burt, untitled reminiscence; Crawford, "Story of a Scout."

8. DeBarthe, *Life and Adventures of Frank Grouard*, pp. 161–62; Darlis A. Miller, *Captain Jack Crawford: Buckskin Poet, Scout, and Showman* (Albuquerque: University of New Mexico Press, 1993), p. 62.

9. Crawford, "Story of a Scout"; James E. Smith, *A Famous Battery and Its Campaigns, 1861-'64—The Career of Corporal James Tanner in War and in Peace—Early Days in the Black Hills, with Some Account of Capt. Jack Crawford, the Poet Scout* (Washington: W. H. Lowdermilk & Co., 1892), p. 229; DeBarthe, *Life and Adventures of Frank Grouard*, p. 162.

10. DeBarthe, *Life and Adventures of Frank Grouard*, pp. 162–63.

11. Crawford, "Story of a Scout."

12. Ibid.; Paul L. Hedren, "Garrisoning the Black Hills Road: The United States Army's Camps on Sage Creek and Mouth of Red Canyon, 1876–1877," *South Dakota History* 37 (Spring 2007): 25.

13. Crawford, "Story of a Scout."

14. Crawford to Crook, [24] Sept. 1876; Paul L. Hedren, *Fort Laramie in 1876: Chronicle of a Frontier Post at War* (Lincoln: University of Nebraska Press, 1988), pp. 166–67; Greene, *Slim Buttes*, pp. 130–31. The newspapers had remarked on Sheridan's hurried trip from Chicago to Fort Laramie, with the *Bee* noting his passage through Omaha on 14 September and the *Cheyenne Daily Leader* observing his trip through Cheyenne on the fifteenth.

15. [Reuben B. Davenport], "Crook's Victory" and "A Forlorn Hope," *New York Herald*, 17 Sept. 1876, [Cuthbert Mills], "The Indian Campaign," *New York Times*, 17 Sept. 1876, "Despatches from Crook," (San Francisco) *Daily Alta California*,

17 Sept. 1876, all in *Newspaper Chronicle of the Indian Wars*, comp. and ed. Abrams, 7:102–8, 112–13; [Robert Strahorn], "Caught Napping," *Chicago Tribune*, 17 Sept. 1876, reprinted in *Bighorn Yellowstone Journal* 2 (Spring 1993): 16–21.

16. DeBarthe, *Life and Adventures of Frank Grouard*, p. 162; William P. Hall, Acting Regimental Quartermaster, Fifth Cavalry, Report of Persons and Articles Employed and Hired, Big Horn and Yellowstone Expedition, Sept. 1876, Records of the Office of the Quartermaster General, Record Group 92, National Archives, Washington, D. C.

17. [Reuben Davenport], "Crook's Campaign," *New York Herald*, 2 Oct. 1876, in *Newspaper Chronicle of the Indian Wars*, comp. and ed. Abrams, 7:175.

18. Knight, *Following the Indian Wars*, pp. 172–73, 282–85.

19. Crawford to Crook, [24] Sept. 1876; Miller, *Captain Jack Crawford*, pp. 63–64.

20. Miller, *Captain Jack Crawford*, p. 63.

21. "Newspaper Enterprise," *Omaha Daily Bee*, 22 Sept. 1876.

22. Crawford's ornate lap desk is today on exhibit at the Autry National Center, Griffith Park, Los Angeles.

Chapter 9. Loose Ends

1. [Reuben B. Davenport], "Crook's Victory," *New York Herald*, 17 Sept. 1876, in *Newspaper Chronicle of the Indian Wars*, comp. and ed. Marc H. Abrams, 16 vols. (Brooklyn: Abrams Publications, 2010), 7:108.

2. Reports of the Warbonnet Creek skirmish appeared in the *Omaha Daily Bee* on 19, 20, and 24 July 1876. Yellow Hair's scalp is first mentioned in the *Bee* under the headline "Buffalo Bill's Trophies" on 7 August 1876.

3. Paul L. Hedren, "The Contradictory Legacies of Buffalo Bill Cody's First Scalp for Custer," *Montana The Magazine of Western History* 55 (Spring 2005): 21; Louis S. Warren, *Buffalo Bill's America: William Cody and the Wild West Show* (New York: Alfred A. Knopf, 2005), pp. 172–73.

4. "Buffalo Bill's Trophies," 7 Aug. 1876, and "Newspaper Enterprise," 22 Sept. 1876, *Omaha Daily Bee*.

5. "Captain Jack Crawford," ibid., 10 Nov. 1876.

6. "Indian Wigwam," ibid., 30 Oct. 1876.

7. "Personal Paragraphs," ibid., 27 Nov. 1876.

8. Ibid., 25 Nov. 1876; Paul T. Nolan, *John Wallace Crawford* (Boston: Twayne Publishers,1981), p. 35; E. J. Kahn, Jr., *The Merry Partners: The Age and Stage of Harrigan & Hart* (New York: Random House, 1955), p. 170; Sandra K. Sagala, *Buffalo Bill on Stage* (Albuquerque: University of New Mexico Press, 2008), pp. 87–88.

9. William F. Cody, *The Life of Hon. William F. Cody, Known as Buffalo Bill, The Famous Hunter, Scout, and Guide: An Autobiography* (1879; reprint, New York: Indian Head Books, 1991), p. 360.

10. Sagala, *Buffalo Bill on Stage*, pp. 71–73, 212–15; Nolan, *John Wallace Crawford*, pp. 34–35; Warren, *Buffalo Bill's America*, pp. 172–73.

11. "The Red Right Hand," *Omaha Daily Bee*, 16 Jan. 1877.

12. "Capt. Jack," ibid., 28 Feb. 1877.

13. Ibid., 10 Mar. 1877.

14. "The Red Right Hand," ibid., 21 Apr. 1877. *See also* "Academy of Music" and "Personal Paragraphs," ibid., 20 Apr. 1877.

15. Nellie Snyder Yost, *Buffalo Bill: His Family, Friends, Fame, Failures, and Fortunes* (Chicago: Swallow Press, 1979), pp. 97–98.

16. "Personal Paragraphs," *Omaha Daily Bee*, 30 Apr. 1877.

17. Darlis A. Miller, *Captain Jack Crawford: Buckskin Poet, Scout, and Showman* (Albuquerque: University of New Mexico Press, 1993), pp. 72–76.

18. Ibid., pp. 74–75; Nolan, *John Wallace Crawford*, pp. 35–36; Paul T. Nolan, "When the Curtains Rise, Scouts Fall Out," *Southern Speech Journal* 29 (Spring 1964): 179; Sagala, *Buffalo Bill on Stage*, pp. 91–97.

19. Nolan, *John Wallace Crawford*, p. 39; Kahn, *Merry Partners*, p. 203; Miller, *Captain Jack Crawford*, pp. 75–77.

20. Quoted in Sagala, *Buffalo Bill on Stage*, pp. 99–100, and Warren, *Buffalo Bill's America*, p. 173.

21. Miller, *Captain Jack Crawford*, pp. 117–18, 187–89.

22. James O. Aplan, "In Search of the Poet Scout," *11th Dakota History Conference, April 6–7, 1979, Papers*, ed. H. W. Blakely, Karl E. Mundt Historical & Educational Foundation Series, no. 5 (Madison, S.Dak.: Dakota State College, 1980), pp. 384–85; "Now the Troops Will Come," (Rapid City) *Black Hills Journal*, 2 Feb. 1878; "Rockerville," *The Wi-Iyohi* 6 (Dec. 1952): 1–3; Paul Fatout, *Ambrose Bierce and the Black Hills* (Norman: University of Oklahoma Press, 1956), pp. 24–25, 32–33; Miller, *Captain Jack Crawford*, pp. 78–80, 207–10.

23. "Captain Jack Crawford," *Hot Springs Weekly Star*, 13 Mar. 1893.

24. Ibid., 24 Mar. 1893; Miller, *Captain Jack Crawford*, p. 177; Joseph G. Rosa, *They Called Him Wild Bill: The Life and Adventures of James Butler Hickok*, 2d ed. (Norman: University of Oklahoma Press, 1974), pp. 313, 315.

25. Jack Crawford, *The Poet Scout: Being a Selection of Incidental and Illustrative Verses and Songs* (San Francisco: H. Keller & Co., 1879), pp. 61, 65.

26. Miller, *Captain Jack Crawford*, p. 194; Denise Ross, "William Gay, Deadwood's Real Desperado," 4 parts, *Adams Banner Quarterly* 7 (Fall 2006) and 8 (Winter, Spring, Summer, 2007).

27. Annie D. Tallent, *The Black Hills; or, The Last Hunting Ground of the Da-*

kotahs (Saint Louis: Nixon-Jones, 1899), p. 291; Miller, *Captain Jack Crawford*, p. 72; "With Bright Prospects," 4 Apr. 1879, and "Mr. T. J. Fisher," 26 Mar. 1880, both in *Cheyenne Daily Sun*; U. S., Department of the Interior, Bureau of the Census, *Tenth Census of the United States, 1880*, National Archives Microfilm Publication T9, Roll 692.

28. "Mr. Dick Brown," *Cheyenne Daily News*, 30 Nov. 1874.

29. John S. McClintock, *Pioneer Days in the Black Hills: Accurate History and Facts Related by One of the Early Day Pioneers* (Deadwood, S. Dak.: By the Author, 1939), p. 129.

30. "The Gold Room," *Cheyenne Daily Leader*, 27 Nov. 1874; "The Appearance of Mr. Dick Brown," *Cheyenne Daily News*, 23 Oct. 1875; "Dick Brown Kills His Man," *Cheyenne Daily Leader*, 21 Nov. 1876; "Dick Brown and Billy Nuttall," *Black Hills Pioneer*, 20 Jan. 1877.

31. Richard B. Hughes, *Pioneer Years in the Black Hills* (Glendale, Calif.: Arthur H. Clark Co., 1957), pp. 114, 117; "Dick Brown Kills His Man"; "The Shooting of Shaughnessy by Brown," 30 Nov. 1876, "In the Homicide Case," 5 Dec. 1876, and "A Word from Fanny and Dick," 16 Dec. 1876, all in *Cheyenne Daily Leader*; "Dick Brown Kills Ed. Shaughnessy," *Laramie Daily Sentinel*, 22 Nov. 1876; "Comique," *Ford County* (Kansas) *Globe*, 30 July 1878.

32. *Laramie Daily Sentinel*, 21 Oct. 1878, quoting the *Cheyenne Daily Leader*.

33. "Another Victim," *Dodge City Times*, 5 Oct. 1878; "Dick Brown," *Cheyenne Daily Sun*, 19 June 1879; "The Stage," (San Francisco) *Daily Alta California*, 8 June 1879.

34. Alfred Sorenson, *History of Omaha from the Pioneer Days to the Present Time* (Omaha: Gibson, Miller & Richardson, 1889), pp. 210–13; "Edward Rosewater," in *Dictionary of American Biography*, vol. 16, ed. Dumas Malone (New York: Charles Scribner's Sons, 1935), pp. 171–72.

35. "The New Eldorado," 18 Sept. 1876, J. C. Wilcox, "The Black Hills," 21 Sept. 1876, and "A Big 'Stake'," 22 Sept. 1876, all in *Omaha Daily Bee*; Steven T. Mitchell, *Nuggets to Neutrinos: The Homestake Story* (N.p.: By the Author, 2009), pp. 108–9. One thousand forty pounds troy was the equivalent of 12,480 ounces troy.

36. "Returned Black Hillers," 18 Dec. 1876, and "Black Hills Nuggets," 3 Jan. 1877, both in *Omaha Daily Bee*; Mitchell, *Nuggets to Neutrinos*, p. 107. The $72.47 nugget weighed 3.6 troy ounces, while the $34.80 nugget weighed nearly 1.75 ounces.

37. Wilcox, "The Black Hills."

38. Jeffrey Ostler, *The Lakotas and the Black Hills: The Struggle for Sacred Ground* (New York: Viking Penguin, 2010), pp. 98–100; Edward Lazarus, *Black Hills, White Justice: The Sioux Nation versus the United States, 1775 to the Present* (New York: HarperCollins Publishers, 1991), p. 452; Watson Parker, *Gold in*

the Black Hills (1966; reprint ed., Pierre: South Dakota State Historical Society Press, 2003), p. 201; Mitchell, *Nuggets to Neutrinos*, p. 558.

39. "Personal Paragraphs," *Cheyenne Daily Leader*, 30 Sept., 17 Oct., 8 Nov. 1876; Oliver Knight, *Following the Indian Wars: The Story of the Newspaper Correspondents among the Indian Campaigners* (Norman: University of Oklahoma Press, 1960), p. 319; Dan L. Thrapp, *Encyclopedia of Frontier Biography*, 3 vols. (Glendale, Calif.: Arthur H. Clark Co., 1988), 1:377; Davenport to Crawford, 7 Mar., 8 July 1877, Box 2, Jack Crawford Papers, WH89, Western History Collection, Denver Public Library, Denver; Harry H. Anderson, "Some Footnotes to Charles King's 'Campaigning with Crook'," *Historical Messenger of the Milwaukee County Historical Society* 29 (Spring 1973): 16–25; "Brave as the Bravest," (Milwaukee) *Evening Wisconsin*, 2 Feb. [1891], "Clippings, 1890–1892," Jack Crawford Materials, Box 2, Darlis A. Miller Papers, MS 218, Rio Grande Historical Collections, New Mexico State University Library, Las Cruces.

40. Nolan, *John Wallace Crawford*, pp. 37–41; Darlis A. Miller, "Captain Jack Crawford: A Western Military Scout on the Chautauqua Circuit," *South Dakota History* 21 (Fall 1991): 230–46. On *Fonda* and Crawford's other plays, *see* Paul T. Nolan, *Three Plays by J. W. (Capt. Jack) Crawford* (The Hague: Mouton & Co., 1966).

41. Quoted in Miller, *Captain Jack Crawford*, pp. 193–94.

42. Ibid., pp. 107–8, 275–76.

43. "Jack Crawford, 'Poet Scout,' Dies," *New York Sun*, 1 Mar. 1917.

44. Quoted in Miller, *Captain Jack Crawford*, p. 271.

BIBLIOGRAPHY

Archives and Manuscript Collections

Burt, Andrew S. Papers. United States Army Military History Institute, Carlisle, Pa.

Crawford, Jack. Papers. Western History Collection. Denver Public Library, Denver, Colo.

Fort Laramie Post Returns, 1876. National Archives and Records Service, Washington, D.C. National Archives Microfilm Publication M617, Roll 596.

Hall, William P., Acting Regimental Quartermaster, Fifth Cavalry. Report of Persons and Articles Employed and Hired, Big Horn and Yellowstone Expedition, Aug.–Sept. 1876. Records of the Office of the Quartermaster General. Record Group 92. National Archives and Records Service, Washington, D.C.

Miller, Darlis A. Papers. Rio Grande Historical Collections. Hobson-Hunter University Archives. New Mexico State University, Las Cruces.

United States. Department of the Interior. Bureau of the Census. *Tenth Census of the United States*, 1880. Kansas City, Missouri. National Archives Microfilm Publication T9, Roll 692.

Newspapers

Black Hills Pioneer, 1876–1877.
Cheyenne Daily Leader, 1874–1876.
Cheyenne Daily News, 1874–1875.
Cheyenne Daily Sun, 1876, 1879–1880.
Dodge City Times, 1878.
Ford County (Kansas) *Globe*, 1878.
Hot Springs Weekly Star, 1893.
Laramie Daily Sentinel, 1876, 1878.
New York Herald, 1876.
New York Sun, 1917.
Omaha Daily Bee, 1875–1877, 1896.
(San Francisco) *Daily Alta California*, 1879.
Sidney Telegraph, 1876.

Books and Articles

Abel, Annie Heloise, ed. *Tabeau's Narrative of Loisel's Expedition to the Upper Missouri*. Norman: University of Oklahoma Press, 1939.

Abrams, Marc H., comp. and ed. *Newspaper Chronicle of the Indian Wars*. 16 vols. Brooklyn, N.Y.: Abrams Publications, 2010.

Anderson, Grant K. "Samuel D. Hinman and the Opening of the Black Hills." *Nebraska History* 60 (Winter 1979): 520–42.

Anderson, Harry H. "A Challenge to Brown's Indian Wars Thesis." *Montana The Magazine of Western History* 12 (Jan. 1962): 40–49.

———. "Some Footnotes to Charles King's 'Campaigning with Crook'." *Historical Messenger of the Milwaukee County Historical Society* 29 (Spring 1973): 16–25.

Aplan, James O. "In Search of the Poet Scout." In *11th Annual Dakota History Conference, April 6–7, 1979, Papers*. Ed. Herbert W. Blakely. Karl E. Mundt Historical & Educational Foundation Series, no. 5. PP. 379–93. Madison, S.Dak.: Dakota State College, 1980.

Bourke, John G. *On the Border with Crook*. New York: Charles Scribner's Sons, 1891.

Briggs, Harold E. "The Black Hills Gold Rush." *North Dakota Historical Quarterly* 5 (Jan. 1931): 71–99.

Brown, Jesse, and A. M. Willard. *The Black Hills Trails*. Ed. John T. Milek. Rapid City, S.Dak.: Rapid City Journal Co., 1924.

Brown, Mark H. "A New Focus on the Sioux War." *Montana The Magazine of Western History* 11 (Oct. 1961): 76–85.

Bryant, Jerry. "The Wives and Times of Al Swearengen—Part I." *Adams Banner* 5 (Fall 2004): 1, 4.

Buecker, Thomas R. *Fort Robinson and the American West, 1874–1899*. Lincoln: Nebraska State Historical Society, 1999.

———. "Red Cloud Agency Traders, 1873–1877." *Museum of the Fur Trade Quarterly* 30 (Fall 1994): 4–14.

———, ed. "Letters of Carolyn Frey Winne from Sidney Barracks and Fort McPherson, Nebraska, 1874–1878. *Nebraska History* 62 (Spring 1981): 1–46.

Clow, Richmond L. "Timber Users, Timber Savers: Homestake Mining Company and the First Regulated Timber Harvest." *South Dakota History* 22 (Fall 1992): 213–37.

Cochran, Alice. "The Gold Dust Trail: Jack Langrishe's Mining Town Theaters." *Montana The Magazine of Western History* 20 (Spring 1970): 58–69.

Cody, William F. *The Life of Hon. William F. Cody, Known as Buffalo Bill, The Famous Hunter, Scout, and Guide*. Facsimile ed. New York: Indian Head Books, 1991.

Conard, Jane. "Charles Collins: The Sioux City Promotion of the Black Hills." *South Dakota History* 2 (Spring 1972): 131–71.

Crawford, Jack. *The Broncho Book, Being Buck-Jumps in Verse*. East Aurora, N. Y.: The Roycrofters, 1908.

———. *Camp Fire Sparks*. Chicago: Charles H. Kerr & Co., 1893.

———. *From Darkness into Light and Other Poems*. Chicago: R. R. McCabe & Co., 1886.

———. *Lariattes: A Book of Poems and Favorite Recitations*. Sigourney, Iowa: William A. Bell, 1904.

———. *The Poet Scout: A Book of Song and Story*. New York: Funk & Wagnalls, 1886.

———. *The Poet Scout: Being a Selection of Incidental and Illustrative Verses and Songs*. San Francisco: H. Keller & Co., 1879.

———. *Whar' the Hand O' God is Seen and Other Poems*. New York: New York Lyceum Publishing Co., 1913.

Curley, Edwin A. *Edwin A. Curley's Guide to the Black Hills*. 1877. Facsimile ed. Mitchell, S.Dak.: Dakota Wesleyan University Press, 1973.

DeBarthe, Joe. *Life and Adventures of Frank Grouard*. Norman: University of Oklahoma Press, 1958.

Dickson, Ephriam D., III. "Capturing the Lakota Spirit: Photographers at the Red Cloud & Spotted Tail Agencies." *Nebraska History* 88 (Spring–Summer 2007): 2–25.

Dippie, Brian W., comp. *Bards of the Little Big Horn*. Bryan, Tex.: Guidon Press, 1978.

Dodge, Richard I. *The Black Hills: A Minute Description of the Routes, Scenery, Soil, Climate, Timber, Gold, Geology, Zoology, etc.* New York: James Miller, 1876.

Eriksson, Erik M. "Sioux City and the Black Hills Gold Rush, 1874–1877." *Iowa Journal of History and Politics* 20 (July 1922): 319–47.

Fatout, Paul. *Ambrose Bierce and the Black Hills*. Norman: University of Oklahoma Press, 1956.

Finerty, John F. *War-Path and Bivouac; or, The Conquest of the Sioux*. Chicago: Donohue & Henneberry, 1890.

Flannery, L. G. ("Pat"), ed. *John Hunton's Diary: Vol. 2, 1876–1877*. Lingle, Wyo.: By the Editor, 1958.

"Gold Nuggets." *Black Hills Engineer* 19 (Nov. 1931): 362.

Grafe, Ernest, and Paul Horsted. *Exploring with Custer: The 1874 Black Hills Expedition*. Custer, S.Dak.: Golden Valley Press, 2002.

Gray, John S. "News from Paradise: Charley Reynolds Rides from the Black Hills to Fort Laramie." *By Valor & Arms: The Journal of American Military History* 3, no. 3 (1978): 37–45.

Greene, Jerome A. *Slim Buttes, 1876: An Episode of the Great Sioux War*. Norman: University of Oklahoma Press, 1982.

Grossman, James R., ed. *The Frontier in American Culture: An Exhibition at the Newberry Library, August 26, 1994–January 7, 1995*. Berkeley: University of California Press, 1994.

Hedren, Paul L. "The Contradictory Legacies of Buffalo Bill Cody's First Scalp

for Custer." *Montana The Magazine of Western History* 55 (Spring 2005): 16–35.
———. *First Scalp for Custer: The Skirmish at Warbonnet Creek, Nebraska, July 17, 1876*. Rev. ed. Lincoln: Nebraska State Historical Society, 2005.
———. *Fort Laramie in 1876: Chronicle of a Frontier Post at War*. Lincoln: University of Nebraska Press, 1988.
———. "Garrisoning the Black Hills Road: The United States Army's Camps on Sage Creek and Mouth of Red Canyon, 1876–1877." *South Dakota History* 37 (Spring 2007): 1–45.
———. *The Great Sioux War, 1876–77: The Best from* Montana The Magazine of Western History. Helena: Montana Historical Society Press, 1991.
———. *Great Sioux War Orders of Battle: How the United States Army Waged War on the Northern Plains, 1876–1877*. Frontier Military Series, no. 31. Norman, Okla.: Arthur H. Clark Co., 2011.
———. "Persimmon Bill Chambers: The 'Scourge of the Black Hills Trail'." *Annals of Wyoming* 81 (Autumn 2009): 2–10.
Hughes, Richard B. *Pioneer Years in the Black Hills*. Glendale, Calif.: Arthur H. Clark Co., 1957.
Irvine, Leigh. "Biographical Sketch." In *The Poet Scout: A Book of Song and Story*, by Jack Crawford. pp. v-xiii. New York: Funk & Wagnalls, 1886.
Isern, Thomas. "The Controversial Career of Edward W. Wynkoop." *Colorado Magazine* 56 (Winter/Spring 1979): 1–18.
Jackson, Donald. *Custer's Gold: The United States Cavalry Expedition of 1874*. New Haven, Conn.: Yale University Press, 1966.
Jennewein, J. Leonard, and Jane Boorman, eds. *Dakota Panorama*. Mitchell, S.Dak.: Dakota Territory Centennial Commission, 1961.
Jenney, Walter P. *The Mineral Wealth, Climate and Rain-Fall, and Mineral Resources of the Black Hills of Dakota*. Washington, D.C.: Government Printing Office, 1876.
Jensen, Richard C., ed. *The Indian Interviews of Eli S. Ricker, 1903–1919*. Voices of the American West, vol. 1. Lincoln: University of Nebraska Press, 2005.
———., ed. *The Settler and Soldier Interviews of Eli S. Ricker, 1903–1919*. Voices of the American West, vol. 2. Lincoln: University of Nebraska Press, 2005.
Kahn, E. J., Jr. *The Merry Partners: The Age and Stage of Harrigan & Hart*. New York: Random House, 1955.
Kappler, Charles J., comp. and ed. *Indian Affairs: Laws and Treaties*. Washington: Government Printing Office, 1904.
Kime, Wayne R., ed. *The Black Hills Journals of Colonel Richard Irving Dodge*. Norman: University of Oklahoma Press, 1996.

King, Charles. *Campaigning with Crook and Stories of Army Life*. New York: Harper & Bros., 1890.
King, James T. "The Sword and the Pen: The Poetry of the Military Frontier." *Nebraska History* 47 (Sept. 1966): 229–45.
Knight, Oliver. *Following the Indian Wars: The Story of the Newspaper Correspondents among the Indian Campaigners*. Norman: University of Oklahoma Press, 1960.
Kolbe, Robert, with Brian Bade. *They Captured the Moment: Dakotas Photographers, 1853–1920*. Sioux Falls, S.Dak.: By the Authors, 2006.
Kovats, Nancy Niethammer. "*Black Hills Pioneer*: First Newspaper of Deadwood, Dakota Territory, 1876–1877." *South Dakota History* 8 (Summer 1978): 193–220.
Kraft, Louis. *Ned Wynkoop and the Lonely Road from Sand Creek*. Norman: University of Oklahoma Press, 2011.
Krause, Herbert, and Gary D. Olson. *Prelude to Glory: A Newspaper Accounting of Custer's 1874 Expedition to the Black Hills*. Sioux Falls, S.Dak.: Brevet Press, 1974.
Larsen, Arthur J. "The Black Hills Gold Rush: Letters from Men Who Participated." *North Dakota Historical Quarterly* 6 (July 1932): 302–18.
Lass, William E. *From the Missouri to the Great Salt Lake: An Account of Overland Freighting*. Lincoln: Nebraska State Historical Society, 1972.
Lazarus, Edward. *Black Hills, White Justice: The Sioux Nation versus the United States, 1775 to the Present*. Lincoln: University of Nebraska Press, 1999.
Linde, Martha. *Sawmills of the Black Hills*. Rapid City, S. Dak.: Jessie Y. Sundstrom, 1984.
Ludlow, William. *Report of a Reconnaissance of the Black Hills of Dakota, Made in the Summer of 1874*. Washington, D.C.: Government Printing Office, 1875.
McChristian, Douglas C. *Fort Laramie: Military Bastion of the High Plains*. Norman, Okla.: Arthur H. Clark Co., 2008.
McClintock, John S. *Pioneer Days in the Black Hills*. Deadwood, S.Dak.: By the Author, 1939.
McDermott, John D., ed. *Gold Rush: The Black Hills Story*. Pierre: South Dakota State Historical Society Press, 2001.
McLaird, James D. *Calamity Jane: The Woman and the Legend*. Norman: University of Oklahoma Press, 2005.
———. *Wild Bill Hickok & Calamity Jane: Deadwood Legends*. South Dakota Biography Series, no. 2. Pierre: South Dakota State Historical Society Press, 2008.

Mahnken, Norbert R. "The Sidney-Black Hills Trail." *Nebraska History* 30 (Sept. 1949): 203–25.
Malone, Dumas, ed. *Dictionary of American Biography*. Vol. 16. New York: Charles Scribner's Sons, 1935.
Miller, Darlis A. "Captain Jack Crawford: A Western Military Scout on the Chautauqua Circuit." *South Dakota History* 21 (Fall 1991): 230–46.
———. *Captain Jack Crawford: Buckskin Poet, Scout, and Showman*. Albuquerque: University of New Mexico Press, 1993.
Mitchell, Steven T. *Nuggets to Neutrinos: The Homestake Story*. N.p.: By the Author, 2009.
Nolan, Paul T. *John Wallace Crawford*. Boston: Twayne Publishers, 1981.
———. *Three Plays by J. W. (Capt. Jack) Crawford*. The Hague: Mouton & Co., 1966.
———. "When the Curtains Rise, Scouts Fall Out." *Southern Speech Journal* 29 (Spring 1964): 175–86.
O'Harra, C. C. "The Earliest Mining Laws and Mining Organizations in the Black Hills." *Black Hills Engineer* 12 (Nov. 1924): 239–43.
Ostler, Jeffrey. *The Lakotas and the Black Hills: The Struggle for Sacred Ground*. New York: Viking Penguin, 2010.
Parker, Watson. *Deadwood: The Golden Years*. Lincoln: University of Nebraska Press, 1981.
———. *Gold in the Black Hills*. 1966. Reprint ed. Pierre: South Dakota State Historical Society Press, 2003.
———. "The Majors and the Miners: The Role of the U.S. Army in the Black Hills Gold Rush." *Journal of the West* 11 (Jan. 1972): 99–113.
———, ed. "The Report of Captain John Mix of a Scout to the Black Hills, March–April 1875." *South Dakota History* 7 (Fall 1977): 385–401.
Patrick, Jeffrey L., ed. "To the Black Hills Gold Fields: The Letters of Samuel M. Zent, Hoosier Prospector, 1875–1876." *Indiana Magazine of History* 91 (Sept. 1995): 262–87.
Paul, Rodman. *California Gold*. Cambridge, Mass.: Harvard University Press, 1947.
Powers, Thomas. *The Killing of Crazy Horse*. New York: Alfred A. Knopf, 2010.
Prucha, Francis Paul. *American Indian Treaties: The History of a Political Anomaly*. Berkeley: University of California Press, 1994.
Robinson, Charles M., III. *The Diaries of John Gregory Bourke*. Vol. 2, July 29, 1876–April 7, 1878. Denton: University of North Texas Press, 2005.
"Rockerville." *Wi-Iyohi* 6 (Dec. 1952): 1–8.
Rosa, Joseph G. *Jack McCall, Assassin: An Updated Account of His Yankton*

Trial, Plea for Clemency, and Execution. N.p.: English Westerner's Society, 1999.
———. *They Called Him Wild Bill: The Life and Adventures of James Butler Hickok*. 2d ed. Norman: University of Oklahoma Press, 1974.
Ross, Denise. "William Gay, Deadwood's Real Desperado." *Adams Banner Quarterly* 7 (Fall 2006): 1, 7; 8 (Winter, Spring, & Summer 2007): 4–5 each.
Russell, Don. *The Lives and Legends of Buffalo Bill*. Norman: University of Oklahoma Press, 1960.
Sagala, Sandra K. *Buffalo Bill on Stage*. Albuquerque: University of New Mexico Press, 2008.
Schmitt, Martin F., ed. *General George Crook: His Autobiography*. Norman: University of Oklahoma Press, 1960.
Secrest, William B., ed. *I Buried Hickok: The Memoirs of White Eye Anderson*. College Station, Tex.: Creative Publishing Co., 1980.
Smith, James E. *A Famous Battery and Its Campaigns, 1861–'64—The Career of Corporal James Tanner in War and in Peace—Early Days in the Black Hills, with Some Account of Capt. Jack Crawford, the Poet Scout*. Washington: W. H. Lowdermilk & Co., 1892.
Sorenson, Alfred. *History of Omaha from the Pioneer Days to the Present Time*. Omaha: Gibson, Miller & Richardson, 1889.
Spring, Agnes Wright. *The Cheyenne and Black Hills Stage and Express Routes*. Glendale, Calif.: Arthur H. Clark Co., 1949.
Stands in Timber, John, and Margot Liberty. *Cheyenne Memories* (New Haven, Conn.: Yale University Press, 1967.
[Strahorn, Robert]. "Caught Napping." *Bighorn Yellowstone Journal* 2 (Spring 1993): 16–21.
Tallent, Annie D. *The Black Hills; or, The Last Hunting Ground of the Dakotahs*. Saint Louis, Mo.: Nixon-Jones, 1899.
Thrapp, Dan L. *Encyclopedia of Frontier Biography*. vol. 1. Spokane, Wash.: Arthur H. Clark Co., 1990.
Triggs, J. H. *History of Cheyenne and Northern Wyoming Embracing the Gold Fields of the Black Hills*. Omaha, Nebr.: Herald Steam Book and Job Printing House, 1876.
Turchen, Lesta V., and James D. McLaird. *The Black Hills Expedition of 1875*. Mitchell, S.Dak.: Dakota Wesleyan University Press, 1975.
Utley, Robert M. "Origins of the Great Sioux War: The Brown-Anderson Controversy Revisited." *Montana The Magazine of Western History* 42 (Autumn 1992): 48–52.
VanEpps-Taylor, Betti. *Forgotten Lives: African Americans in South Dakota*. Pierre: South Dakota State Historical Society Press, 2008.

Warren, Louis S. *Buffalo Bill's America: William Cody and the Wild West Show*. New York: Alfred A. Knopf, 2005.

Wells, John H. *Placer Examination: Principles and Practice*. Portland, Oreg.: North American Geology Publications, 1975.

Whitley, Fred W. "A History of Custer City, South Dakota, 1874–1900." *South Dakota Historical Collections* 37 (1974): 234–343.

Whitlock, Flint. *Distant Bugles, Distant Drums: The Union Response to the Confederate Invasion of New Mexico*. Boulder: University Press of Colorado, 2006.

Yost, Nellie Snyder. *Buffalo Bill: His Family, Friends, Fame, Failures, and Fortunes*. Chicago: Swallow Press, 1980.

Young, Harry ("Sam"). *Hard Knocks: A Life Story of the Vanishing West*. Reprint ed. Pierre: South Dakota State Historical Society Press, 2005.

Young, Jr., Otis E. *Western Mining: An Informal Account of Precious-Metals Prospecting, Placering, Lode Mining, and Milling on the American Frontier from Spanish Times to 1893*. Norman: University of Oklahoma Press, 1970.

INDEX

C

H

I